967.5
Cro

102463

Crowe.
The Berlin West
African Conference.

Date Due

WITHDRAWN
The Library
Nazareth College of Rochester, N.Y.

PRINTED IN U.S.A.

The
Berlin West African Conference
1884 - 1885

BY

S. E. CROWE

M.A., PH.D.
Tutor in Politics, St. Hilda's College, Oxford

WITH THREE MAPS

NEGRO UNIVERSITIES PRESS
WESTPORT, CONNECTICUT

NAZARETH COLLEGE LIBRARY

Originally published in 1942
by Longmans, Green and Company, New York

Reprinted 1970 by
Negro Universities Press
A DIVISION OF GREENWOOD PRESS, INC.
WESTPORT, CONN.

SBN 8371-3287-8

PRINTED IN UNITED STATES OF AMERICA

TO THE MEMORY OF
MY FATHER

PREFACE

IT is to the late Professor Temperley that I owe the initiation of this study. To Professor Lillian Penson I must express my gratitude for the very active help which she gave me during the short time that I worked under her direction in London. Of the interest and encouragement shown me by Professor Walker, who was responsible for the direction of the major part of my studies at Cambridge, I cannot speak too appreciatively. I am also under a debt of gratitude to Professor Newton for valuable assistance in my researches in London which I have acknowledged in more detail in another part of this book.

Without the financial aid so generously provided by the authorities of Girton College it would have been impossible for me to undertake the writing of it at all. By a further act of generosity, particularly appreciated in war-time, they helped to make publication possible for me. I should like to express my sincere gratitude to them, and to Miss Jones and Miss Cam in particular for their continuous interest and help. To M. Emile Cammaerts I am indebted for his advice and help with books; to the Royal Geographical Society for the loan of maps; and to the officials of the Public Record Office for their friendly helpfulness during the long period that I worked there.

Finally, I would like to express my appreciation of the generous grant made me by the Imperial Studies Committee. The arrangements were carried through under great difficulties caused by the severe bombing of the house of the Royal Empire Society in the spring of 1941. To Miss Gladys Buhler, Assistant Secretary of the Imperial Studies Committee, I am much indebted for assistance and advice in the preparation of the book.

S. E. CROWE.

February, 1942.

" Kein Mensch, selbst der böswilligste Zweifler von Demokrat, glaubt es, was für Charlatanerie und Wichtigthumerei in dieser Diplomatie steckt."—BISMARCK.

" No one, not even the most malevolent democrat, has any idea how much nullity and charlatanism there is in this diplomacy."— BISMARCK.

CONTENTS

	PAGE
PREFACE	vii
INTRODUCTION	3

PART I

CHAP.		
I.	THE ANGLO-PORTUGUESE TREATY	11
II.	THE BREAKDOWN OF THE ANGLO-PORTUGUESE TREATY	23
III.	THE ANGLO-GERMAN ESTRANGEMENT	34
IV.	WIDENING OF THE ESTRANGEMENT—ORIGIN OF THE FRANCO-GERMAN ENTENTE (APRIL–JUNE 1884).	50
V.	ENGLAND AND GERMANY—THE FINAL BREACH (JULY 1884)	59
VI.	THE CEMENTING OF THE FRANCO-GERMAN ENTENTE (AUGUST–SEPTEMBER 1884)	62
VII.	WEAKENING OF THE ENTENTE—BISMARCK'S APPROACHES TO GREAT BRITAIN (OCTOBER–NOVEMBER 1884)	72
VIII.	LEOPOLD AND THE POWERS (FEBRUARY–NOVEMBER 1884)	78

PART II

I.	THE CONFERENCE : PROBLEMS AND PERSONALITIES	95
II.	THE FIRST BASIS : FREEDOM OF COMMERCE IN THE BASIN AND MOUTH OF THE CONGO	105
III.	THE SECOND BASIS : FREE NAVIGATION OF THE CONGO AND THE NIGER	119
IV.	THE CONFERENCE RECOGNISES THE ASSOCIATION	142
V.	THE TERRITORIAL NEGOTIATIONS	152
VI.	THE THIRD BASIS : EFFECTIVE OCCUPATION	176
	EPILOGUE	192

CONTENTS
APPENDICES

		PAGE
I.	THE TITLE OF THE CONFERENCE . . .	197
II.	PORTUGUESE CLAIMS ON THE CONGO . .	197
III.	PORTUGAL AND THE SLAVE TRADE IN THE NINETEENTH CENTURY	202
IV.	CAMERON'S OFFER OF THE CONGO TO GREAT BRITAIN	203
V.	THE CONGO NOTE OF MAY 5TH . . .	203
VI.	THE PORTUGUESE PROPOSAL FOR A CONFERENCE .	205
VII.	GERMAN INTERESTS ON THE CONGO OF A SECONDARY NATURE	208
VIII.	BISMARCK'S INQUIRY OF FEBRUARY 1883 .	208
IX.	THE GERMAN TELEGRAM OF APRIL 24TH . .	209
X.	THE MAY 5TH DISPATCH	211
XI.	BISMARCK AND "THE EQUILIBRIUM ON THE SEAS"	219
XII.	THE INVITATIONS TO THE CONFERENCE . .	220
XIII.	THE OIL RIVERS CORRESPONDENCE AND THE ACTIVITIES OF GREAT BRITAIN, FRANCE, AND GERMANY ON THE GUINEA GULF, 1880–5 . . .	221
	NOTE ON SOURCES	224
	BIBLIOGRAPHY	232
	INDEX	238

MAPS

AFRICA IN 1885	8 and 9
THE CONGO BASIN, 1885 . . .	90 and 91
THE GULF OF GUINEA, 1885 . .	*facing* 120

INTRODUCTION

THIS study is primarily a diplomatic not a legal one, its object being to set[1] the Berlin West African Conference of 1884-5 in its true relation to contemporary history. The importance of the conference[2] as a landmark in international law, has in fact been exaggerated, for when its regulations are studied it can be seen that they all failed of their purpose. Free trade[3] was to be established in the basin and mouths of the Congo; there was to be free navigation of the Congo and the Niger.[4] Actually highly monopolistic systems of trade were set up in both these regions.[5] The centre of Africa was to be internationalised.[6] It became Belgian.[7] Lofty ideals and philanthropic intentions were loudly enunciated by delegates of every country to the conference.[8] Only the vaguest and most unsatisfactory resolutions were passed concerning the internal slave trade, the one humanitarian question of any importance to be discussed at its sittings; whilst the basin of the Congo, if not of the Niger, became subsequently, as every-

[1] cf. Appendix I.
[2] cf. J. S. Reeves, *The International Beginning of the Congo Free State*, p. 50 (though afterwards he contradicts himself, p. 65). H. E. Yarnall, *The Great Powers and the Congo Conference, 1884 to 1885*, pp. 76, 78. A. B. Keith, *The Belgian Congo and the Berlin Act*, p. 57. E. Banning, *Le Partage Politique de l'Afrique*, pp. 5-6, 91-2, 154-5.
[3] cf. General Act, Chapters iv and v. (Accounts and Papers LV, 1884-5: C. 4361 : C. 4739. Documents Diplomatiques—Affaires du Congo et de l'Afrique Occidentale, 1885 (Livre Jaune). E. Hertslet, *Map of Africa by Treaty*, Vol. I, pp. 21-45).
[4] General Act, Chapter ii.
[5] cf. For *Congo*—J. S. Keltie, *The Partition of Africa*, pp. 215-16, 219-22. Reeves, p. 8. Keith, pp. 79, 81-2. H. H. Johnston, *Colonisation of Africa by Alien Races*, p. 348.
For *Niger*—Johnston, p. 192. Keltie, pp. 274-5. W. N. M. Geary, *Nigeria under British Rule*, pp. 183, 187-8.
[6] cf. Protocols of Conference (Accounts and Papers LVI, 1884-5: C. 4361), Protocols IX and X. L.J., Congo, 1885. cf. also Reeves, pp. 73-4. Keltie, p. 214. Keith, pp. 64-5.
[7] Keltie, pp. 201-2, 215-16. Keith, pp. 66-7, 137-44.
[8] General Act, Chapter ii. cf. below, p. 103.

4 THE BERLIN WEST AFRICAN CONFERENCE

one knows, the scene of some of the worst brutalities in colonial history.

As regards the more distant future, it was originally stipulated that the Conventional Basin of the Congo,[1] a huge area, which, besides the Congo Free State, comprised parts of French Equatorial Africa, of German Cameroons, of Portuguese Angola, of the future British colony of Rhodesia, of Italian Somaliland, and of territories of the Sultan of Zanzibar (which later became British and German East Africa),[2] should be neutralised in time of war. Actually it was found necessary to make neutrality optional. Only the Congo Free State opted for neutrality,[3] and this neutrality was violated by Germany in 1914.

Last but not least, and this is the feature of international law most commonly associated with it, the conference made an attempt to regulate future acquisitions of colonial territory on a legal basis. But here again, its resolutions, when closely scrutinised, are found to be as empty as Pandora's box. In the first place,[4] the rules laid down concerning effective occupation, applied only to the *coasts* of West Africa, which had already nearly all been seized, and which were finally partitioned during the next few years; secondly, even within this limited sphere the guarantees given by the powers amounted to little more than a simple promise to notify the acquisition of any given piece of territory, *after* it had been acquired, surely on every ground a most inadequate piece of legislation.

Important questions of a territorial nature which may have avoided serious conflict,[5] and in this sense made a real contribution to international law, were undoubtedly settled whilst the conference was sitting. But they were officially outside its programme, were not once mentioned during its meetings, and formed no acknowledged contribution to the act which embodied its results.[6] It is true that the conference also facilitated, *after* it had broken up, a series of bi-lateral agreements made between 1885 and 1886 by powers interested in Africa. These

---

[1] cf. G. L. Beer, *African Questions at the Peace Conference*, pp. 196–7. Banning, *Partage*, p. 90.
[2] cf. below, pp. 135–9.
[3] cf. Beer, p. 263.
[4] General Act, Chapter vi.
[5] cf. below, Part II, Chapter v, pp. 152–75.
[6] cf. Banning, *Partage*, pp. 8–88.

INTRODUCTION

agreements may also have avoided friction, and may therefore also be considered to form a contribution to international law. But they were essentially a continuation of the earlier " ex officio " achievements of the conference, not of its actual work. Besides this they covered a very short span of time, and must not be confused with any far-reaching effect which the conference may have had, even *indirectly*, on international rivalry in Africa during the next fifty years or so. This appears to have been negligible.

The legal significance of the conference, therefore, *dwindles*, when viewed in true historical perspective. But what, for want of a better term, must be styled its immediate diplomatic and political significance, seems, on the contrary, to grow in importance, the closer it is examined, throwing valuable light on historical problems of the first magnitude, and it is for this reason that it has been chosen as the subject of the present study.

This will be divided into two parts :

I. The history of events leading up to the conference.
II. The history of the conference itself.

Certain main threads will be found running through both, the essentials of the situation being these :

The conference, the first big colonial one in modern times, was held at Berlin between November 15th, 1884, and February 26th, 1885, to discuss outstanding problems connected with West Africa. It was attended by every power in Europe (except Switzerland) as well as by the United States—in all, fourteen powers. Of these fourteen powers only five were of real importance. These were—France, Germany, Great Britain, Portugal, and an ambiguous body called the International Association of the Congo, which had no legal representation there at all, and which was in reality only a cloak to hide the ambitions of Leopold II, King of the Belgians. Its history, therefore, resolves itself principally into the interplay of these five powers. Of these five again, three are more important than the rest. They are France, Germany, and Great Britain. The period under consideration is one in which African and colonial questions generally are still subordinate to European in world diplomacy, colonial issues being more affected by

European than European by colonial. Consequently the part played by the *major* European powers is of *major* interest, that of the *minor* ones of *minor* interest.

Amongst these powers again Germany held the commanding position. Hence the importance of an understanding of the policy of Germany, whose immediate interest in the issues at stake is not always clear. The dominating figure in Europe at the time was Bismarck, and it was Bismarck who held the balance between France and England. Not only was Germany dominant in Europe, she was desirous in Africa, and it is in this combination of circumstances that the *raison d'être* of the conference must be found.

Its history bears an intimate relation to the Anglo-German colonial quarrel of 1884-5, and its corollary, the Franco-German entente of the same year (the first and last since 1870), from which the conference sprang. Its conception, it is no exaggeration to say, evolves literally step by step with the growth of friction between England and Germany. It is at once the epitome of, and the index to the outcome of that friction. Each successive stage of Anglo-German tension produced first vague, then ever more determined approaches of Germany to France. These at first took the form of projects concerned entirely with a conference on the Congo; they were then extended to the Niger; then to the general question of effective occupation on the coasts of West Africa; and finally to an understanding (of which the acknowledged " Anknüpfungspunkt "[1] was hostility to England) on the double basis of Egypt and West Africa.

The Anglo-German quarrel of 1884-5[2] was not only unfortunate but unnecessary. This being so, it is to be expected that the history of the conference should reflect something of its superfluous—perhaps even its mistaken nature—and this is indeed what it does. Arising out of a misunderstanding based on false postulates, it is itself an illustration of the mistakes of that misunderstanding. Its diplomatic results were the exact opposite of what had been contemplated. It was the fruit of a Franco-German entente directed against England. It resulted in a weakening of that entente, and, within the charmed walls

[1] cf. below, p. 63.
[2] cf. below, Chapter iii, pp. 34-49.

of the conference room,[1] though without them the colonial conflict still raged, of a rapprochement between England and Germany on all the most important points at issue, it being discovered, when the representatives of the two countries sat down calmly at a conference table to discuss them, that their interests were practically identical.

This aspect of the conference is of course not the only one of diplomatic significance, but it does seem to be the most important, and the one of greatest general interest, and will for this reason occupy the fullest attention here. The part played by Leopold of the Belgians will take a second place not only because it has hitherto been much more fully dealt with by historians, but also because it is considered that this is where it really belongs. By this it is not meant to minimise, or in any way to overlook, Leopold's rôle, in the history of the conference. He emerged from it, as Bismarck did not, as a real, perhaps its greatest victor (although this was only realised later). That he did so was due to the mixture of astuteness and energy, comparable in quality, though not, by the necessities of the case, in actual power, to Bismarck's own, with which he succeeded in deceiving all the great powers, including Germany, as to the real nature of his aims. Owing to the skill with which he did this, his sometimes appears as the guiding hand in the very complicated negotiations from which he gained so signal a triumph. Nevertheless his activities were always on a secondary plane.

Ultimately the deciding factor in the whole situation was the general trend of Bismarck's policy, both colonial and European. It was no accident that the conference should have been held at Berlin : no accident either that German restlessness should have been the yeast fermenting the mixed African and European leaven in the years 1884-5. Germany, at that time, was the arbiter, in a very real sense, of colonial destinies. With this Ariadne-like caution the reader is now invited to enter the diplomatic labyrinth, where, if he does not succeed as seeing himself as Theseus, he will at least, it is hoped, be prepared to find the Minotaur wearing a Pickelhaube.

[1] cf. R. S. Thomson, *Fondation de l'Etat Indépendant du Congo* (who also comments on this). Also G. Königk, *Die Berliner Kongo Konferenz, 1884-5*, p. 185.

AFRICA
in 1885

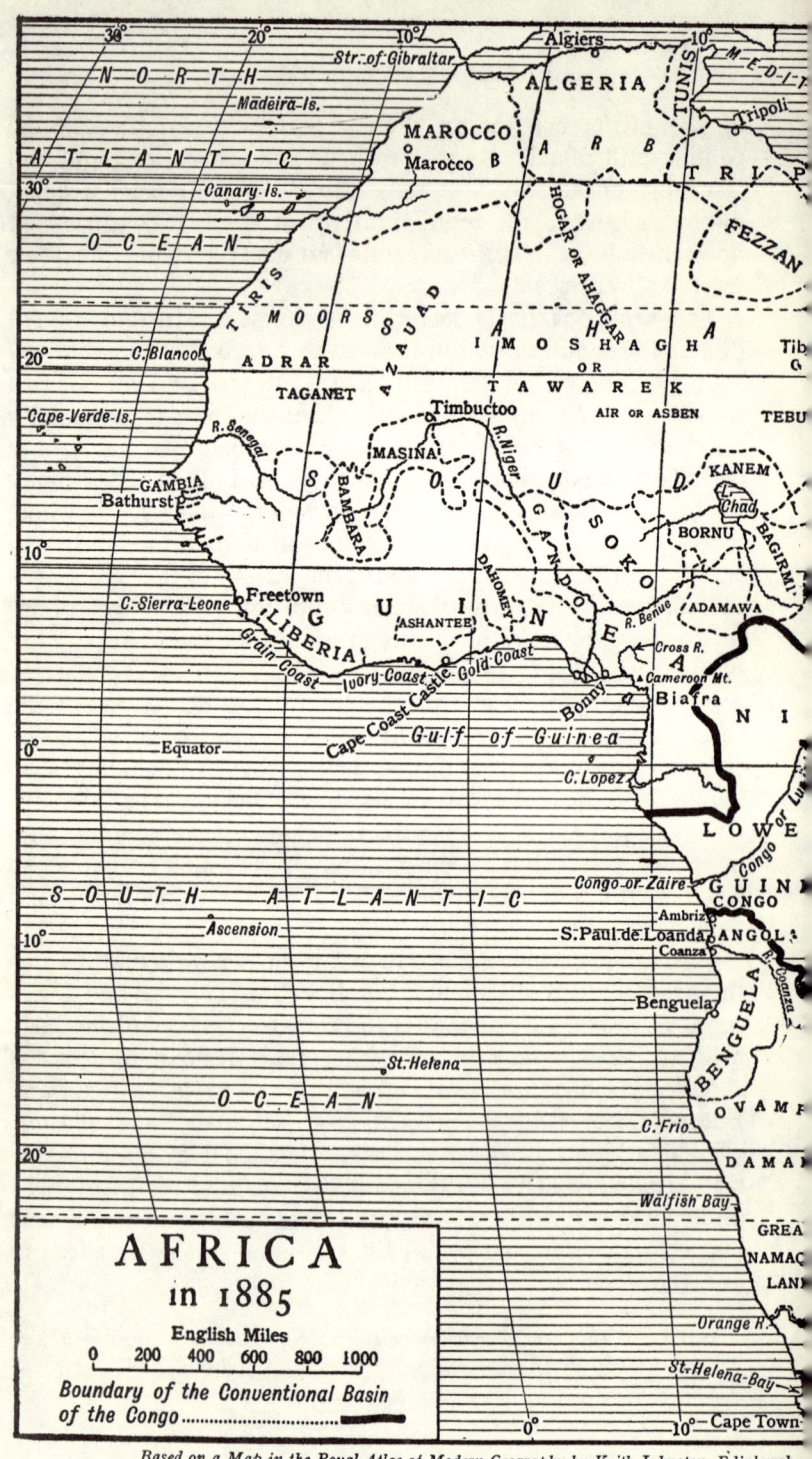

English Miles
0 200 400 600 800 1000

Boundary of the Conventional Basin
of the Congo ....

Based on a Map in the Royal Atlas of Modern Geography by Keith Johnston, Edinburgh,

g Stanley's Line of the Conventional Basin of the Congo as determined by the Conference.

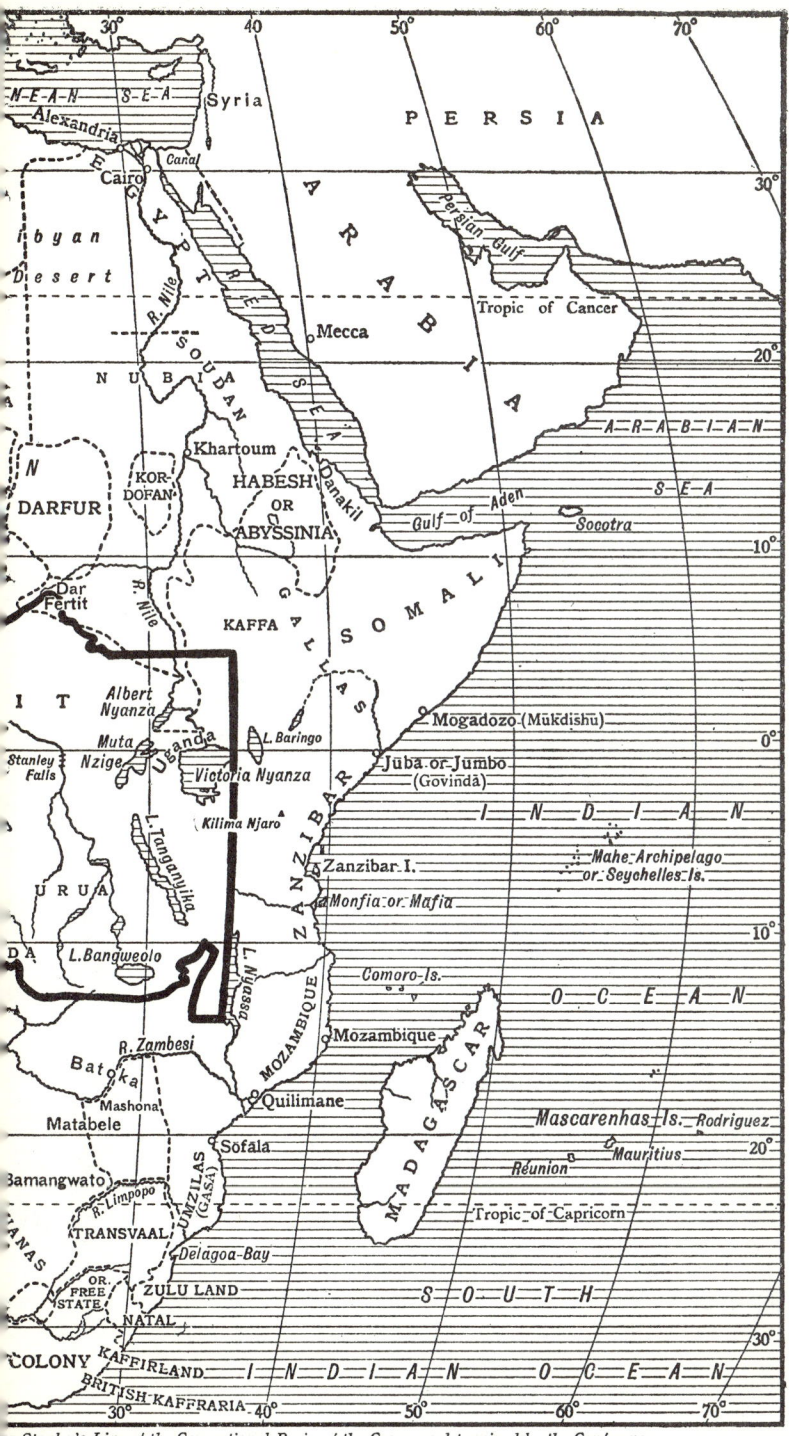

CHAPTER I

THE ANGLO-PORTUGUESE TREATY

THE idea of a conference was at first solely concerned with the Congo and only later extended to include other questions. It arose directly out of the breakdown of a treaty signed, but never ratified, between England and Portugal on February 26th, 1884. This treaty, nominally an affair concerning England and Portugal only, actually involved a third power, France, very closely : whilst in its origin, which must be related to the peculiar conditions prevailing at that time on the Congo, it touched four out of the five powers already mentioned in the introduction to this study, namely—France, Great Britain, Portugal, and the International Association of the Congo.

Portugal[1] was the oldest-established power in the neighbourhood, but her claims to any authority in the regions immediately bordering on the river, were of the vaguest, and were not substantiated by any effective administration. Moreover her interests[2] had for four centuries been those of a slave-trader, and in 1815[3] the Congress of Vienna passed a resolution for the suppression of the slave trade. This explains the attitude of the powers when the nineteenth century opens,[4] their complete apathy, namely, with regard to this part of the coast of Africa and their lack of any serious attempt either to dislodge or to confirm Portugal in a position where the only extensive profits to be made came from a trade universally condemned, for

[1] H. H. Johnston, *George Grenfell and the Congo*, Vol. I, Chapter v, p. 76 : *Colonisation*, pp. 80, 85–9. 70–8. Keltie, pp. 39, 41–3, 45–9, 65–6, 74–5, 76–8, 89–91, 139–41. Keith, pp. 19–25. Reeves, pp. 8–16, 22–3. Stanley, *The Congo*, Vol. I, pp. 1–2, 9–13. Thomson, pp. 120–7. M. Koschitzky, *Deutsche Kolonialgeschichte*, p. 224. Evans Lewin, *The Germans and Africa*, p. 147. Königk, pp. 47–52. cf. Appendix II.
[2] Keltie, pp. 59–74. Keith, p. 19.
[3] Thomson, p. 123. Keltie, p. 84. Keith, pp. 22–3. Reeves, p. 42. cf. Appendix III.
[4] Keltie, pp. 90, 93–4.

which she and she alone, was brazen enough to demand special privileges and exemptions.[1]

At the same time,[2] partly to protect whatever small trade of an ordinary nature existed at the mouth of the river, but chiefly to prevent the expansion of a power whose illicit slave traffic was the object of her constant supervision and control, Great Britain, at first in conjunction with France, exercised strong pressure on Portugal to keep her away from it, as well as from both banks and the adjacent coast-line, between 5° 12′ and 8° South Latitude.

These regions[3] came in this way to constitute a sort of no-man's-land, not owned by any civilised state, where European trade, such as it was, was free to develop under a régime of absolute liberty.

Up to about 1850[4] the volume of this trade was small. Merchants did not wander much from the coast and they displayed little curiosity as to possible developments inland. About this date[5] however it began to grow. It was discovered[6] that rubber, ivory, palm-oil, and ground-nuts could be obtained through middlemen from the interior, and that the increased demand for raw materials in Europe,[7] particularly for palm-oil, which was used in ships' engines and for sewing-machines, as well as for the manufacture of soap and candles, made these products valuable assets in the international market. Big commercial houses[8] began, in consequence, to be established at

[1] H. C. F. Bell, *Life of Palmerston*, Vol. I, pp. 234-5. Keith, pp. 22-4. Reeves, pp. 13-16. Thomson, pp. 123-7. Stanley, I, pp. 15-16. Keltie, pp. 112, 139. Johnston, *Colonisation*, pp. 157-9. cf. Appendix III.
[2] Reeves, pp. 13-15. Keith, pp. 23-4. Johnston, *Grenfell*, I, pp. 83, 91: *Colonisation*, pp. 94-5. Thomson, pp. 123-7. Königk, pp. 49-52. Bell, pp. 234-5. Stanley, I, pp. 15-16. cf. Appendix III.
[3] E. Fitzmaurice, *Life of Lord Granville*, Vol. II, pp. 342-3. Keltie, pp. 89-90. Keith, pp. 23-5, 28-9. Stanley, I, p. 17. Thomson, p. 127. Johnston, *Grenfell*, I, p. 83. Reeves, pp. 16, 23. Banning, p. 96.
[4] Keith, pp. 28-9. Keltie, p. 89.
[5] Keith, p. 28. Johnston, *Grenfell*, I, p. 91. Fitzmaurice, II, p. 342. Stanley, I, p. 91. Koschitzky, p. 225. Slave Trade Papers relating to Congo and West African Conference, F.O./84/1809/Memo. Phillips, October 14, 1883.
[6] Senate Executive Document, No. 196, 49th Congress, 1st Session, Washington, 1886: No. 105, Tisdel to Frelinghuysen, Nov. 23, 1884: No. 107, Tisdel to Bayard (Lisbon), April 25, 1885.
[7] cf. Sylvia Masterman, *Origins of International Rivalry in Samoa*, pp. 57-8. Johnston, *Colonisation*, p. 183.
[8] S.E.D., 196: Nos. 107 and 108 (as above). Johnston, *Grenfell*, I, p. 91. Keith, p. 28. F.O./841/1810/ Petre to Granville, April 13, 1884, Africa, 27. (Enclosure, List of Factories established on Banks of Congo, February 1883.) F.O./84/1811/ Holman Bentley to Alfred Baynes, April 21, 1884.

THE ANGLO-PORTUGUESE TREATY 13

the mouth of the river. At the same time[1] the activities of explorers in central Africa were stimulated and increased by the new commercial demands, and it was these activities which finally brought the Congo into the sphere of international interest. It appears to have been the discoveries of a British explorer, Cameron,[2] who visited the Congo in 1874, after a fruitless search for Livingstone, who had died the year before, and whose offer of the Congo to Great Britain was refused,[3] which were responsible for arousing those budding jealousies on the part of the King of the Belgians, of France, and of Portugal, which were to culminate successively in the formation of the International African Association, the journeys of Stanley and De Brazza on the Congo and the Anglo-Portuguese Treaty. Cameron returned to England in 1875. In 1876[4] Leopold of the Belgians founded the International African Association at Brussels. This association must not be confused with the International Association of the Congo, which was one of the many subsidiary bodies to be evolved out of it later. It was an association formed by the powers convened by Leopold in 1876 at Brussels, for discussing and devising means of opening up equatorial Africa to European civilisation. Its first act[5] was to form an International Commission with an executive committee of four, of which Leopold was elected head, and national committees,[6] which were formally organised between 1876 and 1877, when another conference[7] was called at Brussels to discuss the situation. Great Britain[8] from the first stood

[1] Fitzmaurice, II, p. 342. Keith, pp. 25-8. Keltie, pp. 104, 114-17. Johnston, *Colonisation*, pp. 308, 322 : Grenfell, II, cf. especially pp. 80-4, 91. Stanley, *The Congo*, 2 vols. Koschitzky, pp. 225-7. Thomson, pp. 38-40. Königk, pp. 5-6. Evans Lewin, pp. 147-8. W. L. Langer, *European Alliances and Alignments*, pp. 289-90.
[2] Johnston, *Grenfell*, II, pp. 81-3 : *Colonisation of Africa*, pp. 322-5, 328-30, Keith, pp. 27-8. Fitzmaurice, II, p. 343. Thomson, pp. 39-40.
[3] cf. Appendix IV.
[4] Reeves, pp. 17-18. Thomson, pp. 41-7. Keltie, pp. 116-17. Keith, pp. 31-34. Koschitzky, pp. 225-6. Johnston, *Grenfell*, I, p. 408 : *Colonisation*, pp. 342-3. Stanley, I, pp. 33-8. Banning, *Partage*, p. 4. Königk, pp. 23-31. Langer, p. 291. Yarnall, p. 9.
[5] Reeves, p. 17. Keltie, p. 119. Keith, pp. 33, 34. Thomson, pp. 46-7, 56. Königk, pp. 26-7.
[6] Reeves, pp. 17-18. Keltie, pp. 119, 120. Keith, p. 33. Thomson, pp. 47, 49-53. Stanley, I, pp. 33-6. Johnston, *Colonisation*, p. 342. Königk, p. 27.
[7] Reeves, pp. 18-19. Keltie, p. 120. Keith, pp. 35-6. Königk, p. 30.
Keltie, p. 120. Keith, pp. 33-4. Stanley, I, pp. 34, 36. Thomson, pp. 47-9. Königk, pp. 27-8.

aloof from the movement, refusing to form a committee affiliated to the Association, and founding instead the Royal Geographical Society in 1877, as an entirely independent body. But Germany, France, Austria-Hungary, Spain, the United States, Italy, Holland, Russia, Switzerland, and Belgium all formed national committees.[1] The important thing to realise about these committees[2] is that they were as jealously nationalistic, probably more so, than if they had never been brought together by an international association, localising their energies, and appropriating funds accordingly, almost as soon as they had been formed. The foundation of the International Association may in fact be said to have stimulated, not alleviated, as it professed to do, the keenness of international rivalry in Africa.

There is no clearer illustration of this[3] than the story of the rivalry of Stanley and De Brazza on the Congo,[4] between the years 1879 and 1883. Lieut. Savorgan de Brazza (an Italian by birth, but who had long been in the service of the French Government) was the agent of the French national committee of the International African Association ; Stanley (English born, but an American citizen), of the " Comité d'Études du Haut Congo ",[5] a special body formed by Leopold after Stanley's return from the Upper Congo in 1877, to deal exclusively with that region. In 1879 Stanley agreed to undertake an expedition to the Congo as the agent of this committee, and early in the year he left for Africa. But De Brazza, starting a few months earlier for the same destination, succeeded in stealing a march on him by securing, before his arrival, an important stretch of territory on the Upper Congo. In 1883, however, De Brazza, who had hurried home to report on his treaties, was in turn forestalled by Stanley, who annexed the valuable districts watered by the Niari Kwilu on the north bank of the Congo.

[1] Keltie, p. 120. Keith, p. 34. Stanley, I, pp. 35–6.
[2] Keith, pp. 33–4, 35–6. Keltie, pp. 119–20, 122–3. Thomson, Chapter i (pp. 49–52). Johnston, *Grenfell*, pp. 408–9.
[3] cf. Keltie, p. 138.
[4] Keith, pp. 37–49. Keltie, pp. 124–38. Johnston, *Colonisation*, p. 343. Koschitzky, pp. 226–7. Reeves, pp. 20–5. Stanley, Vol. I, Chapters v–xxv : Vol. II, Chapters xxv–xxxiii. Yarnall, pp. 9–10. Königk, pp. 40–5. Thomson, pp. 76–101.
[5] Keith, pp. 38–40. Keltie, pp. 125–8, 343, 409. Koschitzky, p. 226. Reeves, p. 19. Stanley, I, pp. 38, 50. Thomson, pp. 65–8. Yarnall, p. 10.

THE ANGLO-PORTUGUESE TREATY

Both expeditions[1] had been organised with the utmost secrecy. In Belgium[2] the commercial character of the " Comité d'Études " was loudly advertised, its political aims severely concealed, whilst Leopold kept a tight hold on the Press. The political character[3] of De Brazza's mission was also successfully hidden from the public eye in France. But in fact, the political nature of the programme decided upon[4] was responsible for a secret meeting of the French committee shortly before De Brazza left Paris, in which it took steps to establish its national independence, severing all connection with the International African Association, whilst at the same time more or less affiliating itself to the French Government. Thus De Brazza, when he left France, was in reality in the service of the French Government, not of Leopold's Association at all. Stanley's position was even more peculiar. He had, as has been seen, undertaken his expedition under the auspices of the " Comité d'Études du Haut Congo."[5] But on November 17th, 1879,[6] this committee (without Stanley's knowledge) was actually dissolved by Leopold, who took advantage of its financial embarrassments to suggest a kind of voluntary liquidation, in which he played the part of monetary " deus ex machina " and succeeded in placing himself in the legal position of sole director of Stanley's activities. This transaction was naturally kept secret. But in the same month,[7] the name of the " Comité d'Études du Haut Congo " began gradually to be dropped by those connected with it and that of " The International Association of the Congo " substituted in its stead. The transaction once known, it is of course clear, in what overwhelming sense Leopold was the driving power behind this newly-titled organisation.

It was the territorial acquisitions of De Brazza[8] which were immediately responsible for the Anglo-Portuguese Treaty.

[1] Keltie, pp. 126–7. Keith, p. 39. Thomson, p. 69.
[2] Thomson, p. 69.
[3] Thomson, p. 81.
[4] Thomson, p. 80.
[5] cf. above, p. 14.
[6] Thomson, pp. 73–5, 77.
[7] Thomson, pp. 89, 93, 161–2. Keith, p. 45.
[8] Accounts and Papers, Vol. LVI, 1884 : C. 3885. No. 1, Serpa to d'Antas, Nov. 8, 1882. Documents Diplomatiques-Affaires du Congo et de l'Afrique Occidentale (Livre Jaune), 1884 : No. 15, Laboulaye to Ferry, March 15, 1884, p. 30. Keltie, p. 139. Thomson, p. 128. Evans Lewin, p. 148.

This treaty,[1] which was generally considered to establish a veiled British protectorate over the Congo, recognised long-disputed Portuguese claims to the territories lying between 5° 12 and 8° South Latitude, in return for what was considered a low tariff of 10 per cent *ad valorem* on imported goods, and most-favoured-nation treatment for British subjects. It also stipulated that an Anglo-Portuguese Commission should be set up on the river, to control its traffic.

It was Portugal[2] who actually opened the negotiations at the end of 1882; but the idea of an agreement was not new. Already,[3] under the Beaconsfield Government, Sir Robert Morier, then British minister at Lisbon, had advocated a large settlement of West African affairs, in which the Congo was to form a leading chapter. His suggestion was that Great Britain should recognise the claims of Portugal northwards from Ambriz (8° South Latitude), to the south bank of the Congo, that the north bank should become British; and that the river itself should be placed under international control, consisting, in the first instance, of representatives of riverain states. But the British Government at first showed little interest in the matter.[4] Morier[5] was also anxious for a *quid pro quo*, however, and was eventually allowed to open negotiations with the Portuguese on this basis, in order to induce them to agree to the concessions regarding Delagoa Bay in return for concessions on the Congo. But on the latter point the Portuguese proved obstinate; so the idea of compensation on the East coast had to be abandoned. Discussions[6] on the Congo, however, still continued, and in October 1881[7] views were again interchanged at Lisbon on this subject between Morier and the Portuguese Government.

[1] A. and P., LVI, 1884: C. 3885: C. 4023. For text see A. and P., LVI, 1884: C. 3886. Hertslet, *Map of Africa by Treaty*, Vol. II, No. 147, pp. 913–14. State Papers, Vol. LXXV, p. 476 ff. Keltie, pp. 139–44. Keith, pp. 50–2. Fitzmaurice, II, pp. 344–5. Johnston, *Colonisation*, p. 343. Koschitzky, pp. 227–9. Reeves, p. 25.
[2] C. 3855, No. 1, Serpa to d'Antas, Nov. 8, 1883.
[3] Fitzmaurice, II, p. 343. Gwynn and Tuckwell, *Life of Dilke*, II, p. 84.
[4] Fitzmaurice, II, p. 343. Yarnall, p. 10.
[5] Dilke Papers, Vol. LVII, VIII, 43930: *Memoir*, Chapter xxii, 1883, pp. 28–9.
[6] Ibid.
[7] C. 3885, No. 5, Serpa to d'Antas, Nov. 26, 1882. Thomson, p. 128.

THE ANGLO-PORTUGUESE TREATY

There is no doubt that fear of France,[1] and of the exclusive commercial policy of her traders, was the motive power at work in the minds of British statesmen. Already[2] in the '70's French traders had been pushing down towards the Congo from their own colony of Gaboon, and in 1876 the British consul, Hewett, acting under orders from his government, had made a treaty with certain Congo chiefs giving Great Britain most-favoured-nation treatment as a safeguard against possible French penetration. Portugal,[3] alarmed for some time now by the increasing interest of European powers in the Congo, was determined[4] to seize this opportunity to extend her rule, at least to the *south* bank of the river,[5] but was still hesitating as to whether she should try to come to an agreement for this purpose with France or with Great Britain.

That she eventually turned to Britain seems to show that she considered her the least territorially ambitious of the two powers—which indeed she was.

It was the activities[6] of De Brazza, themselves stimulated as has been seen by the foundation of the International African Association, which finally brought matters to a head by inducing Senhor de Serpa, the Portuguese Foreign Minister, to make definite advances to the British Government. On November 18th, 1882,[7] De Brazza's famous Makoko treaties were submitted to the French chambers for ratification. On the same day Serpa wrote to d'Antas,[8] the Portuguese minister in London, instructing him to ask Lord Granville, the British Foreign Secretary, for a settlement of Portuguese claims on the Congo between 8° and 5° 12′ South Latitude. Without recognising the historical or legal validity of these claims,[9] which she had persist-

[1] Dilke, *Memoir*, Chapter xxii, 1883, p. 28. Gooch and Temperley, *British Documents on the Origin of the War, 1898-1914*, Vol. III : Memorandum, Jan. 1, 1907. E. A. Crowe, p. 409. F.O./84/1809/Meade to Cohen, Grievances of British Traders in the Gaboon, Jan. 23, 1884. Memo. Kennedy, March 11, 1884. Fitzmaurice, II, pp. 343, 344. Thomson, p. 128.
[2] Dilke, *Memoir*, Chapter xxii, 1883, pp. 27–8.
[3] cf. Keltie, pp. 139–41. Keith, p. 50.
[4] Johnston, *Grenfell*, p. 91.
[5] Banning, p. 99.
[6] cf. above, p. 15.
[7] Documents Diplomatiques Français, Origines de la Guerre de 1914. Série I, Vol. IV, No. 560, Duclerc to Ménéval, Nov. 18, 1882.
[8] C. 3885, No, 1, Serpa to d'Antas, Nov. 18, 1882. Thomson, p. 128.
[9] Ibid., No. 4, Granville to d'Antas, Dec. 15, 1882. cf Evans Lewin, p. 148. Keith, p. 50. Thomson, p. 129. cf. Appendix II, pp. 200–1.

ently denied for over forty years, Great Britain, on the 15th of December expressed her willingness to recognise them in principle, in return for certain commercial concessions. The negotiations were now launched. But it was to take fourteen months before they were finally brought to a conclusion, this long lapse of time being itself an indication of the difficulties attending them.

It is clear that both England and Portugal entered into the treaty through fear of France. England certainly made it entirely out of fear of French encroachments and of the high protective tariffs which always followed them. The same was true of Portugal—with a reserve—it being important to realise that after, as before the initiation of the negotiations, her fear and distrust of England were almost as great as her fear and distrust of France. These two powers were for her the Scylla and Charybdis of the Congo. It was impossible to steer clear of both. She must use them—one against the other. They were powers, therefore, which she alternately regarded either as the greatest potential menace to, or the strongest bulwark for her traditionally powerful, but practically ineffectual pretensions, whilst all the time seeking to play her own rôle, that of the pawn triumphantly metamorphosed into king—checkmate. Her turn to one or the other, therefore, was never wholehearted. She was always in a state of latent vacillation between the two. It is hardly surprising in these circumstances to find that she never burns her boats, that her entry into negotiations with one power is an almost certain symptom of an increase, rather than a decrease, in the liveliness of her relations with the other, whilst difficulties with the first breed advances to the second, and vice versa.

Even before opening negotiations with England[1] she had made tentative approaches to France, which failed, because the French refused to recognise her territorial pretensions on the north bank of the Congo. Then the intended ratification of the De Brazza treaties swung her right over to England again. But in the opening months[2] of the Anglo-Portuguese negotia-

[1] Banning, *Partage*, p. 99.
[2] Livre Jaune Congo, 1884, No. 15, Laboulaye to Ferry, March 15, 1882 : Extracts from Portuguese White Book, II, d'Azevedo to Serpa Pimentel, Nov. 20, 1882, III, Ménéval to Antonio de Serpa, Nov. 20, 1882, IV, d'Azevedo to Serpa Pimental, Nov. 24, 1882, VI, d'Azevedo to Serpa Pimentel, Dec. 7, 1882, VIII, d'Azevedo to Serpa Pimentel, Dec. 10, 1882. Thomson, pp. 131–2.

THE ANGLO-PORTUGUESE TREATY 19

tions, that is to say in November and December 1882, there was a regular rain of French notes at Lisbon, giving assurances about De Brazza's treaties, which was not without its effect. A détente[1] was produced in Franco-Portuguese relations, and by the end of December[2] France was being kept informed of the progress of the negotiations with England. The year 1882 thus closed under favourable auspices for Portugal. The possibility of a settlement with England seemed well in sight, whilst France appeared content with the rôle of confidante to a potential sister. But things soon took a different turn. Difficulties[3] with England increased during the spring and summer of 1883,[4] though France, on the other hand, still continued to give assurances about the De Brazza treaties and to maintain a friendly attitude. This accounts for what happened in the middle of the year, namely that Portugal,[5] halfway through the negotiations for the treaty with England, tried to negotiate one with France instead. She failed, because once more France proved more exigeant than England, refusing to recognise that which was the very basis of the Anglo-Portuguese treaty—the recognition of Portuguese claims between 8° and 5° 12′ South Latitude. The matter was therefore dropped, though not without causing the resignation[6] of de Serpa, the Portuguese Foreign Minister, in October 1883.

The treaty with England (this country of course knowing nothing of the secret overtures to France) was then carried through by his successor, Du Bocage.[7] In view of the difficulties attending it,[8] however, there is no doubt that as remarkable as its conclusion was the fact that it was ever concluded at all.

[1] D.D.F., IV, No. 575, Laboulaye to Duclerc, Dec. 10, 1882.
[2] Ibid., No. 583, Laboulaye to Duclerc, Dec. 22, 1882.
[3] C. 3885, Nos. 8–13.
[4] D.D.F., V, No. 15, Laboulaye to Challemel-Lacour, April 1, 1883. No. 54, Silva Mendes de Léal to Ferry, June 25, 1883.
[5] L.J., Congo, 1884, No. 7, Laboulaye to Challemel-Lacour, July 18, 1883. No. 9, Challemel-Lacour to Laboulaye, Aug. 16, 1883 (Annex 1—Laboulaye to Serpa Pimentel, Aug. 9, 1883), (Annex 2—Serpa Pimentel to Laboulaye, Aug. 13, 1883). D.D.F., V, No. 79. Annex. Laboulaye to Challemel-Lacour, Aug. 16, 1883. F.O./84/1810/ French Note of Remonstrance on Anglo-Portuguese Treaty, March 18, 1884, F.O. to Petre, Africa, 30, April 8, 1884. Petre to Granville, Tel. 29, April 16, 1884. Ibid., Africa, 30, April 17, 1884. Granville to Petre, Africa, 38, April 29, 1884. Thomson, pp. 132–3. Keltie, p. 144. Banning, *Partage*, pp. 27–8, 99.
[6] L.J., Congo, 1884, No. 15, Laboulaye to Ferry, March 15, 1884, p. 33.
[7] Ibid.
[8] C. 3885.

20 THE BERLIN WEST AFRICAN CONFERENCE

There were four main points of controversy with Britain :[1] the question of transit dues ; the question of the limits to be set to Portuguese sovereignty on the river ; the question of the eastern boundary of the Congo (the western boundary, that is to say, of Mozambique, Portugal in the treaty being given a potential right of expansion to the limits of her eastern colony) ; and the question of whether there should be an international or an Anglo-Portuguese commission on the river. Over all these questions, except the last, Portugal was forced to give way. She had to concede absolute freedom of transit for goods inland,[2] as well as on the coast, and also to extend this freedom to land as well as to water transit on both the upper and lower reaches of the Congo. She was forced[3] to accept Nokki, instead of Vivi, higher up the river as the limit to her sovereignty on it. With regard to the Mozambique boundary,[4] she was made to respect British interests in the region of the great lakes, by accepting a point sixty miles above the confluence of the Shiré and the Zambesi as its western limit. But she had her way over the Anglo-Portuguese commission,[5] which was a question of great significance for the future. Great Britain had from the beginning stipulated that there should be an International not a Dual Commission on the river,[6] on the ground that any other arrangement would arouse almost universal antagonism among the powers, and had only consented to an Anglo-Portuguese one under strong pressure from Portugal. This is of particular interest, since it was indeed the Anglo-Portuguese Commission[7] which proved the principal point of attack from the powers when the treaty was published.

Enough, it is hoped, has now been said, to make it clear that

---

[1] Ibid.
[2] Ibid. cf. Nos. 5, 14-15, 16, 17, 19. F.O./84/1809/ Goldsmid to F.O., Feb. 9, 1884. Granville to d'Antas, Feb. 11, 1884.
[2] C. 3885, Nos. 10, 11, 20, 21, 22, 23, 24, 25. F.O./84/1809/ Fitzmaurice to Petre, Feb. 23, 1884. Granville to Petre, Feb. 23, 1884. L.J., Congo, 1884, No. 15, Laboulaye to Ferry, March 15, 1884, p. 34.
[4] C. 3885, Nos. 4, 5, 10, 11, 12, 13, 14, 15, 16, 17, 18, 20, 21, 22, 23. L.J., Congo, 1884, No. 15, Laboulaye to Ferry, March 15, 1884, pp. 32-3.
[5] C. 3885, Nos. 4, 8, 11, 20, 21.
[6] Ibid., No. 8. cf. Thomson, p. 138. Keith, pp. 51-2. Keltie, p 143. Evans Lewin, p. 149. Banning, *Partage*, pp. 111-12.
[7] cf. F.O./84/1810/ Petre to Granville, March 27, 1884, Africa, 24. cf. also French Protest v. Treaty, March 13, 1884 (p. 26, note 10). For German Protest cf. Aktenstücke Betreffend die Kongo—Frage, 1885 (Weissbuch) No. 9, Hatzfeldt to Schmidtals, April 18, 1884.

the Anglo-Portuguese treaty was made out of fear of France ; that the French activities which immediately led to it were in turn stimulated by the foundation of the International African Association, and that this association was itself a crystallisation of the growing rivalry, as well as of the growing interest among European nations at this time, in the unexplored and unexploited regions of Central Africa. Portugal occupied at once a central and a subordinate position with regard to France and England on the Congo, and pursued a vacillating policy towards these two powers. The history of the treaty illustrates very strongly the purely negative and defensive attitude of Great Britain with regard to it, which contrasts strongly with that of France, the active aggressor in this field. All that the former wanted was free trade for her nationals.[1] She saw this threatened by France, and therefore made the treaty with Portugal, considering the Portuguese tariff a lesser evil than a possible French one, and Portuguese rule a less expensive proposition than consular supervision.[2] Her demand for an international commission was only another illustration of her lack of any desire for exclusive commercial control. Had this been more generally realised, had it been grasped that Portugal made the treaty with England as an *alternative* to one with France, precisely because she was the least territorially ambitious of the two powers ; had the French danger been better understood, Britain's rôle would not have been so misinterpreted.

As it was she emerged—falsely—in the public eye—as a power with dangerous territorial and commercial ambitions on the Congo, the deceptively positive appearance given to her policy being accentuated by the incongruity existing between the territorial pretensions of Portugal, her treaty-partner, and the latter's actual rank as a minor power in the councils of Europe. This does much to explain what ultimately happened, namely that France, with the co-operation of Germany, succeeded in summoning a conference whose aim was avowedly to put England in her place, and to check what were considered her dangerous territorial and commercial ambitions in central

[1] cf. Thomson, p. 145.
[2] For her ideas on this question cf. W. H. Scotter, International Rivalry in the Bights of Benin and Biafra (unpublished Thesis—London). M. A. Adams, The British Attitude to German Colonial Development, 1880-5, pp. 225-8 (unpublished Thesis—London).

Africa; whilst at the conference itself, France and Portugal were seen to be the two powers, which, besides the International Association of the Congo, really had such ambitions.

Consequently, like two burglars preparing to rob the same house, they found wisdom in acting together; whilst Great Britain and Germany, who wished for nothing better than free trade internationally controlled, in this hope supported Leopold's so-called " international " association.

CHAPTER II

THE BREAKDOWN OF THE ANGLO-PORTUGUESE TREATY

THE Anglo-Portuguese Treaty[1] was signed on February 26th, 1884. But it was never ratified.[2] This was due to the opposition of numerous interested powers, of which France was the chief ;[3] wherein Holland took a second place,[4] owing to her large commercial interests, though her political rôle was small ; where Leopold of the Belgians was very active ;[5] and which included the United States,[6] but which was eventually canalised, directed, controlled and rendered peremptory and decisive by the action of Germany.[7] The German refusal to recognise the treaty,[8] which was what finally killed it, was made on June 7th in a note delivered to the British Government on June 14th. Prior to this date,[9] the opposition of the powers, headed by France, had led Portugal, as well as Great Britain,

[1] A. and P., LVI, 1884 : C. 3886. Hertslet, II, p. 713. F.O. /84/1809/ (C. 4023.) No. 8, F.O. to Cohen, Feb. 29, 1884. cf. also Keltie, pp. 142-3. E. Banning, *Mémoires*, pp. 1, 5 : *Partage*, p. 102. Koschitzky, p. 228. Stanley, II, p. 381. Yarnall, p. 11. Thomson, p. 139. Evans Lewin, p. 148. Langer, p. 380.
[2] W.B., Congo, No. 29. Münster to German F.O., June 26, 1884. cf. Banning, *Mémoires*, p. 5 : *Partage*, pp. 102, 113. Yarnall, p. 21. Koschitzky, p. 233. Gwynn and Tuckwell, *Dilke*, II, p. 84. Evans Lewin, p. 149. Langer, p. 300.
[3] cf. below, p. 24. Also Koschitzky, pp. 228-33. Banning, *Partage*, p. 112. Stanley, II, p. 381. Johnston, *Colonisation of Africa*, pp. 278, 343. Königk, p. 88. Adams, p. 178. Langer, p. 300. Wienefeld, *Franco-German Relations, 1878-85*, p. 141.
[4] F.O./84/1810/1811/. Thomson, pp. 143, 200. Yarnall, p. 20. Banning, *Partage*, p. 112. Koschitzky, p. 229. Königk, pp. 91-2.
[5] F.O./84/1809/ Memo., Anderson, March 2, 1884. Keith, p. 53. Thomson, pp. 141-2. Königk, p. 88.
[6] Thomson, p. 143. Banning, *Partage*, p. 112. Stanley, II, p. 382. Koschitzy, p. 230.
[7] cf. below, pp. 28-33. Reeves, pp. 29-30. Keltie, pp. 144-5. Yarnall, p. 21. Koschitzky, p. 233. Adams, p. 178. Wienefeld, pp. 141-2.
[8] W.B., Congo, No. 2, Bismarck to Münster, June 7, 1884. F.O./84/1811/ Bismarck to Münster, June 7 (communicated June 14), (shown to Queen and Gladstone). Accounts and Papers, LV, 1884-5 : C. 4205, No. 2. Ibid. (date of delivery, June 14, not given). cf. Keltie, pp. 145-6. Stanley, II, pp. 384-5.
[9] Thomson, pp. 144-5. Keith, pp. 54-5. cf. below, pp. 24-8.

24   THE BERLIN WEST AFRICAN CONFERENCE

to consider substantial modifications in it and to delay its ratification. But there was no question of abandoning the treaty altogether before the arrival of the German veto.

France,[1] as might have been expected, was the first power to make a protest against it, and her protest was addressed to Portugal. This was on March 13th. She was afraid of England,[2] but evidently did not despair[3] of the possible fruitfulness of pressure on Portugal, no doubt encouraged in this by inside knowledge[4] of some of the many difficulties which had attended the course of the recent Anglo-Portuguese negotiations. She made formal reserves[5] with regard to any clauses of the treaty infringing French interests or previous Franco-Portuguese agreements, implying by this a definite refusal to accept either the 10 per cent tariff or the Anglo-Portuguese Commission. She also specifically stated her refusal to recognise Portugal's claims to the territories lying between 8° and 5° 12′ South Latitude. In reply[6] the Portuguese Government fastened particularly on this latter point, vigorously defending their territorial claims.

Throughout Portugal remained adamant about these,[7] for her the most important part of the treaty. But she very early[8] showed herself ready for other concessions, and seems from the first[9] to have realised that it would not be possible to maintain the Anglo-Portuguese Commission. Indeed the French protest[10] of March 13th appears to have been made with the knowledge that Du Bocage would see without regret any efforts made at London either by France or by Holland to obtain a modification in the constitution of the commission. On March 27th,[11] the day

---

[1] L.J., Congo, 1884, No. 14, Ferry to Laboulaye, March 14, 1884 (Annex). F.O./84/1810/ Petre to Granville, March 23, 1884, Africa, 23. cf. also W.B., Congo, No. 11, Hatzfeldt to Hohenlohe, April 17, 1884. E. Banning, *Partage*, p. 112. Keith, p. 53.
[2] cf. D.D.F., V. No. 214, Waddington to Ferry, March 4, 1884.
[3] cf. Ibid., 218. Laboulaye to Ferry, March 12, 1884.
[4] cf. above, Chapter i, pp. 19–20.
[5] L.J., Congo, 1884, No. 14, Ferry to Laboulaye, March 14, 1884 (Annex). F.O./84/1810/ Petre to Granville, March 23, 1884, Africa, 23.
[6] F.O./84/1810/ Granville to Petre, April 29, 1884 (text enclosed), Africa, 38. L.J., Congo, 1884, No. 16, Laboulaye to Ferry, March 29, 1884.
[7] F.O./84/1810/ Granville to Petre, April 29, 1884, Africa, 38.
[8] D.D.F., V, No. 218, Laboulaye to Ferry, March 12, 1884. F.O./84/1810/ Fitzmaurice to London Chamber of Commerce, March 24, 1884.
[9] F.O./84/1810/ Petre to Granville, March 27, 1884, Africa, 24.
[10] D.D.F., V, No. 218, Laboulaye to Ferry, March 12, 1884.
[11] F.O./84/1810/ Petre to Granville, March 27, 1884, Africa, 24.

BREAKDOWN OF ANGLO-PORTUGUESE TREATY 25

before answering the French note, Du Bocage suggested to Petre, the British minister at Lisbon, that these two countries should be admitted to it. Petre not unnaturally reminded him[1] that a mixed commission was what Great Britain had always asked for, and that she would therefore be only too pleased to concur in this suggestion. This statement,[2] however, received no official confirmation from London for over another month. The exchange of notes[3] between France and Portugal in March 1884 had led to the discovery by Great Britain of the secret negotiations which had passed between them in July and August 1883 (in the midst of those for the Anglo-Portuguese Treaty), these being openly referred to both in the French protest of March 13th and the Portuguese answer of March 28th. Not unnaturally this aroused a deep distrust of Portuguese diplomacy in the minds of British statesmen,[4] coupled with a suspicion that the same kind of thing might actually be going on at that moment, a suspicion enhanced rather than alleviated by the unsatisfactory attempts made by the Portuguese to try and explain away the events of 1883. Consequently most of April passed in acrimonious discussions[5] between members of the British and Portuguese governments on this head, the atmosphere thus produced not being very favourable to a joint consideration of modifications in the treaty, avowedly to be made as a result of French protests, even although the most important one at issue,[6] that of the International Commission, was one which Great Britain had always advocated.[7]

Towards the end of the month, however, another question came to the fore, which caused more active developments in the negotiations for the proposed amendments in the treaty. This was the question of ratification. On April 23rd,[8] Lord Edmond Fitzmaurice, the British parliamentary Under-Secre-

[1] Ibid.
[2] F.O./84/1811/ Granville to Petre, May 10, 1884, Africa, 44.
[3] F.O./84/1810/ Petre to Granville, March 23, 1884, Africa, 23 : F.O. to Petre, April 8, 1884, Africa, 30 : Petre to Granville, April 17, 1884, Africa, 30 : April 25, 1884, Africa, 33 : Memo., Lord E. Fitzmaurice, May 2, 1884 : Granville to Petre, April 29, 1884, Africa, 38.
[4] Ibid. cf. especially F.O. to Petre, April 8, 1884, Africa, 30 : Petre to Granville, April 25, 1884, Africa, 33 (Comment, Anderson) : Granville to Petre, April 29, 1884, Africa, 38.
[5] Ibid.—as above. Note 2.
[6] cf. F.O./84/1810/ Petre to Granville, March 27, 1884, Africa, 24.
[7] cf. Chapter i, p. 20.
[8] F.O./84/1810/ Fitzmaurice to Granville, April 23, 1884.

tary for Foreign Affairs, wrote to Lord Granville, declaring that there was grave danger of the government being beaten in parliament over the treaty. He advised playing for time, therefore, informing parliament that negotiations were still pending with Portugal over the Mozambique tariff and the Dual Commission, and urging upon them that it would be better for the government to postpone asking their opinion on the treaty until it could inform them more fully on the subject. This it would be in a position to do after it had communicated with the other interested powers and ascertained their probable course of action. There is no doubt that it was the almost universal opposition to the treaty *abroad*[1] which caused Fitzmaurice to take so grave a view. It is true that the treaty[2] had never been popular in England, chiefly for the same reason as in other countries, that the danger from France had not been fully realised ; but Fitzmaurice himself later gave it as his opinion[3] that if the political horizon had been otherwise clear there would have been no difficulty in carrying it through on this account.

Almost immediately after he had written to Granville[4] he received a visit from d'Antas, the Portuguese minister in London, who asked him what the prospects were for discussion in the House. Fitzmaurice told him, and then asked him whether he would prefer postponement or defeat. Somewhat disconcertingly, d'Antas replied, the latter, " pour avoir une situation nette." He had always feared, he said, that the present treaty was destined to die "ou de violence ou d'anémie." He himself preferred violence to anæmia. His statement, however, should probably be taken more as an expression of pique, than as a considered opinion, subsequent events showing that the Portuguese were in fact very unwilling to abandon the treaty.

It is true that Fitzmaurice's attitude[5] caused great annoyance at Lisbon. Du Bocage began to threaten that if the House of

[1] Fitzmaurice, *Granville*, II, p. 346.
[2] cf. F.O./84/1809/ Memo. Kennedy, March 11, 1884. F.O./84/1816/ Memo. Holmwood, May 6, 1884. F.O./84/1816/ Richards to Fitzmaurice, Nov. 28, 1884. Fitzmaurice, II, pp. 345–6   Yarnall, p. 20. Keith, p. 53. C. 4023, Nos. 10, 24–46.
[3] Fitzmaurice, II, p. 346.
[4] F.O./84/1810/ Fitzmaurice to Granville, April 23, 1884—additional note.
[5] F.O./84/1810/ Petre to Granville, April 25, 1884, Africa, 33.

BREAKDOWN OF ANGLO-PORTUGUESE TREATY 27

Commons did not ratify, the Cortes would not ratify, and that if the Cortes did not ratify, the non-completion of the treaty might compel Portugal to come to an agreement with France and the Belgian Association, an arrangement, he declared, that would not be advantageous to Portugal, but which she might be obliged to make. But it is clear that these threats were largely bluff. When it came to the point Portugal knew that she stood to gain more from England than from any other power, and this accounts for her acceptance,[1] at the beginning of May, of what would otherwise seem an almost incredible proposition on the part of the British Government,[2] namely, that Portugal should ratify the treaty before the month was out, though Great Britain herself could not do so.

All seemed going well—from the British point of view—when on May 9th,[3] the date fixed for ratification in Portugal, Fitzmaurice himself upset the apple-cart by making a speech in the House of Commons on the need for postponing ratification in England. In this speech he went in great detail into the motives of the government for advocating such a step. The terms of his appeal,[4] which were immediately wired to Lisbon, caused such offence to Du Bocage, that he forthwith adjourned the proposed ratification in the Cortes. The next morning when Petre came to see him, he informed him that as the parliamentary session in Portugal ended on May 17th, it would be impossible to discuss the question again before the new Cortes should meet. This would be early in July, when they could ratify the treaty "should the circumstances then render it expedient to ratify it." On May 25th[5] he informed Petre that the meeting of the new Cortes was further adjourned till November, and with it consequently the discussion of the Congo treaty.

Meanwhile conversations had been proceeding between England and Portugal over the question of modifications in the treaty. On May 2nd,[6] Petre, seeking confirmation for his state-

---
[1] F.O. /84/1811/ Petre to Granville, May 7, 1884, Africa, 42.
[2] Ibid. F.O. to Petre, May 3, 1884, Africa, 40a.
[3] Ibid. Petre to Granville, May 10, 1884, Africa, 44 : May 11, 1884, Africa, 45.
[4] F.O./84/1811/ Petre to Granville, May 11, 1884, Africa, 45.
[5] Ibid. Petre to Granville, May 25, 1884, Africa, 53.
[6] Ibid. Petre to Granville, May 2, 1884 (confidential), Africa, 37.

ments of March 27th,[1] wrote to Granville, declaring that Du Bocage would like to know the views of the British Government as to the admission of France and Holland to the Anglo-Portuguese Commission, the Portuguese Foreign Minister being definitely prepared to make this concession, if Great Britain agreed to it. Granville answered this note on May 10th,[2] officially stating the willingness of the British Government to agree to a commission of delegates. This important modification having been decided on, it now remained to determine what procedure should be adopted for introducing it into the treaty, together with any others which might be considered advisable. Already on the 9th of May,[3] d'Antas had suggested to Granville that Great Britain should open negotiations with the powers about the proposed amendments. Granville agreed to this in principle, promising to consider in what manner it would be best to approach them, but added that there was a certain difficulty about doing so at the moment, because of the attitude of Germany—which had not yet been defined.

This assurance[4] was evidently considered sufficient by the Portuguese for them to inform France that, on their demand, the British Government had consented to modify the treaty, and to take the initiative in negotiating modifications with the powers. But Granville's difficulty with regard to Germany was a real one. His position was this. He knew Germany's attitude to be important, but had, up to this date, received only one rather vague communication from her about the treaty. On April 29th[5] she had made a simple protest against its application to her nationals. This protest[6] was delivered in London on May 1st, by Count Münster, the German Ambassador, Granville stating in reply that modifications in the treaty were being discussed with Portugal, particularly the substitution of an International for an Anglo-Portuguese Commission on the river. On May 5th a *second* German note was addressed to Münster,[7] saying that Granville's statement

[1] cf. above, pp. 24–5.
[2] F.O./84/1811/ Granville to Petre, May 10, 1884, Africa, 44.
[3] F.O./84/1811/ Granville to Petre, May 9, 1884, Africa, 40b.
[4] D.D.F., V, No. 17, Laboulaye to Ferry, May 11, 1884.
[5] W.B., Congo, No. 17, Hatzfeldt to Münster, April 29, 1884.
[6] Ibid., No. 18, Münster to Bismarck, May 1, 1884. F.O./84/1811/ Granville to Ampthill, May 1, 1884, Africa, 3. (C. 4205, No. 1, ibid., as above—same text).
[7] W.B., Congo, No. 23, Hatzfeldt to Münster, May 5, 1884.

BREAKDOWN OF ANGLO-PORTUGUESE TREATY

of May 1st did not make it clear whether he wished to come to a *new* agreement with Portugal, or whether he was going to seek an understanding with the interested powers for *a new treaty basis*. The moment had now come, it was declared, to tell the London Cabinet of the necessity for the latter course. But this note was never delivered by Münster.[1] Consequently Granville remained in the dark as to Germany's attitude to the proposed modifications. Had he known, at the beginning of May, that these were considered inadequate by Bismarck, and that he insisted on a *new* treaty, it seems probable that he would have acceded to the German demand, and dropped the old one altogether. In this case there might never have been a conference, the matter being settled through the ordinary diplomatic channels.

The proposal for one came originally from Portugal, and was made first to Great Britain, who turned it down. But it was taken up and given reality by Bismarck. Granville's note[2] of May 10th agreeing to an International Commission, also asked Du Bocage what his views were as to the form of the intended modifications, and stressed the necessity for the assent of the powers. When Petre communicated this message[3] to Du Bocage on May 11th, the latter proposed a conference as the best means of doing so. But the British Government refused to consider the idea,[4] on the ground that a conference would probably be "wrecked" by France, and on May 28th a note was dispatched to the Portuguese Government in this sense, suggesting that the best course would be to ascertain first whether other powers would be prepared to sit on a mixed commission, then if they were prepared to do so, for Portugal herself to show her willingness to make reasonable concessions concerning tariffs. In this way it was argued, a general agreement might be reached, to which the French Government might assent. Meanwhile, however, Portugal, *behind* Britain's

---

[1] No record either in German White Book or F.O. documents. Indirect evidence from latter that Granville after this date continued to be in complete ignorance of Germany's attitude. cf. Appendix V.
[2] F.O./84/1811/ Granville to Petre, May 10, 1884, Africa, 44. cf. above, p. 28.
[3] F.O./84/1811/ Petre to Granville, May 11, 1884, Africa, 46.
[4] Ibid. cf. Minutes by Fitzmaurice, Granville, Anderson. Memo., H. P. Anderson. May 23, 1884, Granville to Petre, May 28, 1884.

back,[1] had, on May 13th, addressed a circular to the powers proposing a conference. The proposal was immediately taken up by Bismarck,[2] after he had sounded France as to whether he could count on her support if it were held, and had received a favourable reply. The reason[3] he gave for doing so was that if Portugal were allowed to summon a conference, the initiative would pass from her hands to those of England. Portugal, in other words, might propose, it was important that Germany should dispose.

The extent to which the proposal became almost immediately " de alma " German, if originally " de iure " Portuguese, is made very clear by the attitude adopted by Portugal in her conversations with England between the date of the proposal (May 13th) and its publication to the world at large, in the middle of June. (After the delivery of the German note[4] of June 7th on June 14th.)

On May 28th,[5] the very day on which the British Government replied to the Portuguese proposal of the 11th, Du Bocage,[6] impatient at their delay, asked Petre whether he was not yet in a position to give him information on the precise course which Great Britain intended to adopt in obtaining the assent of the powers to the treaty. " What ", he asked again, " did Granville think about the conference idea?" He, Du Bocage, was anxiously waiting to know his opinion. But he was " by no means wedded to the idea " if Granville saw any objection to it. He had merely thrown it out as a suggestion. On June 5th,[7] when d'Antas, in accordance with the instructions from Du Bocage, again complained on behalf of the Portuguese Government of Granville's non-fulfilment of his promise to

[1] Thomson, pp. 201–3. Accounts and Papers, LV, 1884–5 : C. 4361. Protocols and General Act of Conference : Protocol II. F.O./84/1811/ Bismarck to Münster, June 7, 1884 (C. 4205, No. 2). F.O./84/1812/ Petre to Granville, June 29, 1884, Africa, 75 : Ampthill to Granville, July 25, 1884, Africa, 8 (C. 4205, No. 7). cf. Keltic, p. 208. Keith, p. 55. Reeves, p. 64. Yarnall, p. 41. W.B., Congo, No. 24, Bülow to Bismarck, May 29, 1884. D.D.F., V, No. 275, Courcel to Ferry, May 22, 1884. cf. Appendix VI.
[2] Thomson, p. 202. cf. also C. 4205, No. 5, Lyons to Granville, July 16, No. 1884.
[3] Thomson, p. 201.
[4] W.B., Congo, No. 2, Bismarck to Münster, June 7, 1884. F.O./84/1811/ Bismarck to Münster, June 7, 1884 (C. 4205, No. 2).
[5] F.O./84/1811/ Granville to Petre, May 28, 1884, Africa, 52.
[6] Ibid. Petre to Granville, May 28, 1884, Africa, 55.
[7] Ibid. Bocage to d'Antas, May 29, 1884 (communicated June 5 to Granville).

BREAKDOWN OF ANGLO-PORTUGUESE TREATY

open negotiations with the powers, he again posed the question, should the problem be solved by separate negotiations or by a conference, and again made it clear, that although the second mode of procedure seemed the most natural and the most expeditious to the Portuguese, they would not hesitate to follow the first if Lord Granville in his "haute sagesse" should think it better. On June 14th,[1] when Du Bocage had at last, after a somewhat unaccountable delay,[2] received the British note of May 28th turning down the Portuguese proposal for a conference, he repeated what he had said earlier,[3] namely, that he was not "wedded to the idea," whilst he admitted that the difficulties which the two Governments had to contend with might equally well be met in another way.

There is thus some ground for thinking that the Portuguese proposal of the 13th was originally a more tentative one than the course of events allowed it to become. Otherwise, why was Du Bocage prepared to waive it in face of opposition from England? It is clear that he still attached more value to an understanding with *her*, than to one with any other power, and that it did not occur to him that he had compromised himself in any way by his statements of the 13th. On the other hand, he certainly *did* propose a conference to the powers on that date. It is difficult to read logic into his attitude. Perhaps this would be the greatest mistake of all. He represented, in Portugal, a weak power, rather blindly striking out wherever she could to obtain what she wanted from others stronger than herself. This may explain why her thrusts were often at random.

The comments of the British Foreign Office on the repeated complaints made by Portugal of their delay in opening negotiations with the powers were always the same. Nothing could be done, until it was known what was the attitude of Germany. On the flyleaf of Portugal's original proposal for a conference[4] Granville scribbled—"I should consult Germany first as to what she wishes." Indeed, it is evident, that just as Bismarck's irritation must have been increased by the fact that his note of

[1] Ibid. Petre to Granville, June 16, 1884, Africa, 62.
[2] Ibid. cf. also Petre to Granville, June 6, 1884, Africa, 59.
[3] Ibid. Petre to Granville, June 16, 1884, Africa, 62.
[4] F.O./84/1811/ Petre to Granville, May 11, 1884, Africa, 46. Minute, Granville.

May 5th had received no answer, so the effect of its non-delivery on the British Foreign Minister was greatly to augment the latter's perplexities. On May 26th,[1] still hearing nothing from Berlin, Granville finally addressed an inquiry to Bismarck asking whether Germany would co-operate with the powers in appointing a delegate to an International Commission, and whether she would support the treaty with this important modification, together with a guarantee that the *absolute* value of the Mozambique tariff should not exceed 10 per cent *ad valorem* on all articles except tobacco, brandy, guns, and gunpowder. Everything now hung for Granville on the answer to this note. Against Petre's report of his conversation of May 28th[2] with Du Bocage he wrote simply—" We must wait for the German Government's answer before considering any course of action." When d'Antas again pressed him on June 5th,[3] to open negotiations with the powers, Anderson, the head of the African department, this time anticipated him in his minute—" Wait for an answer from Berlin."

But the German reply to the British inquiry of May 26th was the note of June 7th[4] refusing to recognise the treaty in any form. It also sprung the news of Portugal's proposal for a conference to Germany upon the astonished Granville, and announced Germany's willingness to participate in it if other powers concurred. Granville made no attempt to oppose this decision. On the afternoon of June 20th,[5] when d'Antas called to see him, he showed him Bismarck's dispatch, saying that it appeared to him to put an end to the treaty. D'Antas agreed, and Granville wired to Petre the same day, in this sense. On the 23rd[6] he telegraphed to him once more giving him definite instructions to communicate Bismarck's dispatch to Du Bocage and to tell the Portuguese Government that there was now no hope for the treaty as a whole, and that ratification was useless.

[1] F.O./84/1811/ Granville to Ampthill, May 26, 1884, Africa, 5. (C. 4205, No. 1, Granville to Ampthill, May 26, 1884) (full text).
[2] Ibid. Petre to Granville, June 16, 1884, Africa, 62.
[3] Ibid. Bocage to d'Antas, May 29, 1884 (communicated June 5 to Granville). Minute, Granville.
[4] W.B., Congo, No. 2, Bismarck to Münster, June 7, 1884. F.O./84/1811/ Bismarck to Münster, June 7, 1884. (C. 4205, No. 2. Date of delivery not given.) cf. also Keltie, pp. 145-6. Stanley, II, pp. 384-5.
[5] F.O./84/1811/ Granville to Petre, June 20, 1884, Africa, 65.
[6] F.O./84/1812/ Granville to Petre, June 23, 1884, Africa, 67.

BREAKDOWN OF ANGLO-PORTUGUESE TREATY 33

This was done by Petre,[1] who confirmed his action by a written note to Du Bocage on June 28th.[2] Meanwhile June 26th passed,[3] the day finally fixed for ratification in England, without any steps being taken to ratify it. Bismarck's hatchet had indeed carried the " coup de mort " to the treaty. It was now dead—of violence as well as of anæmia. It remained only to complete its obsequies—and to nurture its illegitimate offspring—the Portuguese proposal for a conference.

[1] Ibid. Petre to Granville, June 24, 1884, Africa, 70.
[2] Ibid., Petre to Bocage, June 28, 1884.
[3] W.B., Congo, No. 29, Münster to German F.O., June 26, 1884. Banning, *Mémoires*, p. 5 ; *Partage*, p. 102. Yarnall, p. 21. Koschitzky, p. 233. Gwynn and Tuckwell, *Dilke*, II, p. 84.

CHAPTER III

THE ANGLO-GERMAN ESTRANGEMENT

BEFORE discussing the history of the diplomacy leading up to the conference, it seems necessary to account for the intervention of Germany. It is clear that French opposition to the Anglo-Portuguese treaty was inherent in the circumstances of its origin. But German opposition, which was what finally wrecked it, was due to extraneous causes, German interests on the Congo being of a secondary nature.[1] The question therefore arises—What was it which induced Germany to adopt such a hostile attitude to Great Britain with regard to the treaty, and to co-operate with France in summoning a conference to nullify its results?

The answer to this inquiry must be sought in the Anglo-German estrangement of 1884-5,[2] which was also the background to Germany's acquisition of colonies. It is the tempting, because the easiest solution of the problem, to imagine that a clash between the two countries may have been inevitable: that there may have been some deep-seated and fatally destined antagonism: that as Bismarck was bound to fight Austria in 1866, and France in 1870, in order to achieve the unity of Germany in Europe, so he may equally have been impelled in 1884, to have friction with Britain, the greatest colonial power in the world, when he was embarking Germany, for the first time, on her career as a world power. But this view of the case is not borne out by the facts. There seems indeed no reason why England and Germany should have fallen out over questions whose nature was not such as to warrant the friction they

[1] W.B., Congo, 1884, No. 5, Report of Solingen Chamber of Commerce, April 1, 1884 (English interests admittedly greater than German there). cf. Appendix VI.
[2] cf. M. E. Townsend, *Rise and Fall*, pp. 84–110. Fitzmaurice, II, p. 346. Gooch, *Franco-German Relations, 1871–1914*, p. 21.

THE ANGLO-GERMAN ESTRANGEMENT 35

generated. It is true that a certain amount of commercial rivalry existed between them both in the South Seas[1] and in Africa[2] between 1870 and 1884 : but it was not of a kind to justify an open breach. Some ill-feeling also arose against England in Germany over two South Sea questions—Samoa and Fiji—before 1884. But the one did not figure at all, the other played a manifestly subordinate rôle in the history of the estrangement.

That Samoa did not enter into the Anglo-German quarrel must be attributed chiefly to the presence of important American,[3] as well as British and German interests[4] on the island, although the latter[5] were by far the largest there, and also the most powerful which Germany possessed in the South Seas. When in 1879[6] the Hamburg house of Godeffroy, which had a practical monopoly of them, unexpectedly went bankrupt, and threatened to sell its shares to a British bank, Bismarck himself testified to the value which he set on them, by attempting to come to the rescue with a State subsidy. This was refused him by the Reichstag,[7] but was in fact given privately by another German firm, with the more or less official support of the chancellor.[8] But after the first outburst of publicity,

[1] *C.M.H.*, Vol. XII, Chapter xx. M. E. Townsend, *Origins of Modern German Colonisation*, pp. 39–42, 113–35, 150–1, 161–3 : *Rise and Fall of Germany's Colonial Empire*, pp. 47–50. A. L. Hodge, *Angra Pequena*, pp. 12–13. M. Adams, *The British Attitude to German Colonial Development*, pp. 28–69. G. H. Scholefield, *The Pacific, its Past and the Future, and the Policy of the Great Powers from the Eighteenth Century*, pp. 97–167. Yarnall, pp. 18–19, 25. Sylvia Masterman, *Origins of International Rivalry in Samoa*, pp. 51–198. Fitzmaurice, II, pp. 338–9, 354. Granville Papers, G.D./29/206/, G.D./29/178/.
[2] *C.M.H.*, Vol. XII, Chapters xx, vi. Townsend, *Origins*, pp. 37–9, 163–9 : *Rise and Fall*, pp. 45–7. Hodge, *Angra Pequena*, p. 354. Adams, pp. 28–69, Chapter vi., pp. 83–94, 523–5, 533–6. Holland Rose, *The Development of European Nations, 1870–1900*, pp. 515–18, 523, 525, 533, 536. Aydelotte, *Bismarck and British Colonial Policy*. Evans Lewin, *The Germans and Africa*, pp. 69–97, 131–3. Keltie, pp. 159–71. R. L. Lowell, *The Struggle for South Africa*, pp. 75–107. Stanley, *Congo*, II, pp. 385–6. Gooch, *History of Modern Europe*, pp. 99–113. W.B., *Angra Pequena*. Accounts and Papers, LV, 1884–5 : C.4279. LVI, 1884 : C. 4190. Granville Papers, G.D./29/206/, G.D./29/170.
[3] Masterman, pp. 106–30, 189–92.
[4] Masterman, pp. 45–57. Scholefield, p. 148.
[5] Townsend, *Origins*, pp. 38–49 : *Rise and Fall*, p. 48. Adams, p. 69. Hodge, p. 12. Masterman, pp. 57–9, 155, 162, 179, 189, 196. Scholefield, pp. 97, 99, 148–9.
[6] Townsend, *Origins*, pp. 113–17, 129.; *Rise and Fall*, pp. 72–3. Hodge, p. 12. Masterman, pp. 160–1. Scholefield, p. 100.
[7] Townsend, *Origins*, pp. 128–32: *Rise and Fall*, p. 74. Masterman, p. 161. Scholefield, p. 102.
[8] Townsend, *Origins*, pp. 129, 150: *Rise and Fall*, pp. 76, 145. Masterman, p. 161.

necessarily tinged with anti-English sentiment,[1] attending the introduction of Bismarck's subsidy bill into the Reichstag in 1880, no more was destined to be heard of Samoa,[2] either in the state-rooms or the diplomatic couloirs of Europe for another decade. Events elsewhere show that Bismarck did not care to what lengths he went with England, once he had decided to quarrel with her. But his abstention from any political action in Samoa in 1884, seems evidence, not only that he was *not* prepared to do the same with another power, like the United States, with whom he had *no* quarrel, but also of the deliberate nature of that which he had engaged on with England, with which the existence of important German interests in Samoa obviously had no connection.

The grievances of German settlers in Fiji,[3] who in 1874 had been evicted without compensation from their holdings, as the result of a debt regulation, passed by Great Britain after her annexation of the island, played a certain part in the Anglo-German estrangement of 1884-5. But a study of their history shows it to have been a minor one. It seems doubtful whether their claims[4] were as large as the German Government made out ; and it is at any rate certain that Bismarck manipulated the agitation about them to suit his own purposes,[5] so that thus handled by him it assumes more importance as a by-product of his general colonial policy, than as a contributory factor in the evolution of that policy.

It was in fact not a South Sea, but an African question which caused the rift between England and Germany in 1884, although the relations of the two countries in Africa[6] had hitherto been those of entirely peaceful, though in some places growing

---

[1] cf. Masterman, pp. 190-2. Townsend, *Origins*, pp. 125-6 : *Rise and Fall*, pp. 73-4.
[2] Masterman, pp. 190-2. Gooch, *Modern Europe*, pp. 305-6.
[3] Townsend, *Origins*, pp. 56-8, 64, 62. Langer, pp. 288-9. Yarnall, pp. 18-19. Scholefield, p. 126. Fitzmaurice, pp. 338-9.
[4] G.D./29/206/ Granville to Ampthill, April 23, 1884. G.D./29/178/ Ampthill to Granville, March 15, 1884. *Grosse Politik*, IV, No. 760, p. 103, Herbert Bismarck to Bismarck, May 7, 1885. Fitzmaurice, pp. 338-9. A. J. P. Taylor, *Germany's First Bid for Colonies*, p. 32. Scholefield, p. 126.
[5] Townsend, *Origins*, pp. 79, 160-1. Scholefield, pp. 126-7. Fitzmaurice, pp. 338-9.
[6] cf. Townsend, *Rise and Fall*, pp. 45-7 : *Origins*, p. 160. Keltie, pp. 159-71. Stanley, II, pp. 385-6. Evans Lewin, pp. 69-97, 131-3. Langer, p. 287. C. 4279. C. 4190. W.B., Congo. W.B., *Angra Pequena*.

commercial competition. There were parts of the West coast,[1] like the Cameroons, where German interests had even outstripped older-established British ones, but in spite of this, British and German traders appear to have been on the most friendly terms. The mere fact that German trade could develop in this way side by side with British, and under the ægis of British authorities, shows of course how little it was hampered by them, and how unnecessary it was that there should be any friction between two countries which were both advocates of the principle of free trade—though it was far otherwise with the French.[2] The Germans themselves seemed to have realised[3] this, for the Hamburg Senate in 1883, in reply to an inquiry of Bismarck's as to what measures they would like to be taken for the more effective protection of their commercial interests on the West Coast of Africa, declared that " they had no complaints about districts occupied by the British," though their " traders disliked the treatment they received from the French, especially in the Gaboon."

In any case it was not over the Cameroons, nor any place where keen commercial rivalry existed with England in Africa, nor in fact where it could be said to exist at all, that trouble originated. The Anglo-German estrangement[4] seems to have arisen entirely out of a series of unfortunate, and quite unnecessary misunderstandings connected with Angra Pequena,[5] an insignificant strip of territory on the South-West coast, reputed one of the poorest and most barren in all Africa, whose trifling value was quite out of proportion to the storm of controversy which it raised.

After these misunderstandings had occurred, Bismarck proceeded to seize more valuable booty, the Cameroons,[6] Togo-

---
[1] C. 4279, No. 14, Memo. Hewett, Dec. 17, 1883. Evans Lewin, pp. 131–2.
[2] cf. especially for this G.D./29/269/, F.O./146/ Vol. 2680/ Confidential Prints No. 2680, Memo. June 11, 1883—Anderson.
[3] Adams, pp. 154-5.
[4] cf. Townsend, *Origins*, pp. 165, 169 : *Rise and Fall*, pp. 88–91. Yarnall, pp. 19, 25. Fitzmaurice, p. 346. Thomson, p. 192. *C.M.H.*, Vol. XII, Chapter vi, p. 160. Evans Lewin, p. 146. Keltie, p. 189. Adams, p. 83. Gooch, *Franco-German Relations*, p. 21.
[5] Evans Lewin, pp. 78–9. Adams, pp. 60–2. Keltie, p. 172. Fitzmaurice, II, p. 346. Aydelotte, pp. v–vi, 2.
[6] C. 4279. Townsend, *Rise and Fall*, pp. 98–9. Keltie, pp. 191–2, 198–204. Evans Lewin, pp. 133–5, 137–45. Gooch, *Modern Europe*, p. 106. Fitzmaurice, pp. 339–41, 367–8. Adams, pp. 139, 154–9.

land,[1] part of New Guinea[2] in the South Seas (although Germany had hardly set foot in the island before 1884), and later (whilst the West African Conference was actually sitting), part of future German East Africa.[3] His opposition to the Anglo-Portuguese treaty was an offshoot of the same deliberately anti-English policy, of which these seizures were the result, and the idea of a conference on the Congo (later extended to the Niger and other West African questions), summoned in conjunction with France, was only a further evolution of the same deliberately pursued antagonism to English interests. Its origin, like the other manifestations of his anger against England, can be directly traced to the dispute over Angra Pequena.

Why, it may be asked, should this uninviting and uninteresting piece of territory have aroused passions strong enough to lead to an estrangement between two of the most powerful nations in the world ? Germany's interest[4] in the country may be accounted for by the very attributes which would at first sight appear to belie it ; namely, its poverty and the savage nature of the tribes dwelling there, which by removing it from the sphere of all serious international rivalry, made it virgin soil for political, as well as economic penetration. Her entry into the colonial field, in the nineteenth century, has been compared to that of Schiller's poet into the halls of heaven, when the rest of the world had already been parcelled out by the master of Olympus.

" Ganz spät nachdem die Theilung längst geschehen,
   Naht der Poet, er kam aus weiter Fern,
Ach, da war überall nichts mehr zu sehen,
Und alles hatte seinen Herrn.

Was thun ? spricht Zeus—die Welt ist weggegeben—
   Der Herbst, die Jagd, der Markt, ist nicht mehr mein.

---

[1] Evans Lewin, pp. 136-7. C. 4279. Townsend, *Rise and Fall*, p. 99. Keltie, pp. 200-1. Gooch, *Modern Europe*, p. 106. Fitzmaurice, II, p. 341. Adams, pp. 156-7.

[2] Scholefield, pp. 117-43. Adams, pp. 139, 145, 161-76, 186-7. Fitzmaurice, pp. 338-9. Townsend, *Rise and Fall*, pp. 99-100, 106, 106-8. Gooch, *Modern Europe*, pp. 106-7, 366, 371-4.

[3] Keltie, pp. 226-33. Evans Lewin, pp. 168-76. Townsend, *Rise and Fall*, pp. 99, 105-6, 109, 131-3. Holland Rose, pp. 516-19. Gooch, *Modern Europe*, pp. 109-10.

[4] *C.M.H.*, Vol. XII, Chapter vi. H. Oncken, *The German Empire*, p. 159.

THE ANGLO-GERMAN ESTRANGEMENT 39

"Willst du in meinem Himmel mit mir leben,
So oft du kommst, er soll dir offen sein."[1]

To compensate him for his losses in the earthly sphere, Zeus gave the poet a free pass to heaven, as often as he cared to come. The Germans, after 1870, may be said to have had something like a similar option over those unexploited regions of the earth not already seized upon or regarded as falling under the ægis of other powers. But their choice so limited was in fact very restricted—and far from Elysian. This accounts for its including places like Angra Pequena.

Unfortunately even here it proved impossible to escape altogether the interference of another power. Though not considered of sufficient *commercial* importance[2] to Great Britain to justify the assumption by her of any political authority before 1884, Angra Pequena was yet of enough *strategic* value[3] to her colony at the Cape, to warrant by implication a kind of tacit claim to suzerainty on the part of the Mother Country,[4] which was one of Bismarck's prime sources of irritation[5] against her in that year. Opposed to German *commercial*, therefore, was British *strategic* interest in Angra Pequena.

But this does not in itself explain Anglo-German friction. Angra Pequena did not really matter very much to Great Britain. So little, in fact, did it occupy the attention of her politicians, that in 1884,[6] after all the trouble there had been over it, one of her cabinet ministers still confessed that he did not know where it was! Fundamental misunderstandings arose between the two countries over the whole question, whose immediate cause was accidental, but whose deeper origin must be sought in the British Government's ignorance of the real nature of Bismarck's intentions, the irony of the situation lying

---

[1] Not quoted by Oncken. To be found in any edition of Schiller's works and *Oxford Book of German Verse*, pp. 157-8—"Die Teilung der Erde".
[2] Keltie, pp. 172, 173-8. Fitzmaurice, pp. 346-8. Evans Lewin, pp. 69-88. Hodge, pp. 7-14. Adams, pp. 62-6. Townsend, *Origins*, p. 39.
[3] cf. Aydelotte, pp. 33, 35.
[4] C. 4190, No. 30. W.B., *Angra Pequena*, Nos. 7, 9, 14, 19. Keltie, pp. 185-6. Fitzmaurice, p. 349. Evans Lewin, pp. 92-3. Hodge, p. 28. Lovell, p. 84. Adams, p. 89. Townsend, *Rise and Fall*, p. 90. Wienefeld, pp. 137-8. Aydelotte, p. 36.
[5] *Grosse Politik*, Vol. IV, No. 743, Bismarck to Münster, June 1, 1884, p. 61. Evans Lewin, p. 97. Wienefeld, p. 138. Aydelotte, p. 36.
[6] Ibid., No. 747, Herbert Bismarck to Bismarck, June 22, 1884, p. 74. (The Minister was Harcourt.)

40 THE BERLIN WEST AFRICAN CONFERENCE

in the fact that Bismarck himself was not too sure of them, that he made up his mind to events, as they went along, and that they assumed an anti-English character largely as a result of this ignorance.

At the beginning of 1883,[1] he addressed a demand to the British Government for *British* protection of a *German* settlement made by a certain Herr Lüderitz at Angra Pequena Bay. Only in the event of a refusal did he not claim, but merely "reserve to himself the right" to take it under German protection. The British Government, therefore, had not the slightest suspicion that he ever contemplated such a step. Nor in fact is there any evidence that he originally did so. He lost patience because, after a formal and elaborate repetition of his demand,[2] in December 1883, the British Government kept him waiting six and a half months for an answer,[3] whilst in the meantime making vague and irritating assertions about their own still unsubstantiated claims to the whole district.[4] This infuriated Bismarck, who meanwhile decided to do what he quite clearly had not intended earlier—namely, annex it himself.

The reason for the British delay[5] was a genuine difficulty with the Cape. The authorities there were willing enough for annexation, but wanted Great Britain to defray the costs. But this was impossible. The situation was further complicated[6] by a change of ministry at Cape Town, in the spring of 1884, which tied the ministers hand and foot, till the elections were over. It was not till the end of May[7] that the newly formed

---

[1] W.B., *Angra Pequena*, No. 2, Hatzfeldt to Herbert Bismarck, Feb. 4, 1883. Keltie, pp. 179-80. Evans Lewin, p. 88. Fitzmaurice, p. 348. Hodge, p. 16. Lovell, pp. 81-2. Townsend, *Origins*, pp. 165-6: *Rise and Fall*, p. 88. Adams, p. 85. Langer, p. 292. Aydelotte, pp. 28-30, 31. cf. Appendix VIII.

[2] C. 4190, No. 38, F.O. to C.O., Jan. 19, 1884 (Enclosure, Münster to Granville, Dec. 31, 1884). W.B., *Angra Pequena*, No. 8, Busch to Münster, Dec. 27, 1883. Keltie, p. 185. Fitzmaurice, p. 349. Evans Lewin, pp. 92-3. Aydelotte, p. 37. Hodge, p. 20. Adams, p. 88. Lovell, pp. 84-5. Townsend, *Rise and Fall*, p. 90.

[3] W.B., *Angra Pequena*, No. 22. C. 4190, No. 55. cf. Aydelotte, pp. 37, 38.

[4] W.B., *Angra Pequena*, Nos. 9, 14, 19. Keltie, pp. 185-6. Fitzmaurice, p. 349. Evans Lewin, pp. 92-3. Hodge, p. 28. Lovell, pp. 84-6. Adams, p. 89. Aydelotte, pp. 64-6. cf. below, pp. 50-1, 56-7.

[5] C. 4190, Nos. 45, 54. Keltie, p. 175. Aydelotte, pp. 49-50.

[6] W.B., *Angra Pequena*, No. 14, Münster to Bismarck, May 17, 1884. Evans Lewin, p. 93. Hodge, p. 35. Adams, pp. 97-8. Wienefeld, p. 138.

[7] Evans Lewin, pp. 93-4. Hodge, p. 40. Lovell, p. 92. Adams, p. 101. Wienefeld, p. 138. Aydelotte, p. 74.

THE ANGLO-GERMAN ESTRANGEMENT

cabinet was able to wire its decision to London, not only to undertake control of the whole coast-line, from the Orange River to Walfisch Bay, but to pay for it. But it was now too late. Bismarck had meanwhile taken action. On March 14th, 1884,[1] he had already granted " Reichsschütz " to Lüderitz, and on April 24th,[2] he sent a telegram to the German consul at Cape Town, declaring all German establishments north of the Orange River to be under the official protection of the German Government. The British Government were informed of his decision,[3] but completely failed to grasp its significance,[4] partly because of the ambiguous wording of the message which reached them, partly because Bismarck, *at the same time*, continued to press through Count Münster, his ambassador in London, for an answer to his *original* inquiry as to whether *they* would be prepared to undertake annexation. Münster himself did not understand the decision and belittled its importance ; whilst Lord Ampthill, the British Ambassador at Berlin, further fortified the British illusion by continually harping at this time on repeated assurances[5] made by Bismarck to *him*, to the effect that he did not want and never would want colonies for Germany.

It is impossible to exonerate Bismarck from the charge of a certain duplicity in the whole affair,[6] as well as with regard to colonial questions generally,[7] a duplicity which can only be fully understood in relation to the German colonial movement

[1] Hodge, pp. 35–6.
[2] W.B., *Angra Pequena*, No. 12, Bismarck to Lippert, April 24, 1884. Hodge, p. 36. Adams, p. 96. Keltie, p. 197. Fitzmaurice, p. 350. Evans Lewin, p. 94. Townsend, *Origins*, p. 169 : *Rise and Fall*, pp. 62, 91. Adams, p. 96. Aydelotte, pp. 54–5. cf. Appendix IX.
[3] C. 4190, No. 43. F.O. to C.O., April 25, 1884 : No. 50, Sir H. Robinson to Derby, April 29, 1884. W.B., *Angra Pequena*, No. 13, Bismarck to Münster, April 24, 1884. Adams, pp. 96–7. Lovell, pp. 93–4. Aydelotte, p. 55. cf. Appendix IX.
[4] C. 4190, No. 43, F.O. to C.O., April 25, 1884 : No. 51, F.O. to C.O., May 22, 1884 : No. 50, Robinson to Derby, April 29, 1884 : No. 53, F.O. to C.O., May 29, 1884 : No. 55, F.O. to C.O., June 2, 1884 : W.B., *Angra Pequena*, Nos. 14, 16, 19, 20, 23, Münster to German F.O. (May 17, 21, 26, 27 ; June 7). Aydelotte, pp. 29, 55, 59–60, 64–70, 73–4, 80–3 (June 7, 1884). Lovell, p. 94. Adams, pp. 97–101. Keltie, pp. 187–8. cf. Appendix IX.
[5] G.D./29/178/ Ampthill to Granville, March 15, May 31, June 7–14, 28, 1884. C. 4190, No. 58, F.O. to C.O., June 10, 1884 (Enclosure, Ampthill to Granville, May 30, 1884). Adams, pp. 100, 103, 93, 33. Lovell, p. 105. Aydelotte, pp. 41–3, 76–7.
[6] cf. Townsend, *Rise and Fall*, pp. 88–9.
[7] Townsend, *Origins*, pp. 128–31, 151–64. Aydelotte, pp. 28–30, 31, 128–9, 133–4.

as a whole, and to his own attitude to it. The characteristics of this movement[1] were an interest in colonial matters, not only out of proportion to their existing value, but one more artificially stimulated at home than fostered locally by natural growth; an exaggerated sense of national prestige; a prolific use of the most up-to-date methods of political propaganda, and an intense self-consciousness. They are to be explained chiefly by the fact that in Germany in the nineteenth century, in contrast to England and France in the eighteenth, when these two powers first embarked on their colonial careers, her industrial[2] *preceded* instead of *following* her commercial revolution. New markets did not cause an improvement in industrial technique, it was an improvement in industrial technique which caused a demand for new markets. The will to overseas expansion did not produce, it was itself produced by, an increase in industrial output. They are characteristics to be found in an even more extreme form to-day in modern Germany, in Italy, and in Japan. But they made their first somewhat startling appearance in world history at this time.

Of course Germany was not the only power in 1884 to feel the need for markets. But it was precisely because this need was shared by others, including the older colonising powers of France and England, who still forged ahead, that her own was so acute. Her rise to power synchronised with the advent of that new " economic imperialism "[3] of the last quarter of the nineteenth century, of which her own was a peculiar and an exaggerated example. In the commercial competition which ensued, a new-comer like herself, with no colonial traditions, and no jumping-off ground for her ambitions, was naturally handicapped. So great was the gap between these ambitions, and what seemed the possibility of their realisation, that it had to be filled in by a deliberate cult of the colonial spirit, one whose self-consciousness was necessarily in direct proportion to the very limitations which had called it into being, more particularly to the fact that it was not always possible to point to the economic advantages of political colonisation in the

---

[1] Townsend, *Origins*, pp. 85–112, 136–51 : *Rise and Fall*, pp. 77–84, 68–9.
[2] cf. Townsend, *Origins*, pp. 15–16 : *Rise and Fall*, pp. 176–7.
[3] cf. Townsend, *Rise and Fall*, pp. 177–8. Lovell, pp. 75–8. Aydelotte, p. v.

THE ANGLO-GERMAN ESTRANGEMENT 43

only places where it was practicable. This accounts for the element of artificiality in the movement,[1] which expressed itself in an almost feverish desire to have colonies, anyhow, anywhere, and at any price, not always with regard for their actual value, as in Angra Pequena, nor for the nature of previously existing German interests.

It was an element which became very marked after 1880. Growing unity at home,[2] the end of the Kulturkampf,[3] the introduction of the protective tariff in 1879,[4] which by the favourable stimulus which it gave to German trade, enormously increased the already existing volume of over-production, all combined to encourage colonial activities at this time. Bismarck himself gave evidence of his sympathy with them,[5] by his attempt to pass the Samoan Subsidy Bill in 1880. But the Bill failed: and its failure had important repercussions on the colonial movement.[6] In the first place, it greatly increased, after a temporary setback, the activities of the colonial party in Germany, as well as the already existing tendency towards a more highly centralised as well as artificially stimulated interest in colonial affairs. Secondly, it drove Bismarck into an equivocal position with regard to it. There is no doubt that the failure of the Bill was a great disappointment to him. He had counted on a far larger measure of support than he had actually obtained. Having tested public opinion on what he considered an important colonial issue, and found it wanting, he was henceforward almost morbidly chary of giving it his confidence, and began to play a double game of secretly supporting, but publicly repudiating colonial enterprises.

This is illustrated by his subsequent action over Samoa[7]; by his cordial relations with the "Kolonialverein" (founded in 1882)[8]; and by his increasingly friendly attitude towards

[1] cf. Townsend, *Rise and Fall*, p. 55. A. J. P. Taylor, *Germany's First Bid for Colonies*, p. 4.
[2] Townsend, *Origins*, p. 79: *Rise and Fall*, pp. 77, 72, 95–6. Adams, pp. 37–9.
[3] Townsend, *Origins*, pp. 79, 100: *Rise and Fall*, p. 72. Thomson, p. 190.
[4] Townsend, *Origins*, p. 75: *Rise and Fall*, pp. 72, 84–5. Wienefeld, p. 136. Fitzmaurice, p. 347. Yarnall, p. 17. Adams, p. 39. Thomson, p. 100. Aydelotte, p. 21.
[5] cf. above, p. 35.
[6] Townsend, *Origins*, pp. 131–64: *Rise and Fall*, pp. 75–6, 81–4.
[7] Townsend, *Origins*, pp. 129, 150: *Rise and Fall*, pp. 76, 145. Masterman, p. 161. cf. above, pp. 35–6.
[8] Townsend, *Origins*, pp. 152–4. Scholefield, p. 119.

German merchants overseas,[1] of which his support of Lüderitz's enterprise in 1883, was only a further example.[2] Yet all the time he continued to make public and private assurances to the effect that he did not want, and never would want colonies for Germany.[3]

The exact nature of his insincerity is difficult to determine, because there is no doubt that he partly succeeded in deceiving himself. That he played a double game in his relations with the colonial party after 1880, cannot be disputed. But all the evidence goes to show that he made up his mind slowly,[4] through successive stages of determination in detail, to a colonial policy, and the extent to which he himself gauged that he had committed himself at each successive step which he took in favouring commercial projects, was probably not clearly thought out. Habit is also a powerful regulator, and for years[5] he had been officially stating that he would not countenance a colonial policy for Germany. This may also help to explain[6] why right through the Angra Pequena negotiations, when he was actually embarking his country on such a policy, as well as during the first half of his colonial campaign of 1884–5, he continued to make public and private assurances to this effect. A certain confusion[7] also existed in his mind about the meaning of the terms " colonies ", " colonial policy ", " colonial government ", and " colonial protection " which he

---

[1] Townsend, *Origins*, pp. 154–8.
[2] Townsend, *Origins*, pp. 165–6 : *Rise and Fall*, pp. 75–7, 86–7.
[3] C. 4190, No. 58, No. 3, No. 12, Townsend, *Origins*, pp. 130–1, 155, 156, 160 : *Rise and Fall*, pp. 60–1,. 76–7. G.D./29/178/ Ampthill to Granville, March 15, May 31, June 7, 1884. Adams, pp. 28, 33, 93–4, 100, 103. Evans Lewin, pp. 86–7, 91. Fitzmaurice, II, p. 348. Aydelotte, pp. 19–20.
[4] C. 4190, cf. Nos. 15, 29, 58. W.B., *Angra Pequena*, cf. Nos. 2, 5, 8, 12, 13, 22. Hodge, p. 41. Townsend, *Origins*, pp. 151–69 : *Rise and Fall*, pp. 62–7, 88–91. Fitzmaurice, II, pp. 347–8. Adams, pp. 28–39. Aydelotte, pp. 19–20, 21–2. Lovell, pp. 77–8, 80.
[5] C. 4190, No. 3, F.O. to C.O., Sept. 22, 1880 (Enclosure, Russell to Granville, Sept. 18, 1880). No. 12, F.O. to C.O., Sept. 6, 1883 (Enclosure, Walsham to Granville, Aug. 31, 1883). Evans Lewin, pp. 86–7. Adams, pp. 28, 29, 30–31. Townsend, *Origins*, pp. 47–8, 17 : *Rise and Fall*, pp. 60–1. Aydelotte, pp. 18–20. Fitzmaurice, II, p. 337.
[6] G.D./29/178/ Ampthill to Granville, March 15, May 31, June 7, 14, 25, 1884. Lovell, p. 76. Townsend, *Rise and Fall*, p. 77. Adams, pp. 33–7, 93–4. C. 4190, No. 88, F.O. to C.O., June 10, 1884 (Enclosure, Ampthill to Granville, May 30, 1884), pp. 100, 103. Aydelotte, p. 20.
[7] cf. *Grosse Politik*, IV, No. 743, Bismarck to Münster, June 2, 1884, pp. 60 and 61. cf. also No. 745, Herbert Bismarck to Bismarck, June 16, 1884, p. 67. No. 744, Münster to Bismarck, June 7, 1884—Bismarck's Marginal Comments, p. 64, 4—" Was ist Colonialpolitik ? wir müssen unsere Landsleute schützen."

THE ANGLO-GERMAN ESTRANGEMENT 45

used so glibly, which corresponded to a genuine ignorance of the realities which they represented. But behind this lay a real duplicity: a duplicity which played an important part in German politics between 1880 and 1884: which grew with time: and which, in the quarrel with England, undoubtedly assumed on occasions the character of deliberate deception; though here again, owing to the fact that it was persistently dogged by the chancellor's own verbal confusions, it is not always easy to determine when exactly this was the case, and when it was not.[1]

As a personal question his deception is a psychological problem which is probably not capable of definite solution. But there is no doubt about its effect on others. To it more than to any other fundamental cause, must be traced the origin of the misunderstanding with England, and the explanation why not only the British ambassador at Berlin, and the British Government, on their own account, but also his own ambassador in London, failed to understand the trend of his policy, thus hopelessly aggravating the ignorance under which the British Government laboured as to his real intentions. Much has been made of Münster's failure to communicate messages[2] with which he was entrusted by the chancellor, and his slowness in grasping Bismarck's policy was undoubtedly an aggravating factor in the situation. But a close study of the question shows that Bismarck's responsibility for this was *greater*, Münster's *smaller*, than is usually supposed.

When it is remembered that the chancellor's ambiguous attitude[3] towards colonial questions grew *simultaneously* with the strength of the colonial party in Germany after 1880, and the susceptibility of the public to the colonial propaganda by which the party so largely manifested its energies, and when it is seen what a remarkable opportuntty was provided for the manifestation of these energies by the Angra Pequena incident, then it becomes apparent in what way chance played upon the forces of destiny in the crisis of 1884. The state of German

---

[1] cf. Aydelotte, pp. 59, 73, 83, 128.
[2] Fitzmaurice, II, pp. 428–9, 501. Langer, pp. 294–5. Adams, pp. 104–30. Lovell, p. 51. Dugdale, *German Diplomatic Documents*, Vol. I, Preface, Sir R. Rodd, p. vii. Thomson, pp. 193–4. Yarnall, pp. 27–8. Townsend, *Rise and Fall*, p. 103.
[3] Townsend, *Origins*, pp. 136–69: *Rise and Fall*, pp. 75–91.

46 THE BERLIN WEST AFRICAN CONFERENCE

public opinion, at that time, rendered it peculiarly sensitive to able colonial propaganda, and Great Britain, by her delay over Angra Pequena, unexpectedly provided Bismarck with a whipping-post for this propaganda, which, he saw, would give him just the security at home which he needed for a policy of expansion overseas—a security made all the more desirable by the prospect of the coming elections[1] in the autumn of that year.

In so doing there is no doubt that Great Britain fortuitously coloured the tone, as well as forced the pace of what might otherwise have been a far more gradual, certainly a less anti-English development of the German colonial movement. Her difficulties with the Cape, themselves due to an accident, provided Bismarck with a unique opportunity, too fleeting to ponder, too tempting to resist, for furthering the colonial destinies of his country. Like the good opportunist which he was, he therefore promptly seized it, although no evidence exists, before the spring of 1884, of his desire for a quarrel with England. On the contrary, every feature of his policy up to this time reflects a strong wish to be on good terms with her.

Though the international situation, particularly in Egypt,[2] was such as to facilitate the adoption of an anti-English policy by him, should he wish to embark on one, it was not necessarily such as to *cause* it, and there is no sign before 1884 of Bismarck's wishing to embark on such a policy, in spite of Great Britain's embarrassments in Egypt and his own predominant position on the Continent. By a curious concatenation of circumstances,[3] Britain was indeed in a weaker, Germany probably in a stronger, position at this period than at any time before or after in the nineteenth century. As a result of fourteen previous years of amazingly skilful diplomacy, all

---

[1] cf. *Grosse Politik*, IV, No. 743, Bismarck to Münster, June 1, 1884. No. 752, Herbert Bismarck to Granville, Aug. 30, 1884. No. 758, Bismarck to Münster, Jan. 25, 1885, p. 96. G.D./29/178/ Ampthill to Granville, March 25, June 7, 28, Aug. 16, 1884. Fitzmaurice, II, pp. 339, 355, 359, 361. Adams, pp. 35-7. Aydelotte, pp. 25-6.

[2] Grant and Temperley, *Europe in the Nineteenth Century*, pp. 401-2. C.M.H., Vol. XII, Chapter xv, pp. 434-7. Gooch, *Modern Europe*, pp. 73-98. Wienefeld, pp. 97-127. Adams, pp 23-7. Yarnall, p. 31. Langer, pp. 281-3, 298.

[3] cf. Townsend, *Rise and Fall*, pp. 84-6. Adams, pp. 39-41. Thomson, p. 191. Langer, pp. 293, 297. Aydelotte, pp. 27, 132-3. Yarnall, p. 17.

THE ANGLO-GERMAN ESTRANGEMENT 47

the great powers of Europe were now like so many satellites revolving in the diplomatic field, round one focal centre of gravity—Bismarck. Bound to him by the Dreikaiserbund and the Triple Alliance, Austria, Russia, and Italy may be said to have been on an inner ring of this rotating Bündnissystem, France and England, with whom he had no commitments, on an outer. Since 1877[1] Bismarck had persistently pursued a policy of supporting France in her colonial enterprises in Africa, in order to turn her eyes from the " blue line of the Vosges ". It could not be said that there was an entente between the two countries, but there was certainly a friendly understanding on this basis. With England there was no definite understanding;[2] but up to 1884[3] he continued to support her in Egypt, as a kind of makeweight, so it seemed, to his support of France in other parts of North Africa. It may be questioned whether France in 1884 stood in a potentially closer relationship to Germany than England. On the one hand, a more active understanding certainly existed between France and Germany, than between England and Germany, Anglo-Russian tension[4] being a strong deterrent to any close Anglo-German *rapprochement*. On the other must be set the balance of nationalist and patriotic sentiment in France, and the legacies of 1870, rendering any permanent understanding of a close nature with Germany improbable. The odds were about even.

There was no antithesis either for Bismarck between Franco-German and Anglo-German friendship. Indeed, it was largely on account of his understanding with France[5] that he showed himself so anxious to cultivate friendly relations with England,

[1] J. Bainville, Bismarck et la France d'Après les Mémoires du Prince Hohenlohe. Gooch, *Franco-German Relations*, pp. 15–21. Bourgeois et Pagès *Origines et Responsabilités de la Grande Guerre*, Part II, pp. 174, 203–4; Part IV, Nos. 6–8. E. Daudet, *La France et l'Allemagne Après le Congrès de Berlin*. Langer, pp. 297–8, 317–18. *Grosse Politik*, III, pp. 381–409. Yarnall, pp. 14–16. Thomson, p. 191. Townsend, *Rise and Fall*, p. 85. Wienefeld, *Franco-German Relations, 1871–85*, pp. 41–96. D.D.F., II, Sections I, IV. D.D.F., III, Sections III, IV. D.D.F., IV, Sections I, IV.
[2] cf. Adams, pp. 1–7.
[3] G.D./29/22/ Odo Russell to Granville, Sept. 12, 1882 (Enclosure, Bismarck to Crown Prince, Sept. 7, 1882, on Anglo-German Relations). G.D./29/206/ Granville to Ampthill, Nov. 16, 1881. G.D./29/178/ Ampthill to Granville, Feb. 9, 1884. Ampthill to Granville, Jan. 14, 20, 21, 1882. Grant and Temperley, pp. 401–2. *C.M.H.*, Vol. XII, Chapter xv, pp. 436–7. Aydelotte, p. 1.
[4] cf. Adams, pp. 4–8.
[5] cf. Adams, pp. 40, 24. Wienefeld, p. 114.

believing that if France, assured as she was of German cooperation in the colonial field, saw no reason to fear English hostility, she would have no incentive to form the coalition, which of all coalitions he most dreaded—one with Russia—Anglo-German friendship being the best bridge for her to this feeling of security. It was to his advantage, therefore, not only to cultivate the goodwill of the two countries on their own account, but to reconcile their interests wherever they conflicted, and this was an additional reason for his support of England in Egypt after 1882, when her military occupation caused difficulties for her with France. He knew that he could win the goodwill of France by other means, but the help which he could afford England in Egypt was as unique for him as it was invaluable for her. Up to the middle of 1884[1] therefore, he showed himself in every way willing to give it, as well as to do his utmost to bring about a *rapprochement* between England and France.[2]

That he then suddenly reversed his policy must be attributed not to any feature of the international situation, but solely to the misunderstandings which had arisen between him and England over Angra Pequena, leading to further ones concerning his colonial policy as a whole. These misunderstandings brought into play certain features of the German colonial movement, which were inherent in the nature of its growth—an exaggerated interest in any colonial enterprise that offered possibilities of political development, no matter what its real value; an intense susceptibility to colonial propaganda, easily ending itself to diversion against a foreign power; and last but not least Bismarck's own equivocal attitude towards the movement which made his words and his deeds so difficult to reconcile and therefore so mysterious to all around him.

But the immediate cause of the misunderstandings was accidental. They need never have arisen, in the first place, had not Great Britain given Bismarck a unique chance of

---

[1] Gooch, p. 85. Grant and Temperley, p. 402. Thomson, p. 192. Wienefeld pp. 120, 123. G.D./29/22/ Russell to Granville, Sept. 12, 1882. G.D./29/206/ Granville to Ampthill, Nov. 16, 1881. G.D./29/178/ Ampthill to Granville, Feb. 9, 1884.
[2] cf. G.D./29/178/ Ampthill to Granville, Jan. 20, 1882, Jan. 21, 1882. Wienefeld, pp. 120–1.

THE ANGLO-GERMAN ESTRANGEMENT 49

prematurely beating up colonial opinion in his country by their seven months' delay in answering his simple inquiry about Angra Pequena. In this delay the procrastinating tendencies of the British ministers and the naturally difficult nature of their constitutional relations with the Cape played a certain part, but it was aggravated beyond repair by the unfortunate and entirely fortuitous change of ministry in South Africa.

The subsequent estrangement bears the hall-mark of its origin. Riddled as this was with misunderstandings on both sides it inevitably led to tension based on false suppositions. The Franco-German entente, which was a result of this estrangement, necessarily shares its characteristics. It was this entente which was responsible for the Berlin West African Conference, whose conception will now be traced side by side with that of the widening breach between England and Germany, and whose history will be found to be a further illustration of the fundamental illusions on which it was based.

CHAPTER IV

WIDENING OF THE ESTRANGEMENT—ORIGIN OF THE FRANCO-GERMAN ENTENTE (APRIL–JUNE 1884)

APRIL 24th,[1] the day on which Bismarck telegraphed his decision to Cape Town to annex Herr Lüderitz's settlement at Angra Pequena Bay, has been called " the birthday of the German Colonial Empire ". The title is merited—with one qualification—strictly speaking it had two birthdays, one formal and one informal. On March 14th[2] Bismarck had already privately but officially granted " Reichsschütz " to Lüderitz, whilst intimately connected both with his private as well as with his later public announcement of his intention to do so, must be set a series of events, ranging from the middle of March to the end of April 1884, showing that he had now made up his mind to a colonial policy for Germany. These events clearly have their origin in the same source, namely, his irritation over Angra Pequena. They were : the organisation of an expedition to the West Coast of Africa,[3] under the German explorer, Dr. Nachtigal, concerning whose objects Bismarck deliberately deceived the British Government, in order to obtain their official assistance for them : the renewal[4] of

---

[1] Townsend, *Rise and Fall*, p. 61.
[2] cf. above, p. 41.
N.B.—The early date of Bismarck's encouragement of Lüderitz's schemes in Angra Pequena as well as of the initiation of his other colonial schemes, coupled with the very vague nature of his approaches to France, refutes the argument put forward recently by Mr. Taylor (A. J. P. Taylor, *Germany's First Bid for Colonies*, p. 35) that the Franco-German entente was the cause of the Anglo-German estrangement, instead of the Anglo-German estrangement being the cause of the Franco-German entente.
[3] A. and P., LV, 1884–5 : C. 4279, Nos. 16, 17, 18, 19, 20, 25, 31, 33. G.D./29/178/ Ampthill to Granville, May 31, 1884. Fitzmaurice, II, pp. 340–1. Gooch, p. 106. Evans Lewin, pp. 133–4. Adams, pp. 154–6. Keltie, pp. 199–200. Townsend, *Rise and Fall*, pp. 98–9.
[4] G.D./29/178/ Ampthill to Granville, March 15, 1884. G.D./29/206/ Granville to Ampthill, April 23, 1884. Adams, pp. 93–6. Fitzmaurice, II, pp. 338–9. Aydelotte, pp. 52–3.

WIDENING OF THE ESTRANGEMENT

German protests about the Fiji land claims; Bismarck's first protest against the Anglo-Portuguese treaty;[1] and a preliminary exchange of views with France on the Congo.[2]

Bismarck's position was now this. Owing to his pique about Angra Pequena, he had decided to launch his country on a colonial policy in opposition to English interests. This opposition he was prepared to counter, and for this reason synchronised the tone of his policy as a whole, by going out of his way to oppose England on a matter of secondary importance to him like the Congo treaty. At the same time he was not anxious for an open rupture. That is to say, he was determined to have his way in the colonial controversies which, by the direction of his policy, were now made inevitable with England. But his overtures to France[3] were still quite vague, and there is no doubt that he would have preferred to do this on the basis of a direct understanding with her, in which it should be made clear, without any ill-feeling on either side, that the price of German support for England in Egypt was compliance with Germany's demands in the colonial field—whatever these might be—rather than the more extreme alternative of a *rapprochement* with France.

At the beginning of May he endeavoured to make this clear in a celebrated dispatch[4] of the 5th of that month—which was never delivered. Reference has already been made[5] to the note of May 5th about the Congo treaty, which was also never communicated by Münster to the British Government. Its more famous confrère of the same date was concerned with German policy as a whole, and its non-delivery had an even more disastrous effect on Anglo-German relations. Its history

---

[1] cf. above, p. 28.
[2] W.B., Congo, No. 11, Hatzfeldt to Hohenlohe, April 17, 1884 : No. 12, Hohenlohe to Bismarck, April 24, 1884. L.J., Congo, 1884, No. 20, Courcel to Ferry, April 26, 1884. D.D.F., V, No. 244, Courcel to Ferry, April 22, 1884 : No. 249, Courcel to Ferry, April 26, 1884. Koschitzky, pp. 224–56. Banning, *Partage*, p. 112. Thomson, p. 199. Keith, p. 53. Taylor, pp. 29–31, 35.
[3] cf. W.B., Congo, Nos. 11 and 12, Hatzfeldt to Hohenlohe, April 17, 1884 ; Hohenlohe to Bismarck, April 24, 1884. L.J., Congo, 1884, No. 20, Courcel to Ferry, Aprill 26, 1884. D.D.F., V, No. 233, Courcel to Ferry, April 22, 1884. Koschitzky, pp. 224–56. Banning, *Partage*, p. 112. Thomson, p. 199. Keith, p. 53.
[4] G.P., IV, No. 738, Bismarck to Münster, May 5, 1884.
[5] cf. above, pp. 28–9.

has become so famous, controversy has raged,[1] and still rages round it so unceasingly, that it is difficult even now to discuss it freely without raising a hornet's nest of conflicting opinions. It seems clear, however, that Münster was not to blame entirely for its non-delivery. Bismarck must also take a share of the blame for not expressing himself clearly, this lack of clearness on his part being due to the mixture of confusion, of hesitation, and of secretiveness in his mind regarding colonial questions which has already been commented on.[2]

The dispatch of May 5th is in fact an extraordinarily rambling document. It was the chancellor's first serious attempt to explain the issues of his colonial policy as a whole. Yet he does not once mention by name Angra Pequena,[3] the one colonial question which was at that moment gravely troubling him, and to which he attached most importance, though he harps at great length on what had hitherto been for him, and still was, as far as Münster knew, one of entirely secondary consideration—the Anglo-Portuguese treaty. The dispatch[4] then ambiguously introduces the question of Heligoland in such a way as to make it sound probable that Bismarck considered it the main part of the price to be paid by England for German support in Egypt, though it is clear from his subsequent statements that this was not so. The alternative of a *rapprochement* with France, should England not fulfil his (very vaguely expressed) wishes, was indeed threatened, but not in the sense of a definite entente, as Bismarck affirmed later,[5] but as part of a generally anti-English policy to be adopted by Germany in Egypt, in which her influence over Russia was

---

[1] cf Fitzmaurice, II, pp 351, 361–3, 367, 427, 428–9, 501. Adams, pp. 104–32. Gooch, pp. 104–5. Lovell, pp. 102–7. Langer, 293–6. Aydelotte, pp. 62–3, 70–2. Dugdale. Preface, Rennell Rodd, p. vii. Thomson, pp. 193–4. A. J. P. Taylor, pp. 33–5. A. and P., LIV, 1884–5 : C. 4273, No. 148a, Malet to Granville, Jan. 24, 1885 ; No. 176, Granville to Malet, Feb. 7, 1885. Gooch and Temperley, *British Documents on Origin of War*, Vol. III, Memo. Jan. 1, 1907, E. A. Crowe. E. Thimme, Das Berühmte Schwindel-Dokument, E. A. Crowes (*Berliner Monatshefte*, Sept., 1929, Vol. VII, pp. 874–9). cf. Appendix X.

[2] cf. above, pp. 41–6.

[3] cf. Lovell, p. 102 (who mentions this). cf. also Aydelotte, p. 62—not quite such an emphatic emphasis on this point.

[4] cf. Adams, pp. 105–11. Aydelotte, pp. 62–4. Lovell, pp. 102–4. Thomson, pp. 193–4. Langer, pp. 293–4.

[5] C. 4273, No. 148a, Malet to Granville, Jan. 24, 1885. cf. Appendix X, pp. 213–14.

WIDENING OF THE ESTRANGEMENT

mentioned as being just as important. Last, but not least,[1] it was left to Münster's discretion whether he should deliver the contents of the dispatch to Granville at all, or wait for Count Herbert Bismarck to do so, on a forthcoming visit to London.

Is it surprising in these circumstances that he did not do so? Bismarck's reason for not mentioning Angra Pequena in the dispatch, was probably that carrying on, as he was at that moment, a long correspondence with Münster over the whole question, he took it for granted that the latter would realise the connection, which in fact he did not. But it must be remembered that Münster was in a muddle too[2] (and this more through Bismarck's fault than his own) about Angra Pequena, whose importance he did not realise, and that this was an additional reason for his not understanding Bismarck's drift in the May 5th dispatch. He was instructed " to make complaints about German grievances in the South Seas and ... trade interests in Africa." But the only grievances which Germany had at that moment in the South Seas were the Fiji land claims, and, in Africa (apart from Angra Pequena, which he did not connect with them) the Congo treaty. Münster evidently neglected to make the complaints required of him, because he thought the questions at issue comparatively unimportant—which of course they were—in themselves. The cause of his mistake was precisely his failure to understand that Bismarck's policy with regard to them was an offshoot of his annoyance over Angra Pequena, and the ambitious and provocative attitude over colonial affairs which was its result.

But it cannot be said that Bismarck made the connection very clear. It is of course true that he gave Münster a chance of realising the importance which he was beginning to attach to the Anglo-Portuguese treaty, by the Congo note of May 5th.[3]

---

[1] cf. Adams, pp. 105, 124. (She is the only writer who has noticed this.)
N.B.—This part of the dispatch is very foolishly omitted from Dugdale's translation, cf. pp. 170–1.
[2] cf. above, p. 41. Also Appendices VIII, IX. Also Aydelotte, pp. 80–3. Mr. Aydelotte has very forcibly brought out the ambiguity of the tel. of April 24th and Münster's failure to understand it. But he does not, I think, nor does any other account stress sufficiently the *connection* between Münster's misunderstanding of the tel. of April 24th and his misunderstanding of the May 5th dispatch. But behind one lay the other.
[3] cf. above, pp. 28–9.

But since the main reason for Münster's misunderstanding was his failure to *connect* the questions set out in the May 5th dispatch with the general policy which Bismarck was trying to make him understand, this note did not help matters. On the contrary it aggravated them, not only, as has been seen,[1] by creating a misunderstanding on the subject of the Congo itself, but also by of course increasing Bismarck's irritation over Great Britain's *general* misunderstanding of his colonial aims, wherein the Congo now played a part, caused by the non-delivery of the other more famous May 5th dispatch.

The point which immediately misled Münster here was Heligoland.[2] He thought this was the principal concession demanded of Great Britain in return for Germany's goodwill. The moment seemed favourable to him for asking it, and he accordingly wrote home to Bismarck in this sense.[3] Bismarck immediately wrote back to him on May 11th,[4] expressing himself somewhat less ambiguously than before; though still not mentioning Angra Pequena, and this time also omitting any reference to Egypt. But Münster was now at least told definitely to get on with the matter, without waiting for the arrival of Herbert Bismarck, and was also instructed to make his opening in the form of an offer, not a demand; finally it was definitely stated that Heligoland was of less importance than this offer, which was to be one of German assistance to England in her political affairs, on condition that Germany's grievances in the South Seas and in Africa, inclusive of the Anglo-Portuguese treaty, were satisfied, though, it was added, the cession of Heligoland in this connection would also be considered a token of goodwill on the part of England.

Unfortunately Bismarck's earlier ambiguity still pursued him, fatally blurring the issue. Münster still clung to the idea that Heligoland was of great importance, and the expected epitome of English goodwill, and he accordingly made repre-

---

[1] cf. above, pp. 31–2.
[2] cf. Adams, pp. 106–13, 115. Fitzmaurice, II, pp. 351–61, 363. Lovell, pp. 102–4, 106. Thomson, pp. 193–4. Taylor, pp. 34–5. Aydelotte, p. 63.
[3] G.P., IV, No. 739, Münster to Bismarck, May 8, 1884. cf. also Adams, p. 106. Lovell, p. 103. Thomson, pp. 193–4. Taylor, p. 36. Aydelotte, p. 63.
[4] G.P., IV, No. 740. Bismarck to Münster, May 11, 1884. cf. also Adams, p. 106. Thomson, p. 194. Aydelotte, pp. 63–4.

WIDENING OF THE ESTRANGEMENT

sentations to Granville[1] in this sense, without mentioning any other colonial questions. When Bismarck, whose irritation against England was meanwhile growing steadily, as the accumulated result of his annoyance over her failure to communicate with him over Angra Pequena, the propositions of May 5th, and the Anglo-Portuguese treaty, wrote to Münster on May 25th,[2] telling him to say no more about Heligoland because "it would provide an excuse for making the justice of our African claims subservient to our rights regarding Heligoland," Münster thought this meant a *complete* cancellation of the *whole* of the message of May 5th.[3]

On June 1st Bismarck wrote to him again,[4] *for the first time* treating the Angra Pequena and the May 5th correspondence together,[5] and *for the first time* really clearly stating his views. He explained that it was his annoyance over Angra Pequena which was at the root of his threats about colonial questions, and he now urgently pressed Münster to deliver the messages of May 5th and May 11th, whether he had done so earlier or not. But it was now too late. Almost irretrievable mischief had meanwhile been done by Münster's failure to communicate them.

In the first place, together with the non-delivery of the Congo May 5th dispatch, it seems to have been directly responsible for the Franco-German entente, whose basis was laid during this month. It has already been seen how Bismarck took up the Portuguese proposal for a conference[6] made on May 13th. He did this after consulting France on the 18th,[7] as to whether she would co-operate with him over its programme. The French reply,[8] which was given on May 29th, was favourable to the proposal, so long as it was limited to the

---

[1] cf. Fitzmaurice, II, p. 351, Memo., Granville, May 7, 1884. Adams, p. 107. Aydelotte, p. 64. Lovell, p. 103. cf. also Appendix X, p. 212.
[2] G.P., IV, No. 741. Bismarck to Münster, May 25, 1884. cf. also Adams, pp. 112–13. Aydelotte, p. 68.
[3] Fitzmaurice, II, p. 428. cf. Adams, pp. 115, 125. cf. also Appendix X, p. 214.
[4] G.P., IV, No. 743, Bismarck to Münster, June 1, 1884.
[5] This I think has not been commented on before. For general summaries of dispatch cf. Adams, pp. 113–14. Aydelotte, p. 64. Thomson, p. 194.
[6] cf. above, p. 30.
[7] Thomson, p. 202.
[8] W.B., Congo, No. 24, Bülow to Bismarck, May 29, 1884. cf. Thomson, p. 202. Banning, *Partage*, p. 113.

assurance of free trade and free navigation on the Congo, as well as the establishment of an International, instead of an Anglo-Portuguese commission, though expressly stipulating that territorial questions should be excluded from the discussions. On June 5th, having failed in a tentative attempt[1] to extend the entente wider by making it embrace all African questions to the exclusion of England, Bismarck finally accepted it on this basis.[2]

Parallel to these negotiations, and again closely connected with the May 5th dispatch, must be set an alteration made on May 19th[3] in the original instructions of Dr. Nachtigal, which had been somewhat vague, definitely ordering him to annex the Cameroons, and so encroach on British interests on the north-west coast of Africa, but to have scrupulous regard for French interests in the same neighbourhood: and the foundation on May 15th[4] of a German New Guinea Co., followed by the organisation of an expedition to this island under Dr. Finsch, a second Nachtigal of the South Seas and another bird of ill omen for British colonial interests. Taken in conjunction with his exchange of views with France on the Congo, these events show how deeply Bismarck had now committed himself to an anti-English policy.

Finally the Angra Pequena negotiations themselves precipitated a crisis which dealt the last blow to any hope of an amicable understanding between England and Germany. On May 29th,[5] Lord Derby, the Colonial Secretary, at last received the long-awaited answer from the Cape announcing the newly-formed government's decision to undertake the cost, as well as the control of the coast-line of South-West Africa, from the Orange River to Walfisch Bay. On June 2nd[6] he accordingly suggested to the Foreign Office that Bismarck should be informed, and a warship sent to the neighbourhood. Unfortu-

---

[1] Bourgeois et Pagès, *Origines et Responsabilités de la Grande Guerre*, p. 208. Daudet, *Mission de Courcel*, pp. 53–5.
[2] W.B., Congo, No. 25, Hatzfeldt to Bülow, June 5, 1884. Thomson, p. 202. Banning, *Partage*, p. 113.
[3] Adams, p. 156.
[4] Townsend, *Rise and Fall*, pp. 99–100.
[5] C. 4190, No. 54, Sir Hercules Robinson to Derby, May 29, 1884. Adams, p. 101. Lovell, p. 92. Hodge, p. 40. Taylor, p. 38. Wienefeld, p. 138. Aydelotte, p. 74.
[6] C. 4190, No. 55, C.O. to F.O., June 2, 1884. Adams, pp. 101–2. Lovell, p. 92. Fitzmaurice, II, p. 352. Taylor, p. 38. Aydelotte, p. 74.

WIDENING OF THE ESTRANGEMENT

nately the German Government had already heard,[1] on the 3rd, before it had been officially announced to them, of the Cape Government's decision. Instructions were at once telegraphed to Münster,[2] telling him that the German Government were not prepared to recognise the proposed step. This he did on the same day. Bismarck then wrote to him on June 10th,[3] telling him to inform Granville that " vital German interests (Lüderitz's establishment had now grown apparently to this dignity) could not be sacrificed for the sake of English goodwill.

Close on the heels of this dispatch[4] came the chancellor's son himself, whom Bismarck, realising Münster's incompetence, now sent to London to make clear the issues of German policy to Granville. So well did Herbert Bismarck succeed in doing this, and in enforcing his demands with threats about Egypt, that all the colonial questions outstanding between the two governments were for the moment settled by concessions on the part of Great Britain. On June 19th[5] a mixed commission was appointed to inquire into the Fiji land claims: on June 21st[6] the British Cabinet recognised the German protectorate over Lüderitz's settlement in Angra Pequena : and on June 26th,[7] as has been seen, the Anglo-Portuguese treaty was finally abandoned.

These concessions[8] were favourably received in Germany, and it might have been thought that reconciliation would have

---

[1] W.B., *Angra Pequena*, No. 21, Lippert to German F.O., June 3, 1884. Adams, p. 102. Lovell, p. 94. Fitzmaurice, p. 352. Taylor, p. 39. Aydelotte, p. 75.
[2] W.B., *Angra Pequena*, No. 22, Hatzfeldt to Münster, June 4, 1884. Adams, p. 102. Lovell, p. 94. Fitzmaurice, II, p. 352. Taylor, p. 39. Aydelotte, p. 75.
[3] W.B., *Angra Pequena*, No. 24, Bismarck to Münster, June 10, 1884. Adams, pp. 115–16. Aydelotte, pp. 90–1.
[4] G.P., IV, Nos. 745, 746, 747. Herbert Bismarck to Bismarck, June 16, 17, 22. W.B., *Angra Pequena*, No. 25, H. Bismarck to Bismarck, June 14, 1884. C. 4190, No. 69, F.O. to C.O., July 4, 1884 (Enclosure, Granville to Ampthill, June 14, 1884). Lovell, pp. 95–7. Adams, pp. 128–9, 133. Fitzmaurice, pp. 353–4. Yarnall, pp. 23–30. Taylor, pp. 41–2. Aydelotte, pp. 91–8.
[5] Townsend, *Rise and Fall*, p. 87. Adams, p. 133. Fitzmaurice, II, p. 354. Gwynn and Tuckwell, *Dilke*, II, p. 81.
[6] W.B., *Angra Pequena*, No. 27, Münster to German F.O., June 22, 1884. G.P., IV, No. 747. Gwynn and Tuckwell, II, p. 81. Lovell, p. 97. Adams, p. 133. Gooch, p. 103. Keltie, p. 189. Hodge, p. 45. Aydelotte, pp. 97–8.
[7] cf. above, pp. 32–3.
[8] G.D./29/178/Ampthill to Granville, June 28, 1884. Fitzmaurice, II, p. 355. Gooch, p. 106.

been permanent, and the Franco-German entente, which significantly enough, saw no developments during this period, have come to nothing. But it must be remembered that the now inevitable fruits of the policy launched by Bismarck in May[1] were in themselves a latent cause of friction. It was actually further developments in the Angra Pequena question which were responsible for the next, and final breach in Anglo-German relations. But it is difficult to believe that had not these occurred, some other difficulty would not have cropped up—with similar results.

[1] Especially in Cameroons. cf. A. and P., LV, 1884–5: C. 4279. Keltic, pp. 199–204. Evans Lewin, pp. 135–41. Adams, pp. 154–60. Fitzmaurice, II, pp. 340–1, 367–8. Gooch, p. 106.

CHAPTER V

ENGLAND AND GERMANY—THE FINAL BREACH
(JULY 1884)

ON June 21st[1] the British Government had decided not to question Bismarck's claims to a protectorate over German establishments on the coast of Angra Pequena. But this protectorate had so far only been extended to Lüderitz's own settlement at Angra Pequena Bay, and no further claims had as yet been put forward to any wider stretch of territory. Realising this, Lord Derby now made an effort, in co-operation with the Cape, to secure those parts of the coast where British merchants were established.

On July 14th, the same day on which instructions were sent to Lord Ampthill,[2] at Berlin, to give official confirmation to the German Government of the British decision of June 21st, he therefore wired to the Cape authorities,[3] suggesting that they should annex those parts of the coast where British subjects had concessions. The immediate result of his telegram was a resolution,[4] enlarging on his suggestion, passed on July 16th in the Cape parliament, in favour of the annexation to Cape Colony of Bechuanaland and those parts of the south-west coast not already occupied by Lüderitz. By one of those unfortunate accidents which seemed to dog the Angra Pequena negotiations from the beginning to the end of their career, this resolution[5] was published almost immediately in leading news-

---

[1] cf. above, p. 57.
[2] C. 4190, No. 75, F.O. to C.O., July 15, 1884 (Enclosure, Granville to Ampthill, July 14, 1884). Aydelotte, pp. 95, 106–7, 108. Lovell, p. 97. Fitzmaurice, II, p. 354. Evans Lewin, p. 96. Thomson, p. 196.
[3] Ibid., No. 74, Derby to Sir Hercules Robinson, July 14, 1884. Lovell, p. 97. Evans Lewin, p. 96. Fitzmaurice, II, p. 354. Aydelotte, pp. 105–6.
[4] Fitzmaurice, II, p. 354. Lovell, p. 99. Adams, pp. 142–3. Keltie, p. 189. Yarnall, p. 35. Thomson, p. 196. Aydelotte, p. 117.
[5] Lovell, p. 101. Taylor, p. 44.

papers, including the London *Times*, before official notification had even been received by the British Government. Bismarck was furious, and on July 24th[1] he wrote to Münster declaring that Germany refused to recognise the step contemplated by Great Britain; whilst at the beginning of August[2] he followed up his protest by declaring a German protectorate over the whole coast-line of Angra Pequena, from Cape Colony to the Portuguese frontier.

This fresh demonstration of anger on his part had important repercussions, not only on his colonial policy as a whole, but on the Franco-German entente and the future of the West African Conference. The chancellor himself[3] admitted that it was responsible for the strongly hostile attitude which he now adopted towards Great Britain at the Egyptian Conference of June 28th–August 2nd.

This conference[4] had been called to London to discuss Egyptian finance. It was a matter which touched all the great powers, but had a special significance for Great Britain at this moment, on account of her military campaign of 1881-2. Her case was this.[5] The share of revenue of the Egyptian Government assigned to the service of the debt, was in a most prosperous state, promising a surplus of £400,000. But under the terms of the existing law of liquidation, this sum would have to be devoted to the re-purchase of unified stock, no matter what the other needs of the country might be. Great Britain therefore demanded a modification in the law, and a diversion of some part at least of the Egyptian revenue towards defraying the costs of her army of occupation. France, who had refused to take part in the military campaign was of course opposed

---

[1] W.B., *Angra Pequena*, No. 33, Bismarck to Münster, July 24, 1884. Aydelotte, p. 115.
[2] Ibid., No. 39, Commander of *Elizabeth* to Admiralty : Berlin, Cape Town, August 14, 1884. Adams, p. 144. Fitzmaurice, II, p. 354. Keltie, p. 190. Gooch, p. 103. Hodge, p. 63. Aydelotte, p. 118. Langer, p. 300. Lovell, p. 101.
[3] G.P., IV, No. 749, Bismarck to Münster, August 12, 1884, pp. 77–8, N.B. Footnote. G.D./29/122/ Dilke to Granville, Sept. 25, 1884. G.D./29/128/ Gladstone to Granville, Sept. 5, 1884. Adams, p. 136. Wienefeld, p. 139.
[4] G.P., IV, Nos. 748, 749. G.P., III, No. 681, p. 415. Langer, pp. 298–9. Gooch, pp. 90–1. Lovell, p. 98. Adams, p. 136. Yarnall, pp. 33–7. Fitzmaurice, II, pp. 329–34, 358. Thomson, pp. 196–7. Taylor, pp. 45–6. Wienefeld, pp. 127, 143. Aydelotte, p. 113.
[5] Langer, pp. 298–9.

to any such changes, and led the opposition of the other powers to any consideration of them. As a result of his renewed annoyance over Angra Pequena,[1] Bismarck now put into action the threats which he had long been making about Egypt, crossed the diplomatic Rubicon, and supported her at the head of the other powers, in her violent protests against the British proposals. Consequently a deadlock was reached at the conference, which broke up on August 2nd without effecting anything. Its failure was a triumph for Franco-German co-operation. Not only was the achievement of a united Franco-German front on Egyptian questions, of the utmost importance in itself, it also had a decisive influence on that which had already been formed over the Congo. Discussions on this head, which at the request of the French, had now been extended to include the Niger also,[2] had been taking place both before and during the sittings of the Egyptian conference.[3] But it was the breakdown of this conference which, by uniting the question of Egypt to that of West Africa, was finally responsible for cementing the Franco-German entente on this double basis, and in so doing, for ensuring at once the solidity and the definitely anti-English character of the new combination.

[1] cf. G.P., III, No. 681, p. 415 ; IV, No. 749. Langer, p. 299. Lovell, p. 98. Yarnall, pp. 36–7. Fitzmaurice, II, pp. 334, 358. Adams, p. 136. Thomson, pp. 196–7.
[2] W.B., Congo, No. 30, Hatzfeldt to Hohenlohe, July 5, 1884 : No. 31, Hohenlohe to Bismarck, July 9, 1884. Koschitzky, p. 233. Yarnall, p. 41. Thomson, p. 205.
[3] Ibid. cf. also above, pp. 50, 55–6.

CHAPTER VI

THE CEMENTING OF THE FRANCO-GERMAN ENTENTE
(AUGUST–SEPTEMBER 1884)

ON August 7th,[1] Bismarck wrote to Count Hatzfeldt, his Minister for Foreign Affairs, declaring the moment propitious for approaching France, in view of the deadlock which had been reached in the Egyptian question, and suggesting an understanding concerning free trade on those parts of the West Coast of Africa, which were under no definite jurisdiction. Whilst Hatzfeldt was instructed to begin conversations with Baron de Courcel, the French Ambassador in Berlin,[2] Count Hohenlohe, the German Ambassador in Paris, was also told to approach M. Ferry, the French Foreign Minister. But the real author of the entente on the French side, was Courcel, not Ferry, and the conversations which took place at Berlin were consequently the most important. Indeed, so little did Ferry take the initiative,[3] that later in the month Courcel had to pay a flying visit to Paris, in order to convince him of the possibility as well as of the wisdom of an agreement with Germany, and it was due to *his* efforts, and to *his* eloquence, that Ferry finally clinched matters with Bismarck.

On August 4th[4] Hatzfeldt, in accordance with Bismarck's instructions, formally suggested to Courcel the formation of a Franco-German entente on West African affairs. The conversation in which this took place is interesting, because in it nearly all the essentials of the situation are made clear;

---

[1] G.P., III, No. 680, Bismarck to Hatzfeldt, Aug. 7, 1884. cf. Yarnall, pp. 45–6. Adams, pp. 42–3. Thomson, pp. 205–6.
[2] Ibid. Yarnall, p. 46. Wienefeld, p. 143.
[3] cf. below, pp. 64–5. Wienefeld, p. 52.
[4] G.P., No. 681, Hatzfeldt to Bismarck, Aug. 11, 1884. D.D.F., V, No. 361, Courcel to Ferry, Aug. 11, 1884. Bourgeois et Pagès, *Origines et Responsabilités de la Grande Guerre*, pp. 208–9. Wienefeld, p. 143. Adams, p. 43. Thomson, pp. 206–7.

namely, that the initiative in suggesting the entente came from Germany, not France; that what Germany really wanted was the establishment of free trade in the Congo and other unclaimed parts of Africa; that France was from the outset suspicious of the free trade principle and anxious to limit it territorially, and that what she really cared about was Egypt and the advancement of her claims against the English there; that the German Government realised this and were prepared to make concessions in this sense, in order to obtain the desired co-operation in West Africa, but that at the same time there was a tacit struggle with the French, because neither government was willing to take the initiative in opposing England in Egypt, each doing its utmost to push the other to the fore: finally that hostility to England was the acknowledged "Anknüpfungspunkt" of the entente.

From the beginning, Bismarck's idea was that Germany should play France's game in Egypt, and that in return France should play Germany's game in West Africa. But whilst it is true that Egypt was what mattered most to France, and West Africa to Germany, there is no doubt that France actually stood to gain far more from the German proposals, than Germany herself, the reason being that when Bismarck *thought* that he was playing his country's game in bringing international pressure to bear on Great Britain in West Africa, he was in reality playing that of France to an extent which he himself did not realise. In the first place, being ignorant of local conditions, he was unaware of the origin of the Anglo-Portuguese treaty in Great Britain's fear of a French monopoly, and consequently of the existence of French territorial ambitions on the Congo and the lack of any serious British ones there. Secondly, as a result of the *general* misunderstanding with Great Britain, he had by now an altogether exaggerated and erroneous conception of the obstructive nature of British policy; an illustration of this being his belief, expressed to Hatzfeldt on August 7th,[1] that England's adhesion to the conference must be considered doubtful, and that it might be necessary for the other powers to put pressure on her, whilst he cited the Armed Neutrality as a precedent for such a form of coercion. This in turn led him to set such value on French

[1] G.P., III, No. 680, Bismarck to Hatzfeldt. Aug. 7, 1884, p. 414.

co-operation that it eventually caused him to make important concessions to France, in his proposals concerning West Africa itself, in order to obtain her unqualified consent to them.

These proposals were drawn up in the middle of August,[1] and finally given to Courcel on the 17th of the month[2] when he left Berlin for Paris in order to show them to Ferry. Besides asking for free trade on the Congo coast, free navigation of the river, and the establishment of an International instead of an Anglo-Portuguese commission, they also suggested that there should be a reciprocal guarantee between France and Germany for freedom of commerce in any territories which they might in future occupy on the West Coast of Africa, together with an engagement not to recognise the occupations of any other powers on this coast which did not fulfil the same conditions. Bismarck made it clear, that is to say, that he would like the principle of free trade to be linked to that of effective occupation, and to be a condition of it. Out of consideration for France, however, he proposed that this arrangement should be limited to regions south of the equator, not imagining, he declared, that France would wish to subscribe for those in the neighbourhood of Senegal.

When Courcel showed these propositions to Ferry,[3] the latter, who was evidently still in two minds about Bismarck's sincerity, was at first somewhat taken aback, and had many objections to offer. But Courcel seems to have succeeded in talking him round[4] and in convincing him of the wisdom of accepting Germany's offer. The principle of agreement was therefore itself agreed upon—but with considerable modification in detail. The counter-propositions[5] now drawn up at Paris, in every

[1] G.P., III, No 681, Hatzfeldt to Bismarck, Aug. 11, 1884: No. 682, Hatzfeldt to Bismarck, Aug. 14, 1884: No. 683, Bismarck to Hatzfeldt, Aug. 15, 1884: No. 684, Hohenlohe to Bismarck, Aug. 15, 1884. D.D.F., V, No. 365, Courcel to Ferry, Aug. 14, 1884: No. 366, Courcel to Ferry, Aug. 15, 1884 : No. 369, Courcel to Ferry, Aug. 16, 1884.
[2] D.D.F., V, No. 372, Courcel to Ferry, Aug. 17, 1884. G.P., III, No. 685, Hatzfeldt to Bismarck, Aug. 17, 1884. cf. Yarnall, p. 47. Thomson, pp. 207-8. Taylor, p. 48.
[3] G.P., III, No. 686, Hohenlohe to Bismarck, Aug. 23, 1884. D.D.F., V, No. 376, Note : Ferry—On German Propositions (no date) : No. 377, Courcel to Ferry, Aug. 25, 1884. cf. Yarnall, p. 47. Wienefeld, p. 143.
[4] G.P., III, No. 686, Hohenlohe to Bismarck, Aug. 23, 1884. D.D.F., V, No. 377, Courcel to Ferry, Aug. 25, 1884.
[5] G.P., III, No. 687, Hatzfeldt to Bismarck, Aug. 25, 1884. D.D.F., V, No. 377, Courcel to Ferry, Aug, 25, 1884.

CEMENTING OF FRANCO-GERMAN ENTENTE 65

way limited and particularised the original German proposals, especially with regard to the principle of free trade, the essential divergence revealed between the two countries on this point illustrating the erroneous nature of one of the fundamental assumptions on which the entente was based. Germany, as has been seen, wished it to be linked to that of effective occupation, and to be a condition of it ; but France refused to entertain such a suggestion. The German proposals also made what it was imagined would be a welcome concession to France by limiting the application of free trade to regions south of the equator ; but this did not satisfy the French, who demanded the limitation of the principle to the Congo region only. Even this was considered a concession by Ferry,[1] who, in his first criticism of the German proposals had suggested that Bismarck should give a *quid pro quo* in the form of a modification in Article VII of the Treaty of Frankfurt, by which France had ceded Alsace-Lorraine to Germany in 1871. Needless to say,[2] he did not obtain it, but it is possible that the threatened demand may have had some effect on Bismarck by further inclining him to accept the other suggestions made by the French. It is true that, though limiting the principle of free trade in general, it was they who were responsible for demanding free navigation on the Niger:[3] but this was solely out of fear of England, who claimed the lower river, not from any general desire to extend the principle of free trade. A kind of general protest[4] was also entered by them against any too extensive an application of rules about the seizure of unoccupied territories.

It was in fact Germany, not France, who had the most highfaluting ideas about these, and about the possibility of drawing up a sort of international code, which should replace the undignified scramble for territory, in which she herself had recently played such a conspicuous part. This apparent paradox is again to be explained by Bismarck's obsession about England, who was in his eyes the power with at once the great-

[1] D.D.F., V, No, 376, Note : Ferry—On German Propositions, p. 379.
[2] cf. Yarnall, p. 49.
[3] G.P., III, No. 687, Hatzfeldt to Bismarck, Aug. 25, 1884, p. 423. D.D.F., V, No, 376, Note: Ferry—On German Propositions, p. 380 : No. 377, Courcel to Ferry, Aug. 25, 1884, p. 382.
[4] D.D.F., V, No. 376, Note: Ferry—On German Propositions, p. 379: No. 377, Courcel to Ferry, Aug. 25, 1884, pp. 381-2,

est and the most monopolistic ambitions in the colonial field. There is no doubt that his efforts at a general formulation of international principles were directed against *her* ;[1] though here again, as over the question of free trade, he underestimated, in asking for French co-operation in his plans, the importance of France herself as a colonial power, and the extent to which she would be liable to raise objections to them, on account of her *own* interests being adversely affected.

Courcel did not stay long in Paris, and on August 24th[2] he was back in the German capital with the approval of the Government for the proposed plan of co-operation and with the French counter-propositions, in his pocket. After a preliminary interview with Hatzfeldt[3] he went straight to Varzin,[4] where he was very cordially received by the chancellor. Bismarck was profuse in his expressions of goodwill. He stressed the friendly nature of Germany's intentions towards France on the West Coast of Africa, and advanced what was destined to be an interesting corollary to Anglo-German tension[5] in the Gulf of Guinea, namely, a working agreement with France to respect her interests there, and a promise of withdrawal on the part of Germany from any points where Dr. Nachtigal should inadvertently have encroached on their interests. The French propositions[6] regarding the conference were all accepted by the chancellor, becoming with little alteration its official bases, in which, if Germany may be said to have taken the initiative in formulation, there is no doubt that France ultimately played the preponderating part—an important point. These bases as now formulated were three :

---

[1] cf. D.D.F., V, No. 249, Courcel to Ferry, April 25, 1884 (Adams, p. 42). No. 407, Courcel to Ferry, Sept. 21, 1884, p. 424.
[2] G.P., III, No. 687, Hatzfeldt to Bismarck, Aug. 25, 1884. Wienefeld, p. 143. Langer, p. 300.
[3] D.D.F., V, No. 377, Courcel to Ferry, Aug. 25, 1884. G.P., III, No. 687, Hatzfeldt to Bismarck, Aug. 25, 1884. cf. Yarnall, p. 48. Thomson, p. 208.
[4] D.D.F., V, No. 383, Courcel to Ferry, Aug. 30, 1884. G.P., III, No. 685, Bismarck to Busch, Aug. 30, 1884. cf. Wienefeld, p. 144. Daudet, p. 58. Bourgeois et Pagès, p. 209. Langer, p. 301.
[5] cf. above, p. 56. G P., III, No. 688, Bismarck to Busch, Aug. 30, 1884. D.D.F., V, No. 383, Courcel to Ferry, Aug. 30, 1884. cf. also D.D.F., V, No. 395, Courcel to Ferry, Sept. 14, 1884. Evans Lewin, pp. 130, 133–6. Keltie, p. 200. Banning, *Partage*, pp. 121–2.
[6] G.P., III, No. 688, Bismarck to Busch, Aug. 30, 1884. cf. also Thomson, p. 209.

I. Freedom of commerce in the basin and mouths of the Congo.
II. The question of the application to the Congo and the Niger of the principles adopted by the Congress of Vienna, with a view to rendering inviolable the liberty of navigation on several international rivers.
III. The definition of formalities to be observed in order that occupation on the coasts of Africa shall be effective.

The question of invitations to the conference was also discussed at this interview, as well as that of where it should be held, Bismarck suggesting Paris, Courcel Berlin as its meeting-place. But afterwards[1] Bismarck wrote to Hohenlohe declaring that if, as he believed, the French proposal to have the conference at Berlin was really serious, then it should be accepted, and the Kaiser would issue the invitations. It took another month, however, before final agreement was reached.

On September 13th,[2] Bismarck sent a long note to Courcel repeating the assurances which he had given him at Varzin, and asking for formal confirmation from Ferry of the identity of views of the two governments, so that invitations could be issued to the other powers. But Ferry, in reply,[3] though stating his agreement in principle on the question of a general entente, still asked for further assurances with regard to free trade and effective occupation. He appeared to be again suspicious of Bismarck, his suspicions, which had so largely been allayed by Courcel at the time of the latter's visit to Paris, having apparently been revived by the recent meeting of the three emperors at Skiernewice, where they had renewed the Dreikaiserbund, and drawn closer the bonds of Austria, Germany, and Russia,[4] bonds which Courcel himself now believed to be in part a fresh guarantee of the treaty of Frankfurt.

Bismarck seems to have realised this, for, on his return from Poland, on September 21st,[5] he went straight to see Courcel,

[1] G.P., III, No. 688, Bismarck to Busch, Aug. 30, 1884.
[2] D.D.F., V, No. 395, Courcel to Ferry, Sep. 14, 1884. L. J., Congo, 1884, No. 25, Bismarck to Courcel, Sept. 13, 1884. cf. Banning, *Partage*, p. 21. Thomson, p. 209.
[3] D.D.F., V, No. 402, Ferry to Courcel, Sept. 19, 1884.
[4] cf. D.D.F., V, No. 400, Courcel to Billot, Sept. 15, 1884.
[5] D.D.F., V, Nos. 404, 405, 407, Courcel to Ferry, Sept. 21, 23, 1884. cf. Bourgeois et Pagès, pp. 383-4. Gooch, *Franco-German Entente*, p. 21. Langer, pp. 301-2. Daudet, p. 106. Yarnall, p. 52. Taylor, p. 53.

and in a long interview, lasting for over an hour, not only gave full assurances to the French Ambassador on this head, but treated him to a lengthy exposé of his political views as a whole, in which, after launching forth into diatribes against England, he emphatically stressed the need for a common front of France and Germany against her, giving point to his exhortations, by emphasising his willingness to meet her in every way over the West African programme. In fact, the Skiernewice meeting, far from being a political move directed against France, was one calculated, by the increased sense of security which it gave Bismarck in Europe, to strengthen the Franco-German entente, both by lessening his fear of England, and by making him more anxious than before to win the support of France for his policy of planned opposition to English interests.

It was at this interview with Courcel that he first formulated an idea which had evidently been germinating for some time in his mind,[1] and which was in effect what paralysed English policy in the years 1884–5, the possibility, namely, of naval co-operation of the Continental powers against her. " What I wish to establish,"[2] he told Courcel, " is a sort of equilibrium on the seas, and France has a great rôle to play in this matter, if she is willing to concur in our views. Men spoke formerly of a European equilibrium. It is an eighteenth-century expression. But I think it is not obsolete to speak of the equilibrium of the seas. I repeat, I do not want war with England, but I want her to understand that if the navies of the other nations unite they will counterbalance her on the ocean, and will compel her to consider the interests of others. To this she must accustom herself, as well as to the idea that a Franco-German alliance is not an impossibility."

The eloquence of the chancellor appears to have had the desired effect as far as the West African negotiations were

---

[1] cf. D.D.F., V, No. 249, Courcel to Ferry, April 25, 1884. cf. G.P., IV, No. 680, Bismarck to Hatzfeldt, Aug. 7, 1884. The idea of the " armed neutrality," etc., above, p. 68. Langer, p. 301 (Interview, Bismarck with General von Schweinitz, July, 1884). Wienefeld, pp. 145–6. Adams, p. 42. cf. Appendix XI.

[2] D.D.F., V, No. 407, Courcel to Ferry, Sept. 23, 1884, p. 424. A much-quoted passage. cf. Gooch, *Franco-German Relations*, p. 21. Bourgeois et Pagès, pp. 209–10, 383, 386. Langer, pp. 301–2. Daudet, pp. 106, 109–11. Wienefeld, p. 146. Taylor, pp. 53–4. Adams, p. 44. cf. Appendix XI.

CEMENTING OF FRANCO-GERMAN ENTENTE 69

concerned, for a week later[1] he at last received official confirmation from Ferry of the identity of views of the two governments, together with a statement of Ferry's willingness to issue invitations to the conference. It was decided[2] that these should include all the Great Powers of Europe, as well as the United States and the Scandinavian countries, in order to give the strongest validity possible to the resolutions of the conference; it was also agreed that they should be issued in two series, the powers directly interested in the Congo being invited first, in order to save time, as Bismarck was anxious for the conference to meet before the end of October.

September closed, therefore, with the West African question temporarily settled until the conference should meet. But the position with regard to Egypt, "the other side" of the entente,[3] was far less advanced. It had figured constantly in the conversations which had taken place on West Africa since the beginning of August,[4] but so far only a very small measure of agreement had been reached. During the whole of this month the French had persistently pressed Germany to take the initiative in approaching England about what they considered the two outstanding questions of Egyptian finance, the regulation of the Alexandria indemnities, and the debt commission—but without success—the Germans, though recognising in principle the need for giving France support in Egypt, being as loath to take it as they. On the occasion of Courcel's visit to Varzin,[5] at the end of August, Bismarck himself admitted that the matter had been no further advanced since the London Conference. Nevertheless, Courcel left the chancellor more satisfied that he had come,[6] declaring that Bismarck

---

[1] L.J., Congo, 1884, No. 26, Courcel to Bismarck, Sept. 29, 1884. cf. also A. and P., LV, 1884-5 : C. 4205, No. 16, Lyons to Granville, Oct. 15, 1884 (Comments and Extracts). Banning, *Partage*, p. 21. Koschitzky, p. 230. Stanley, II, pp. 389-90.
[2] W.B., Congo, 1885, No. 36, Bismarck to Courcel, Sept. 30, 1884 : No. 37, Courcel to Bismarck, Oct. 2, 1884 : No. 38, Note : On Invitations. L.J., Congo, 1884, No. 27, Bismarck to Courcel, Sept. 30, 1884 : No. 28, Courcel to Bismarck, Oct. 2, 1884. cf. also D.D.F., V, No. 406, Courcel to Ferry, Sept. 22, 1884 : No. 414, Courcel to Ferry, Oct. 1, 1884. Yarnall, pp. 55-6. Reeves, pp. 30-1. Wienefeld, pp. 144, 149. Thomson, pp. 209-10. cf. Appendix XII.
[3] cf. G.P., III, No. 694, Herbert Bismarck to Bismarck, Oct. 6, 1884, p. 432.
[4] cf. G.P., III, Nos. 680, 681, 682, 686, 687, 688, 689, 692, 693. D.D.F., V, Nos. 366, 369, 372, 377, 405. Bourgeois et Pagès, p. 383.
[5] G.P., III, No. 688. Bismarck to Busch, Aug. 30, 1884.
[6] Bourgeois et Pagès, p. 383, Courcel to Ferry, Aug. 30, 1884.

appeared to be taking a keener interest in Egypt than formerly, and seemed disposed " to depart from that Olympian indifference " which he had hitherto displayed regarding it.

During the following month, in accordance with the rising tide of hostility towards England (with whom he was now having bitter controversies over Angra Pequena,[1] the Cameroons,[2] and New Guinea),[3] which especially characterised his policy at this time, Bismarck showed himself increasingly complacent towards French wishes in Egypt as well as in West Africa. In the conversation[4] which he had with Courcel after his return from Skiernewice, he did not enter into any detailed discussion of Egyptian affairs, but he severely criticised England's attitude at the London Conference, dropping a palpable hint for the future, when he declared that he did not fear the opposition of the English " in view of the embarrassments into which their action in Egypt has placed them. They have need of us ; we can bargain with them." Presumably encouraged by this,[5] Courcel wrote the next day to Hatzfeldt, asking for a settlement of the debt question. Hatzfeldt somewhat acridly remarked afterwards[6] that France seemed to be trying to get all, or at least as much as possible, for nothing, in Egypt, and suggested the holding of an Egyptian Conference at Paris. But when he showed his report of the conversation to Bismarck[7] the latter made it clear to him that the French demand must be satisfied. Hatzfeldt therefore had another interview with Courcel, in which he told him this. Courcel came away much pleased, and declared his intention of going shortly to Paris again to discuss the whole question with Ferry.

At the end of September, therefore, there was every sign of growing cordiality in the relations of France and Germany. Final agreement had been reached over the West African programme and the issue of invitations to the conference.

[1] cf. W.B., *Angra Pequena*, Nos. 39–49. Fitzmaurice, II, pp. 354, 359–62. Keltie, pp. 190–2. Aydelotte, pp. 122–3. Adams, pp. 143–9. Taylor, pp. 51–2, 54–5. Hodge, 64–73.
[2] cf. C. 4279, Nos. 26–63. Keltie, pp. 201–4. Evans Lewin, pp. 137, 140–1. Gooch, p. 104. Adams, pp. 157–60.
[3] Adams, pp. 145, 162–6, 172. Gooch, p. 107. Fitzmaurice, II, pp. 371–2. Taylor, pp. 68–9.
[4] D.D.F., V, No. 405, Courcel to Ferry, Sept. 21, 1884.
[5] G.P., III, No. 691, Note : Hatzfeldt, Sept. 22, 1884.
[6] Ibid. G.P., III, No. 691. Note, Hatzfeldt, Sept. 22, 1884.
[7] G.P., III, No. 692, Note : Hatzfeldt, Sept. 24, 1884.

CEMENTING OF FRANCO-GERMAN ENTENTE 71

Plans were under weigh for co-operation in Egypt. Expressions of goodwill on the part of diplomats and military experts[1] in both countries testified to the mutual satisfaction felt with the entente, which, if not an alliance, was, as Hohenlohe somewhat jubilantly remarked on one occasion, a *grosses rapprochement*.[2] Nevertheless it would have been wiser if he had expressed the difference a little differently.

[1] G.P., III, No. 689, Herbert Bismarck, Note, Sept. 7, 1884: No. 690, Rotenhan to Bismarck, Sept. 17, 1884. Gooch, *Franco-German Entente*, p. 22. Yarnall, pp. 50–1. Wienefeld, pp. 144–5.
[2] cf. Langer, p. 301. Wienefeld, p. 143.

CHAPTER VII

WEAKENING OF THE ENTENTE—BISMARCK'S APPROACHES TO BRITAIN
(OCTOBER–NOVEMBER 1884)

IN October, a month before the opening of the conference, there were already signs of a certain weakening in the bonds of the Franco-German entente. It is impossible to dissociate this from the fact that the West African question having been temporarily settled, the time had now come for Egypt, the second basis of the entente to be seriously discussed. Although so many concessions had already been made to them in West Africa the French were now undoubtedly out to claim what they considered the pound of flesh due to them in Egypt, in return for their co-operation over the West African programme. Not unnaturally this caused a certain amount of friction with Bismarck.

So excessive were the French demands, and so anti-English in consequence, that the chancellor began really to be afraid of war between France and England; and was thus forced into the curious position of trying to damp the flame which, up till now, he had been so carefully fanning between the two countries. A Franco-British war,[1] he told his son, Herbert Bismarck, on the occasion of a visit paid by the latter to Paris at the beginning of October, would be a calamity, and he therefore instructed him to tell Ferry that Germany as well as France was anxious for a peaceful solution of the Egyptian problem.

It was not only over Egypt, however, that differences arose between France and Germany in October and November 1884. Latent divergencies in the attitude of the two powers to

[1] G.P., III, No. 693, Bismarck to Herbert Bismarck, Oct. 5, 1884.

WEAKENING OF THE ENTENTE 73

West African questions also began to make themselves apparent. A note of the French Foreign Department of October 23rd[1] on the " Attitude to be Adopted towards England in Supporting the German Propositions," illustrates the constant fear still entertained by the French Government of too wide an extension of the principle of free trade ; whilst Courcel's instructions of November 8th show the great reserve which France still maintained with regard to the entente in general, and to her own position in Africa in particular. Courcel's attitude, it was declared, must be determined by the same considerations which had led the French Government originally to welcome the conference, but at the same time rigorously to limit its programme. The conversations which he had had with Bismarck at Varzin showed that the state of French relations with Germany in no way excluded the possibility of an entente between the two countries on certain definite points, where they had interests in common. But this entente must not be " interpreted as a demonstration directed against other powers, or as the inauguration of a new political system." The same preoccupations which had inspired the terms of the agreement should continue to impose themselves on the French representative during the conference. All territorial questions should be strictly excluded from the discussions, whilst the initiation of any suggestions concerning them should be left as far as possible to Germany. On November 12th,[2] German discontent at France's general attitude made itself felt in an interview between Bismarck and Courcel, in which the former charged France with wilfully maintaining a certain reserve over the Congo Conference.

These signs of a diminution of cordiality between France and Germany must be connected with the course of Anglo-German relations during the same months. At the beginning of October[3] Bismarck deemed the time ripe for letting Great Britain know of the conference, and for issuing an invitation to her. But he did so in the barest manner possible, giving only the simple bases of the conference, dropping the news of the

[1] D.D.F., V, No. 437, Note du Départment pour M. Nisard, Sous-Directeur de la Direction Politique, Oct. 23, 1884.
[2] D.D.F., V, No. 450, Courcel to Ferry, Nov. 12, 1884. Yarnall, p. 65.
[3] F.O./84/1813/ Plessen to Granville, Oct. 8, 1884. (C. 4205, No. 10, Plessen to Granville, Oct. 8, 1884) (full text). Yarnall, pp. 56–7.

74 THE BERLIN WEST AFRICAN CONFERENCE

concoction of its programme jointly by France and Germany like a bombshell into the open trench-line of British bewilderment,[1] and expressing great annoyance when the British Foreign Minister dared to ask for further information regarding it.[2] The history of Anglo-German relations up to the middle of November, therefore, resolves itself principally into that of curt notices of invitation from the German Government, combined with insistence on the need for an early reply; and repeated demands from the British Government for more precise information,[3] which in the end, partially at least, were satisfied.

When Granville first received the German invitation on October 8th,[4] he accepted it in principle,[5] but asked for fuller information on the various points which had been raised, before doing so formally. This request was not answered by the German Government until October 22nd,[6] when meanwhile a second and stronger British demand for fuller information had been made on October 17th,[7] which was not answered till November 2nd[8] by the German Government. The standpoint of Great Britain was this. Not only did she accept the conference, she welcomed it, but she felt it impossible to commit herself definitely, before she knew a little more about its programme. As Granville complained[9] to a Foreign Office

---

[1] F.O./84/1813/ Granville to Malet, Oct. 11, 1884, Africa, 33. (C. 4205, No. 13, Granville to Malet, Oct. 11, 1884) (full text). F.O./84/1813/ Malet to Granville, Oct. 18, 1884, Africa, 24. (C. 4205, No. 21, Malet to Granville, Oct. 18, 1884) (full text). F.O./84/1813/ Granville to Malet, Oct. 19, 1884, Africa, 39. (C. 4205, No. 23, Granville to Malet, Oct. 19, 1884) (expurgated). F.O./84/1813/ Münster to Granville, Oct. 22, 1884, Africa, 46. (C. 4205, No. 25, Münster to Granville, Oct. 22, 1884) (full text).

[2] F.O./84/1813/ Granville to Plessen, Oct. 8, 1884. (C. 4205, No. 11, Granville to Plessen, Oct. 8, 1884) (full text). F.O./84/1813/ Granville to Malet, Oct. 11, 1884, Africa, 33. (C. 4105, No. 15, Granville to Malet, Oct. 11, 1884) (full text). F.O./84/1813/ Granville to Malet, Oct. 17, Africa, 37. (C. 4205, No. 18, Granville to Malet, Oct. 17) (full text). F.O./84/1813/ Granville to Malet, Oct. 19, Africa, 39. (C. 4205, No. 23, Granville to Malet, Oct. 19) (expurgated).

[3] F.O./84/1813/ Münster to Granville, Oct. 22, 1884. (C. 4205, No. 25. Münster to Granville, Oct. 22, 1884) (full text). F.O./84/1814/ Malet to Granville, Oct. 23, 1884, Tel. 29. F.O./84/1814/ Münster to Granville, Nov. 2, 1884. (C. 4205, No. 30, Münster to Granville, Nov. 2, 1884) (full text).

[4] F.O./84/1813/ (C. 4205, No. 6). Plessen to Granville, Oct. 8, 1884.
[5] F.O./84/1813/ (C. 4205, No. 11). Granville to Plessen, Oct. 8, 1884.
[6] F.O./84/1813/ (C. 4205, No. 25). Münster to Granville, Oct. 22, 1884.
[7] F.O./84/1813/ (C. 4205, No. 18). Granville to Malet, Oct. 17, 1884, Africa, 37.
[8] F O./84/1814/ (C. 4205, No. 30). Münster to Granville, Nov. 2, 1884.
[9] F.O./84/1815/ (C. 4205, No. 18). Granville to Malet, Oct. 17, 1884, Africa, 37.

WEAKENING OF THE ENTENTE

official, the knowledge of the views of the German Government as to how to carry out a problem to which Great Britain "*was entirely favourable*", was essential, before instructions could be issued to her representative to the conference. He raised objections[1] therefore to the vagueness of the definition of freedom of commerce in the first basis : to any form of international control of the lower Niger in the second, though he was ready, he declared, to guarantee both free trade and free navigation of the river : and finally to any very full application of the principle of effective occupation, showing great anxiety as to the exact meaning of the term "nouvelles occupations" (future occupations).

Though he vouchsafed no full explanation of the third basis, assurances *were* given by Bismarck regarding this latter point, for in an interview which he had with Malet on October 23rd,[2] he declared that the phrase was only intended to refer to "acquisitions made subsequent to the recent Franco-German negotiations". He also met British objections[3] with regard to the first basis, by declaring in his note of November 2nd, that it was intended to give the widest possible interpretation to the meaning of the term "freedom of commerce". But the claims of Great Britain to the Niger were disputed, and the tone of the note, which was the final answer to her inquiries, was markedly hostile in this connection.

This was the one thing, however, about which the British Government really cared, and they therefore stuck to their guns,[4] resolutely reserving their rights on the river and refusing to consider the possibility of an International Commission, as on the Congo, though at the same time accepting without demur the rest of the programme of the conference. Malet's instructions of November 7th,[5] told him not only to give wholehearted support to the principle of freedom of commerce in the basin of the Congo, but also to advocate as large an exten-

---
[1] F.O./84/1813/ (C. 4205, No. 11). Granville to Plessen, Oct. 8, 1884. F.O./84/1813/ (C. 4205, No. 18). Granville to Malet, Oct. 17, 1884, Africa. 37. F.O./84/1813/ (C. 4205, No. 23). Granville to Malet, Oct. 19, 1884, Africa, 39.
[2] F.O./84/1814/ Malet to Granville, Oct. 23, 1884, Tel. 29.
[3] F.O./84/1813/ (C. 4205, No. 30). Munster to Granville, Nov. 2, 1884.
[4] F.O./84/1814/ Malet's Instructions, Nov. 7, 1884, Africa, 59. (A. and P., IV, 1884–5 : C. 4241, Malet's Instructions, Nov. 7, 1884) (full text).
[5] Ibid.

sion of it as possible to the coast-line ; to press for the extension of free navigation to the other rivers of Africa, but to take a strong line with regard to the Niger. There must be no International Commission there, it was insisted, though Great Britain was herself ready to guarantee free trade and free navigation. No objections finally were raised to the acceptance of the third basis, so long as it was applied only to the future. This was the situation till two days before the opening of the conference.

On that day, November 13th,[1] Bismarck had what was really, in view of the preceding negotiations, an extraordinary interview with Malet. The chancellor first read his opening speech, which Malet discovered to be in complete accordance with the views of the British Government, even down to the wish to extend the principles of free navigation and commerce to the coast-line as well as to the basin of the Congo. He then asked Malet to communicate his instructions, which Malet accordingly did. Bismarck agreed with them throughout, declaring that he had nothing to say to the views of Great Britain with regard to the Niger, if her facts were correct. He then made a proposal for co-operation between France, Germany, and Great Britain, in discussing certain matters outside the stipulated bases of the conference, which might arise in connection with it. No attempt was made to define what exactly these matters might be, but it is clear that what Bismarck was thinking of were the territorial questions expressly excluded by France from its programme.

The whole conversation is most interesting, as it illustrates on the very eve of the conference, something like a *volte-face* in Bismarck's attitude. Here for a whole month and more he had been haggling with England over the bases of the conference, grudging her information, grumbling at her delay in answering his (for the most part) rather rudely worded messages, complaining of her attitude. At last he did vouchsafe a little more information. What was the result ? Great Britain eagerly responded. It was found that there was almost complete identity in the views of the two governments, except over the Niger, where Bismarck was inclined to back the French. He now gave way about the Niger, and invited British as well

[1] F.O./84/1814/ Malet to Granville, Nov. 13, 1884, Tel. 37.

WEAKENING OF THE ENTENTE

as French co-operation in discussing the important territorial questions which, he saw, were bound to arise out of its programme, though expressly excluded from it by France.

It is impossible not to connect this change in his attitude with his conversation of the previous day with Courcel,[1] and his growing realisation of the difficulties inherent in the Franco-German entente, both in West Africa and in Egypt, as well as with his discovery of the fundamental identity of views of the British and German governments over West African questions, and with his recognition of the International Association of the Congo, on November 8th.[2] This introduces another important element into the situation, which will be discussed in the next chapter : the position, namely, which Leopold of the Belgians had managed to secure for his Association before the conference opened, and its bearing on the Franco-German entente.

[1] cf. above, p. 73.
[2] W.B., Congo, 1885, No. 43. Protocols of Conference, Protocol IX, Annex I. cf. Hertslet, *Map of Africa by Treaty*, I, pp. 219–20. Thomson, p. 186. Keith, p. 63. Yarnall, p. 23. Reeves, p. 53. Keltie, p. 210. Banning, *Partage*, p. 93 ; *Mémoires*, p. 36.

CHAPTER VIII

LEOPOLD AND THE POWERS
(FEBRUARY—NOVEMBER 1884)

THE Anglo-Portuguese Treaty[1] was not in any sense directed against the International Association of the Congo, as it was against France. The Association was at that time only a small private organisation, loudly advertising its adhesion to the principle of free trade, in whose entirely beneficent, innocuous, and non-political character every one believed, and whose real ambitions, or perhaps it should be said the ambitions of the driving power behind it, which was that of Leopold of the Belgians, no one even remotely suspected. Throughout the negotiations with Portugal[2] Granville continued to be on the most friendly terms with Leopold, with whom he was carrying on a long correspondence about the contents of the treaty, and to whose insistent and repeated demands for consideration of his interests he always lent an attentive and a deferential ear. At one time,[3] when relations with Portugal were particularly difficult, the British Foreign Secretary seems even to have thought of striking a bargain with the Association, as an alternative to one with Portugal. This idea was never carried out; but Granville showed the respect which he had for Leopold's interests, by important modifications[4] (two of which were

[1] Thomson, p. 140. cf. also above, pp. 17, 18, 20-1.
[2] G.D./29/28/ Memo. King of Belgians, March 11, 1883. G.D./29/156/ Lumley to Granville, Dec. 3, 1882: Malet to Granville, Feb. 10, 1884: Malet to Granville, Feb. 14, 1884: Feb. 21, 1884. G.D./29/198/ Granville to Lumley, May 5, 1883: Granville to Malet, Feb. 20, 1884: Granville to Solwyns, Feb. 21, 1884: Granville to Leopold, Feb. 20, 25, 1884. F.O./84/1809/ Goldsmid to F.O., Jan. 4, Feb. 1, Feb. 9, 1884. cf. also Thomson, p. 140. Fitzmaurice, II, pp. 355-6.
[3] G.D./29/198/ Granville to Lumley, May, 5, 1883.
[4] F.O./84/1809/ Goldsmid to F.O., Feb. 9, 1884: Granville to d'Antas, Feb. 11, 1884: Granville to Petre, Feb. 23, 1884: (also in A. and P., LVI: C. 3885, No. 24). Fitzmaurice to Petre, Feb. 23, 1884. G.D./29/156/ Malet to Granville, Feb. 14, 21, 1884. G.D./29/198/ Granville to Solwyns, Feb. 21, 1884: Granville to Leopold, Feb. 20, 25, 1884. cf. also L.J., Congo, 1884, No. 15, Laboulaye to Ferry, March 15, 1884, p. 34. Thomson, p. 141.

LEOPOLD AND THE POWERS

extracted from Portugal at the last moment), which he made in the treaty at his request, which had regard not only for the general principle of free trade, of which Leopold (because of course he stood to gain by it) from the beginning made himself the determined champion, but also for the actual territorial pretensions of the Association.

Nevertheless, whatever the nature of the guarantees given by Portugal, there is no doubt that the treaty,[1] by placing the control of the mouth, the lower course, and the neighbouring coast-line of the Congo in her hands, effectually barred the way to any wide extension of the power of the Association.

This explains[2] why before, as well as after its signature, Leopold not only tried to influence Granville in his favour, but did all he could to weaken and invalidate it in other ways. Before the treaty had been signed[3] he was most active in his efforts to bring pressure on Granville; *after* its signature, though still endeavouring to wring further concessions from Granville[4] (which he evidently deemed practicable, because of the general opposition of the powers to the treaty), he concentrated[5] more and more on himself contributing to this opposition, as well as doing all in his power to utilise it to his own advantage.

It was in fact the hostility of the powers to the treaty, and its subsequent breakdown, which enabled him to manipulate the international situation in such a way as to place himself in the position which was eventually to win him the Congo. By the time the West African Conference opened he had succeeded, by a series of skilful agreements, in which he successively bamboozled three great powers, the United States, France, and Germany, in obtaining their recognition of the flag of the Association. The first of these agreements was made with the United States on April 22nd ;[6] the second with France

---

[1] cf. Text, Hertslet, *Map of Africa by Treaty*, II, pp. 713–14. Yarnall, p. 21.
[2] cf. above, Note 2. Also G.D./29/156/Leopold to Granville, Feb. 27, 1884, March 6, 1884. F.O./84/1809/ March 2, 1884, Memo., Anderson. Thomson, pp. 141–2. Fitzmaurice, II, p. 356. Banning, *Mémoires*, p. 5. Yarnall, p. 21.
[3] cf. above, Note 2.
[4] G.D./29/156/ Leopold to Granville, Feb. 27, March 6, 1884.
[5] F.O./84/1819/ Memo: Anderson, March 2, 1884. Dilke Papers, Vol. LVII, *Memoir*, Chapter xxii, p. 29. Thomson, pp. 141–2. Fitzmaurice, II, p. 356. Banning, *Mémoires*, p. 5. Yarnall, p. 21.
[6] Protocols of Conference, Protocol IX, Annex I. Hertslet, *Map of Africa by Treaty*, I, pp. 244–6. Thomson, p. 157. Yarnall, p. 22. Keith, pp. 53–4. Banning, *Partage*, p. 93. Keltie, pp. 209–10. Reeves, p. 51.

on April 23rd;[1] the third with Germany on November 8th, 1884;[2] and they are all closely connected with each other.

Leopold's motive[3] in obtaining the recognition of the United States appears to have been not only to strengthen his legal position, but also to advertise to the world at large his adhesion to the principle of free trade, and in so doing, not only to show up in black relief the tariff clauses of the Anglo-Portuguese treaty, thus still further invalidating the position of England and Portugal, but also to win for himself the general sympathy of the powers. That he was audacious enough to do so, in face of the avowed policy of the United States, which was to steer clear of foreign entanglements, was due to his astute knowledge of American psychology. On this, with the help of his competent and unscrupulous agent, General Sanford (former American minister at Brussels and a member, since 1877, of the executive committee of the International African Association), he succeeded in playing with consummate skill. American recognition[4] of the International Association was in fact due to a mixture of three quite erroneous conceptions. The first was a belief that the Free States, which it was the avowed object of the Association to establish on the Upper Congo, would in time be able to govern themselves on the model of the recently established republic of Liberia. The second was trust in the sweeping guarantees given by Leopold concerning free trade on the Congo, as well as in his promise to suppress the slave traffic. The third was pride in the American citizenship of Stanley, which led to a quite vague and illogically reasoned faith in the necessarily beneficent results of the enterprises of the Association for America.

There is no doubt that these conceptions[5] were due to a widespread ignorance of the facts, and that they were deliberately fostered by Leopold in order to further his own ends. There was actually not the slightest analogy between the International Association of the Congo and the Society for American

[1] Hertslet, II, p. 562. Thomson, p. 163. Keith, p. 54. Reeves, p. 52. Keltie, p. 210. Stanley, II, p. 388. L.J., Congo, No. 17, Strauch to Ferry, April 23, 1884.
[2] cf. above, Chapter vii, p. 77, Footnote 2.
[3] Thomson, p. 148.
[4] Ibid., pp. 147-9.
[5] Thomson, pp. 147-62. Yarnall, p. 22.

LEOPOLD AND THE POWERS

Colonisation which had promoted negro settlement in Liberia. The promise of absolute free trade[1] in the territories under his possession which was given by him in the treaty was one which he never fulfilled, and which he could never have had any intention of fulfilling, since his agents[2] were at that moment engaged in making treaties with native chiefs on the Congo (treaties which must surely have been drawn up with his knowledge, if not actually by him), giving them the most exclusive trade monopolies wherever they set up stations. Regarding the slave traffic he knew little, and as subsequent events were to prove, was to do less. As for Stanley, he remained throughout Leopold's faithful henchman, and only served the interests of the United States in so far as these were themselves subservient to those of the King of the Belgians. In fact the States gained nothing, Leopold a great deal, from the treaty of April 22nd. By recognising his private association as a sovereign power[3] the American Government gave real existence to this previously very precariously placed body, and thus enormously strengthened Leopold's international position, a fact which was of the utmost value to him in further engineering the rivalries of other powers to secure his own ends.

The treaty with France was signed the morning after the ratification of that with America. In it France recognised the flag of the Association[4]—but at a price—the right of pre-emption, namely, should the Association ever be forced to sell its possessions. It seems to have been the French[5] who first set the negotiations on foot, by asking for this right; whilst the demand for recognition on the part of Leopold, must, it can only be supposed, have been stimulated, if not suggested, by the signal success attending that which had just been made to the United States. There is no doubt[6] that France made the treaty largely out of fear of England. (The Anglo-Portuguese

---

[1] cf. Text, Hertslet, I, pp. 244–6.
[2] cf. F.O./84/1809/ Wyke to Granville, Feb. 2, 1884. Memo. Anderson, March 2, 1884. G.D./29/156/ Leopold to Granville, March 6, 1884. Thomson, p. 171.
[3] Thomson, p. 159. Yarnall, p. 22.
[4] cf. text, Hertslet, II, p. 562.
[5] Thomson, p. 164.
[6] cf. Thomson, p. 164.

treaty, it must be remembered still stood, though it had not yet been ratified.) She was also firmly convinced[1] that the Association would be forced sooner or later to sell its possessions on account of its precarious financial position, and she therefore imagined, that she had, in the pre-emption clause, successfully outwitted three powers—England, Portugal and the International Association of the Congo.

Actually, she had assisted in setting up a far more serious rival for herself on the Congo than either England or Portugal would ever have proved. The treaty of April 23rd, in which France at first sight, appeared " to gain all for nothing,"[2] since she only recognised an Association which she counted shortly on buying out, was in reality a masterstroke of diplomacy on the part of Leopold in which he succeeded in completely outwitting the French. Not only did he gain her recognition for nothing, since the pre-emption clause represented a purely hypothetical concession[3] which he had never any intention of making, he also by this very clause, which appeared to put France in such a strong position, incalculably strengthened his own, in such a way as really for the first time, to put him in sight of the goal of his ambitions, the control of the whole Congo region.

The French belief that he would soon have to sell,[4] was almost universally shared by the powers. By publicly making her his legatee, therefore, he roused such a fear among them of French dominion on the Congo (which it was now realised would be worse even than Anglo-Portuguese, on account of the nature of French tariffs), that he succeeded in rallying to him, not only their goodwill and their support for the designs of the Association, but also an active desire on their part to see its position (so far as this was possible) politically and financially strengthened in order to prevent such a calamity. Indeed, the pre-emption treaty with France caused a complete change in the international situation regarding the Congo, whose

---

[1] D.D.F., V, Ferry to Strauch, April 28, 1884. cf. Hertslet, II, p. 562. Circular, May 31, 1884. D.D.F., V, No. 299, ibid. L.J., Congo, 1884, No. 23 (slightly expurgated). Keith, p. 54. Thomson, pp. 165–6.
[2] The words are Granville's. cf. F.O./84/1810/ Malet to Granville, April 27, 1884, Minute, Granville.
[3] Thomson, p. 166.
[4] Ibid., pp. 167–8.

consequences only became fully apparent, after the Anglo-Portuguese treaty had finally been shelved (at the end of June). Fear of Anglo-Portuguese control of the Congo having now been definitely removed from the international consciousness, it was replaced by an even stronger one of France, which Leopold, not content with having originated, proceeded to utilise with even greater energy and success than he had done that which had formerly been entertained of England and Portugal.

This fear of France was shared by Germany. But owing to her colonial quarrel with England, the latter was now in a somewhat curious position. By the time Bismarck heard of the pre-emption clause in the treaty of April 23rd, he had already laid the foundation of the Franco-German entente, which, as has been seen, was at first entirely concerned with the Congo, and was based on the supposedly extreme nature of *English* ambitions there. There was an element of (apparently still for Bismarck *unconscious*) irony, in the situation, owing to the fact that it was he who was finally responsible for destroying the Anglo-Portuguese treaty. He had now himself to reckon with the new and greater menace to free trade on the Congo, contained in what he, like everyone else, believed to be Leopold's promise of cession to France ; whilst at the same time developing a policy which was grounded in the older fear of England—which no longer existed— and in the destruction of which he himself had played so large a part.

There was no question of giving up the Franco-German entente, for this, though for the moment dealing only with the Congo, was, as has been seen, very intimately connected with the Anglo-German estrangement as a whole, of which it was but an offshoot, and which was now steadily growing and deepening in intensity. It seems doubtful[1] whether Bismarck yet realised the full illogicality of his position, which only became apparent after the West African Conference had opened. There is at any rate no evidence to show that he did so. For the moment he contented himself with characteristically reconciling conflicting interests by continuing, on the one hand, to develop the entente with France, and on the other by entering into negotiations with Leopold for the recognition of his Association.

[1] cf. Thomson, p. 174.

84 THE BERLIN WEST AFRICAN CONFERENCE

In the middle of May[1] (at the time when the quarrel with England was nearing its first climax), and when he first took up the Portuguese proposal for a conference, he seems even to have thought of annexing the Congo himself. He discussed with the German explorer, Gerhard Rohlfs, the possibility of negotiating with Leopold for this purpose ; preparations were made for the latter's journey to Brussels ; everything was ready, Rohlfs was actually on the point of leaving for Belgium —when suddenly official news arrived of the pre-emption clause in the treaty of France with the Association. Bismarck thereupon cancelled the whole scheme out of deference to French interests, realising, as soon as he read the clause, that France was desirous of establishing *herself* there.

But he was no more anxious than anyone else to see this happen, and it was for this reason that he now opened negotiations[2] with Leopold for the recognition of the Association. On June 4th,[3] he wrote to Count Brandenburg, the German minister at Brussels, instructing him to transmit the conditions on which Germany would be ready to concede recognition. These included not only a demand for absolute freedom of trade in the basin of the Congo, but also a guarantee that this freedom would be maintained by any power to which the Association might in future sell its possessions. Bismarck's prime object[4] in making the treaty being to secure free trade for German nationals, he saw that to do this he must make doubly sure of the guarantees given by the Association, by making them cover the pre-emption clause with France, though of course he did not once mention France by name in his note.

The demand was naturally very distasteful to Leopold, who wrote back on June 12th,[5] ingeniously suggesting (in order to avoid embroiling himself with France) that the best way of securing freedom of commerce in the Congo would be the formation of an entente by Germany, France and England, for the establishment of an Independent State (this implied of course a state formed by the Association) in Central Africa.

[1] Thomson, pp. 173–5.
[2] Ibid., pp. 175–87.
[3] Ibid., p. 180.
[4] Thomson, pp. 180, 186–7.
[5] Ibid.

Bismarck, as might have been expected, rejected the suggestion,[1] declaring not only that diplomatic action would be premature, whilst the Anglo-Portuguese treaty was still pending; but also that England's hostility to German interests on the coast of West Africa made it in any case impossible to approach her; whilst as for France, he could not approach her either, since he had to be very careful not to compromise his present relations with her. It was Leopold's part he said to do this, since he had already negotiated a treaty with France, and it was therefore logically easier for him to broach the subject, especially since he was not bound by the political considerations which hampered Germany.

On June 27th,[2] Leopold gave an audience to Brandenburg, in which he thanked him for his last communication from Bismarck, but without vouchsafing any comments on it. At the same time he handed Brandenburg written propositions which he had drawn up for a treaty with Germany, adding that he had not inserted the desired clause guaranteeing freedom of commerce to German citizens in event of alienation, because of his fear that such a stipulation would be an obstacle for the Association in the future, as France would not then recognise the agreement. Bismarck was very angry when he received these propositions,[3] and criticised them severely, not only on account of the inadequate guarantees which they contained concerning freedom of commerce, but also because of what he considered Leopold's exaggerated territorial claims.

Finally Leopold gave way over the alienation clause,[4] but gained his point about delimitation, which was the inclusion of the south bank of the Congo, at that moment in dispute with France,[5] in the possessions of the Association. A note which he sent on August 8th to Bismarck, via the German banker, Bleichröder, on the whole gave satisfaction to the chancellor. There was still some difficulty, however, about his accepting Leopold's demand for the issue of Association currency in Germany, and he still asked for a more exact delimitation of frontiers. Finally Leopold sent him a map, on September 12th, whose demarcations recognising the claims

[1] Ibid., pp. 180-1.
[2] Ibid., pp. 181-2.
[3] Thomson, p. 182.
[4] Ibid., pp. 183-6.
[5] cf. below, 158-9.

86   THE BERLIN WEST AFRICAN CONFERENCE

of the Association to the left bank of Stanley Pool, were then accepted by Bismarck, and became the territorial basis of the treaty with Germany which was signed on November 8th.[1] In this treaty[2] Bismarck considered it his greatest triumph that he had secured a guarantee of free trade in event of alienation.[3] But, since, as has been seen,[4] Leopold never had any intention of alienating his possessions, and since, moreover, he never established, and apparently never meant to establish, free trade, in any case, the alienation clause in the treaty with Germany was really quite valueless.[5] In fact, Bismarck, like the American President, and the French Foreign Minister, was completely outwitted by Leopold.

The recognition also set the seal on the chancellor's ambiguous position with regard to France. On the other hand, it clearly offered an opportunity for co-operation with England, should he ever wish to take it. It has been seen how in the middle of June[6] Bismarck turned down Leopold's suggestion for taking either England or France into his confidence with regard to the Association, on the ground that the hostility of the one power, and the delicate nature of his relations with the other, did not admit of any such possibility. As a matter of fact, even had he been willing to approach England at that moment, he would probably have found that her antagonism to the real interests of the Association was as great, though for different reasons, as that of France. This was the accumulated result of Leopold's opposition to the Anglo-Portuguese treaty ;[7] of distrust of the honesty[8] if not of his intentions, at least of his methods, after the discovery of the monopolistic nature of the treaties which his agents were making with native chiefs on the Congo ; and of anxiety about the pre-emption treaty,[9]

---

[1] cf. above, Chapter vii, p. 77, Footnote 2.
[2] cf. text, Hertslet, I, pp. 219–20. W.B., Congo, 1885, No. 43. Protocol IX, Annex I.
[3] Thomson, p. 187.
[4] cf. above, pp. 82–3.
[5] pp. 105–6.
[6] cf. above, pp. 84–5.
[7] F.O./84/1809/ Memo. Anderson, March 2, 1884. Thomson, pp. 141–2. Fitzmaurice, II, p. 356.
[8] F.O./84/1809/ Wyke to Granville, Feb. 2, 1884 : Memo., Anderson, March 2, 1884. G.D./29/156/ Leopold to Granville, March 6, 1884. Minute, Anderson, March 8.
[9] F.O./84/1810/ Malet to Granville, April 27, 1884, Africa, 5. F.O. /84/1811/ Granville to Lyons, May 5, 1884, Africa, 75 : Granville to Malet,

England being the only country, apparently, on account of these preconceived prejudices, whose immediate reaction to this treaty was a desire to *weaken*, not to *strengthen* the International Association of the Congo.

Gradually, however, she came to adopt a somewhat different attitude, as a result of *Germany's* relations with the Association. At the end of May,[1] when Münster apparently somewhat inadvisedly mentioned to Granville that Bismarck was considering recognising it, Granville suggested a free interchange of views between the British and German governments about its status, rendered particularly desirable, he declared, by the pre-emption treaty with France. On June 20th,[2] however, following up his refusal to Leopold to take England and France into the secret of his plans, Bismarck sent a message to Granville, via Ampthill, declining to discuss the matter, as the subject, he declared, " had not yet occupied the attention of the German Foreign Office," and he was therefore not yet in a position to answer the British query.

By the end of the month, however, his intentions with regard to the Association were common knowledge. On June 21st,[3] the day after he had made this statement to Ampthill, an article was published at Brussels, in the *Indépendance Belge*, announcing that Germany was in negotiation with the International Association ; and on June 23rd,[4] Bismarck himself courted publicity, by a speech in the Reichstag in which he openly declared his intention of supporting the Association. Realising the importance of his policy,[5] the British Government now began to contemplate a further effort to find out exactly what the attitude of Germany might be. But so much had Great Britain learnt to fear and to distrust Leopold, that it was found difficult to understand what Bismarck's motive

May 5, 1884, Africa, 1 : Memo., Frederic Holmwood, May 6, 1884 : Lister to Granville, July 4, 1884. G.D./29/156/ Leopold to Granville, May 15, 1884, Minutes, May 16–18, by Granville, Fitzmaurice, Anderson, Lister. Leopold to Granville, May 22, 1884, Minutes, May 29, Granville, Anderson, Lister. G.D./29/198/ Granville to Leopold, May 20, 1884 : Memo., Lister, May 20, 1884: Granville to Leopold, Dec. 10, 1884.

[1] F.O./84/1811/ Granville to Ampthill, May 28, 1884, Africa, 5a.
[2] Ibid. Ampthill to Granville, June 20, 1884, Africa, 7.
[3] F.O./84/1812/ Malet to Granville, June 21, 1884, Africa, 9.
[4] Thomson, p. 181.
[5] F.O./84/1812/ Lister to Granville, July 4, 1884: Lister to Granville, July 17, 1884.

really could be in according his recognition, and the question was therefore seriously discussed at the Foreign Office of sending him the pre-emption treaty in order to convince him of the real meaning of its clauses,[1] in case he had either not seen, or had not understood them.

Just at this time,[2] however, rumours also began to be afloat concerning Bismarck's plans for a conference on the Congo, and these were finally responsible for staying the hand of the British Government. As Anderson,[3] the head of the African department in the Foreign Office, pointed out in a minute, which he wrote and sent to Granville on July 14th : if Bismarck were now making overtures for a conference, presumably on the basis of support for the Association, since he had publicly stated his intention of giving this, and Great Britain were to put before him her own suspicions of the constitution and aims of the Association, she would run the risk (as Bismarck doubtless knew all about the Association) of exposing her hostility to it before the conference opened without gaining any corresponding advantages. Granville wrote " suspend " against this minute, and the intended note to Bismarck, which had been drafted at the suggestion of T. V. Lister,[4] an official who had a deep distrust of the Association, and was markedly pro-Portuguese in his sympathies, was therefore cancelled. No further steps were taken therefore either now or later by the British Government, to find out the precise nature of Bismarck's relations with the Association, or to bring influence to bear upon them, in spite of a warning, given on July 25th by Ampthill[5] that the German Government were probably entering into negotiations with it, " with a view to promoting German interests on the Congo," and in spite of continued protests on the part of Lister, against " the filibusterings " of this " irresponsible Association ".

British disquiet concerning the Association was by no means allayed, however, and a conversation which took place between

---

[1] F.O./84/1812/ Lister to Granville, July 4, 1884.
[2] Ibid., Minute, Anderson, July 14, 1884   Ampthill to Granville, July 25, 1884, Africa, 8.
[3] Ibid., Minute, Anderson, July 14, 1884.
[4] cf. above (Note 1). Lister to Granville, July 4, 1884.
[5] F.O./84/1812/ Ampthill to Granville, July 25, 1884, Africa, 8.

Münster and Granville, on August 7th,[1] illustrates very clearly the deep suspicion and hostility with which the British Government still regarded it. On this day,[2] the very one on which Bismarck opened negotiations with France for consolidating the programme of the entente on the double basis of Egypt and West Africa, Münster had with Granville what was destined to be the first and last general discussion on the Congo which took place between England and Germany before Bismarck sprung his preconcerted invitation to the conference on Great Britain in October. Referring to the question of international agreement on the Congo, Münster declared that Bismarck thought it might be advisable to include the Association in any arrangements that might be made, "because it was not desirable, by ignoring the Association, to throw it too much into the hands of France." But Granville declared that the matter was one which needed careful consideration, the status of the International Association being doubtful, its administration questionable, whilst the projected reversion to France made the subject even more thorny, though he stated his willingness in principle to discuss it with Germany in order to come to a decision satisfactory to both countries.

At the end of August the attitude of the British Government was still severely non-committal. When Stanley himself came over on the 29th to see Granville at Walmer,[3] in order to sound him about possible British recognition of the Association, he made no headway at all, Granville declaring that he could as yet express no opinion on the subject. When also urged by Portugal,[4] at this time, to define his attitude to the Association, he similarly declined to give any definite statement of opinion.

It was only at the beginning of November,[5] after the German invitation to the conference had been accepted, and the whole question was clearly growing very imminent, that it began to be the object of serious discussion at the Foreign Office. The realities of the situation had meanwhile become

[1] F.O./84/1812/ Granville to Ampthill. Aug, 7, 1884, Africa, 14a. (C. 4205, No. 8), (expurgated).
[2] cf. above, p. 62.
[3] F.O./84/1812/ Memo., Granville, Walmer, Aug. 29, 1884.
[4] Ibid., Granville to d'Andrade, Sept. 3, 1884.
[5] Ibid., Memo., Anderson, Nov. 6, 1884. Twiss to Pauncefote, Nov. 6, 1884: Nov. 7, Malet's Instructions. (For these cf. also A. and P., LV, 1884–5: C. 4241.)

much clearer to the British Government. Germany, as well as the United States and France had now formally recognised the Association, and they saw that it was a force which must be reckoned with, whether they liked it or not. Part,[1] though by no means the whole truth concerning the Franco-German entente was now known, and more suspected; whilst Great Britain's own growing tension with Portugal must further have increased her sense of isolation, and given her an additional reason for not wishing to make an enemy of Leopold.

The attitude finally adopted by Great Britain towards the Association at the time of her entry into the conference, was defined in instructions sent to Malet on November 15th,[3] Though still non-committal, it was distinctly friendly. In the view of the British Government, it was stated, the Association was not yet a state. At the same time, it clearly had in it the possibilities of becoming one. Great Britain would watch with sympathy therefore any efforts which it made to do so, whilst recognition would follow if it succeeded. But this was a process which must necessarily take time, and the British Government would therefore be in favour of the continuation meanwhile of the present system of consular jurisdiction in the territories under its control, although fully prepared to respect the rights of property acquired by it up to this time.

The combination of Bismarck's *wholehearted* support of the International Association, born out of his fear of French tariffs on the Congo, with Great Britain's *half-hearted* support of it, born out of the *same* fear, qualified by an instinctive mistrust of Leopold, which was due to the intrigues which he had carried on against *her* efforts to circumvent French tariffs—in the Anglo-Portuguese treaty—was destined to have important results at the conference. The measure of *agreement* which it represented was finally responsible for establishing Leopold at the mouth of the Congo. The measure of *disagreement* which it contained, seems to have been the deciding factor in placing

---

[1] F.O./84/1813/ Granville to Walsham, Oct. 10, 1884, Africa, 141. (C. 4205, No. 12, Granville to Walsham, Oct. 10, 1884) (full text.) F.O./84/1813/ Lyons to Granville, Oct. 15, 1884, Africa, 91. (C. 4205, No. 15, Lyons to Granville, Oct. 15, 1884) (full text). cf. also Thomson, pp. 210–11.
[2] cf. F.O./84/1812/1813/1814/.
[3] F.O./84/1814/ Granville to Malet, Nov. 15, 1884, Africa, 78.

England on the Lower Niger, since this was the price which Bismarck showed himself prepared to pay, in order to win her conclusive support for the Association. The two together caused more damage to the aims and purposes of the Franco-German entente, than either could have done alone.

The CONGO BASIN
1885

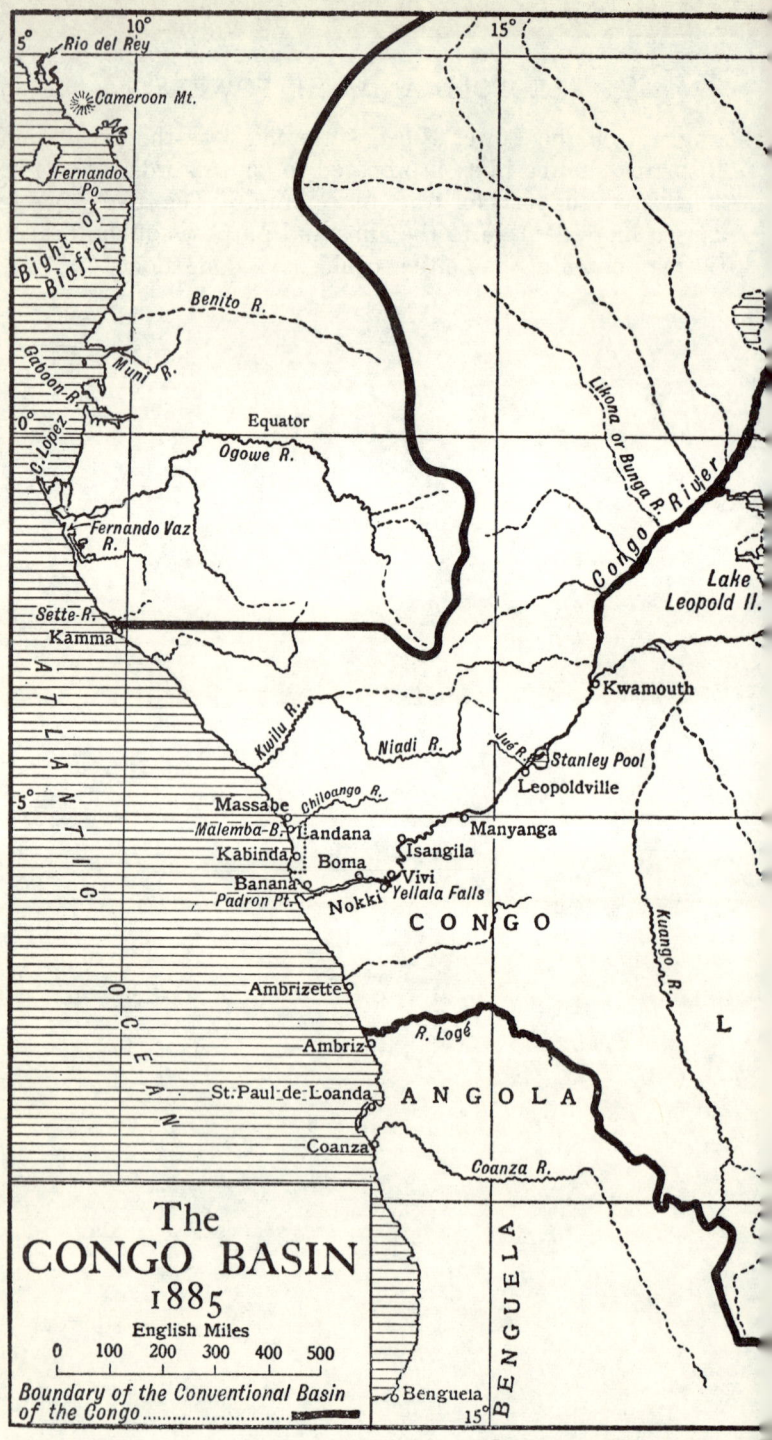

English Miles
0 100 200 300 400 500

Boundary of the Conventional Basin of the Congo ....

Based on a Map in the Royal Atlas

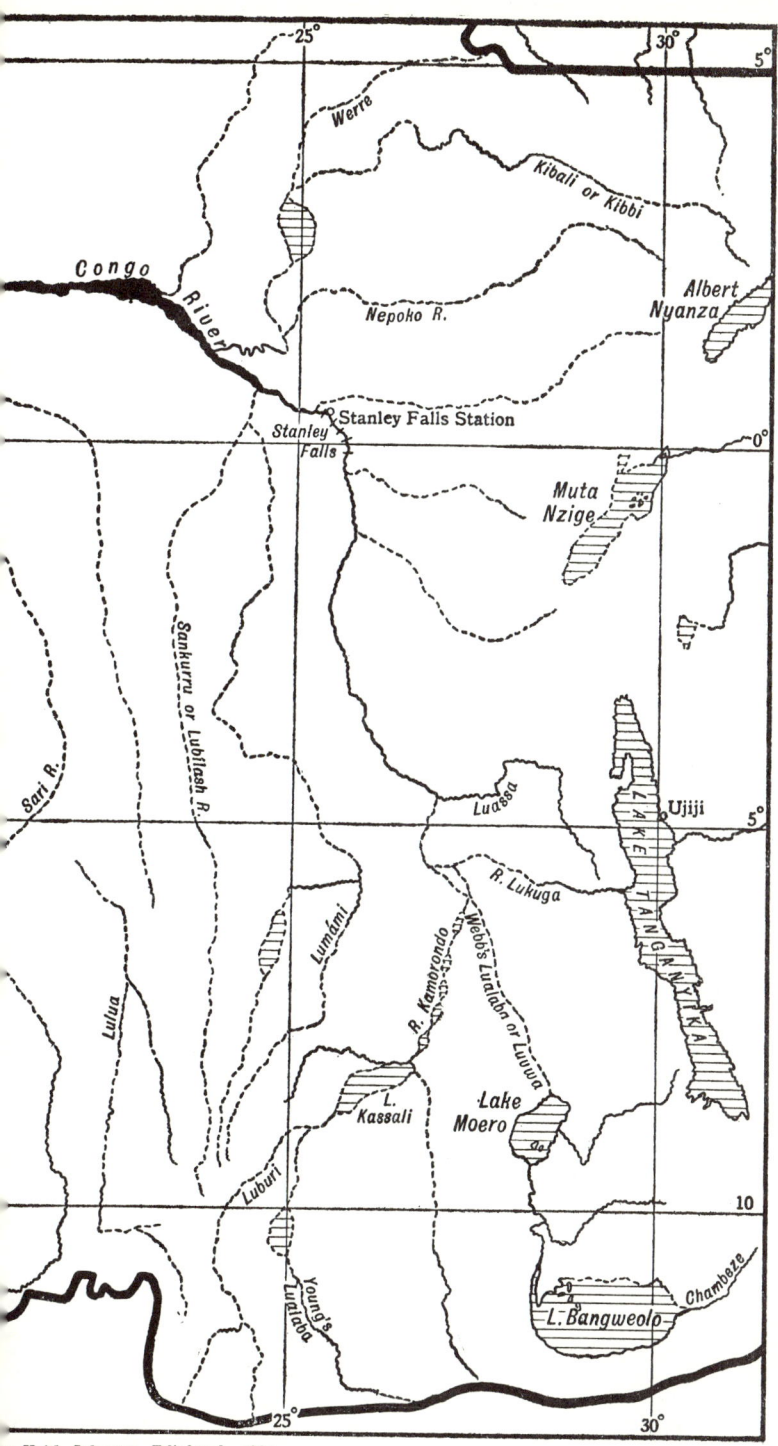

Keith Johnston, Edinburgh, 1885.

CHAPTER I

THE CONFERENCE: PROBLEMS AND PERSONALITIES

THE diplomacy leading up to the conference has now been studied. It remains to analyse that of the conference itself. Fourteen powers[1] were present there, eleven, that is to say (besides Great Britain), being invited by France and Germany to participate in it. These were: Austria-Hungary, Belgium, Denmark, Italy, The Netherlands, Portugal, Russia, Spain, Sweden and Norway, Turkey and the United States. As before, however, it will be found that the policies of only five, France, Germany, Great Britain, Portugal and the International Association (which was not legally represented there at all), are of real importance, and it will be the aim of the following chapters to trace their evolution throughout the tangled and technical subject-matter of the discussions. They form the logical complement to the diplomacy which has already been studied: diplomacy based, as has been seen, upon an unnatural Franco-German entente, itself due to an unnatural Anglo-German estrangement, whose discrepancies become increasingly obvious as the moment for summoning the conference draws near. Put to the acid test of expert investigation the entente now crumbles. Germany draws increasingly away from France, and collaborates to an increasing degree with the Association, effecting in the process a *rapprochement* with England. Portugal orientates her policy more and more closely in accord with that of France.

The ambiguous position of the Association deserves special mention.[2] Not being a state it had no official representatives of its own at Berlin. But its interests were in fact very fully

---

[1] A. and P., LV, 1884–5: C. 4361. Protocols of West African Conference: Protocol I. cf. above, pp. 68–9. Also Appendix XII.
[2] cf. Banning, *Mémoires*, pp. 15–16. Thomson, p. 217.

represented there not only by Colonel Strauch and Captain van der Velde, who, though unable to attend any of the meetings of the conference, were sent to it by Leopold in an unofficial capacity, but also by members of the Belgian and, strangely enough, also of the American delegation. To understand how this was possible it is necessary to see how the delegations of the other powers were constituted. Each of these, except that of Germany, which was headed (after Bismarck) by the German Foreign Minister, was represented in the German capital by its own ambassador or minister there, together with such expert advisers as its government thought fit to send from home. It was the presence of these expert advisers which gave the Association its chance.

It has been seen how the latter was entirely the creation of Leopold. So small a part in fact did Belgium herself play in his Congo ambitions, that, in so far as these were known[1] or even guessed at there, opinion was to a great extent hostile to them. Nevertheless, Leopold managed to effect a link between his own designs and the official representation of Belgian interests at the conference, by sending to the aid of Count van der Straten Ponthoz,[2] the Belgian minister in Berlin, two special envoys of his own. These were Baron Lambermont and Émile Banning, both of whom played an important part in furthering the cause of the Association at the conference. To do this they had to revolutionise the attitude of Belgium, though this did not take place without a preliminary struggle. Before they left for Berlin instructions[3] were actually drawn up for them by the Belgian Government, ordering them to maintain a strictly neutral and non-committal attitude throughout the discussions. But they protested so vigorously against this that finally they were allowed to have their way, and left Brussels fully armed with the most elaborate schemes and propositions regarding the Congo, of which they made full use later.

The representation of the Association's interests in the American delegation was even more curious than in the Belgian.

---

[1] cf. Banning, pp. 14–15. Thomson, pp. 217–18. F.O./84/1812/ Petre to Granville, Aug. 2, 1884, Africa, 83. F.O./84/1813/ Lister to Granville, Oct. 16, 1884. *Dilke Papers*, Vol. LVII, *Memoir*, Chapter xxii, pp. 26–7.

[2] Banning, *Mémoires*, pp. 13–14. Thomson, p. 218.

[3] Banning, *Mémoires*, pp. 14–15. Thomson, pp. 220–1.

THE CONFERENCE

John A. Kasson,[1] the American Ambassador, who appears to have been distinguished more by verbosity than by brains, was an ardent sympathiser with Leopold's designs, as understood in America through the propaganda of Colonel Sanford. He was also anxious for the United States to occupy a position of éclat and prestige at the conference,[2] an ambition which could clearly be more easily realised if she had the advantage of being supplied with really expert advice. For this reason he co-opted on to his staff[3] (entirely, it appears, on his own initiative), not only Sanford himself, but also the explorer, Henry Stanley. Both these men were extremely active in defending the interests of the Association at the conference, and their presence in the American delegation explains why it is so often possible during its discussions, simply to read for the words " International Association " those of the " United States ".

So far as it can be disentangled from this liaison[4] with the Association, the attitude of America and the part played by her at the conference is of some interest but of no practical importance. It is indeed possible to compare it with that taken up by her at Paris in 1918. Secure, then as later, on the other side of the Atlantic, with little or no direct interest in the issues at stake, she could afford, than as later, to be magnificently Utopian in her ideals, but when it came to giving any material pledge of them she at once drew back. Thus her representative at Berlin in 1884 and 1885 is to be found constantly advocating the widest possible application of every possible liberal principle, from free trade and free navigation on the Congo and the Niger, and the abolition of the internal slave trade and the

---

[1] cf. Protocol II: Kasson's Speech, Nov. 19, 1884. S.E.D. 196, No. 34, Kasson to Frelinghuysen, Nov. 20, 1884: No. 36, Kasson to Frelinghuysen, Nov. 24, 1884: No. 47, Kasson to Bayard, Jan. 7, 1885: No. 50, Kasson to Frelinghuysen, Jan. 12, 1885: No. 71, Kasson to Bayard, March 16, 1885: No. 74, Kasson to Bayard, April, 13, 1885. Thomson, pp. 221-3. Reeves, pp. 31-2.
[2] Ibid. cf. also S.E.D. 196, No. 21, Kasson to Frelinghuysen, Nov. 3, 1884.
[3] S.E.D. 196, No. 12, Kasson to Frelinghuysen, Oct. 23, 1884: No. 13, Frelinghuysen to Kasson, Oct. 23, 1884: No. 14, Kasson to Frelinghuysen, Oct. 24, 1884: No. 17, Frelinghuysen to Hatzfeldt, Oct. 30, 1884: No. 23, Frelinghuysen to Kasson, Nov. 6, 1884: No. 32, Kasson to Frelinghuysen, Nov. 17, 1884: No. 36, Kasson to Frelinghuysen, Nov. 24, 1884: Thomson, pp. 221-3. Banning, *Mémoires*, p. 12. Reeves, pp. 33-4. Keltie, p. 207 (but he mentions Stanley only, not Sanford). Keith, Ref., p. 57.
[4] cf. Protocols of Conference. S.E.D. 196, Part I.

liquor traffic, down to international regulation of colonial occupations in Africa ; yet she was the only one[1] who had refused to give a pledge on entering the conference that she would ratify its decisions, and, in fact, she never did ratify them.[2]

The only other powers at the conference, besides the five already mentioned (including Belgium and America as representative of the interests of the Association), whose policies were even occasionally of any moment there, were Holland and Russia. Holland,[3] as a power with considerable trading interests on the Congo, gave substantial support, together with Germany, Great Britain and the agents of the Association, to the claim made by these powers for a large measure of free trade in the Congo : Russia[4] worked with France against them because of her traditional dislike of any extension of the principles of free trade, which was due to the way in which they had proved detrimental to her own interests on the Danube. The rôle of both powers, however, was throughout subordinate to the main conflict which arose between England, Germany and the Association, on the one hand, and France and Portugal on the other, in this question.

Italy was conspicuous throughout the conference[5] as the one power anxious to maintain a consistently friendly attitude towards Great Britain, for its own sake. Partly for this reason, partly no doubt because she was not herself directly affected by the questions discussed, she too joined in the demand for a widespread application of free trade principles in the Congo,[6] and throughout maintained a liberal attitude. But her importance in the conference as a whole was negligible.

So was that of all the other powers present. It is true that

---

[1] S.E.D. 196, No. 7. Frelinghuysen to Alvensleben, Oct. 17, 1884 ; No. 9, Frelinghuysen to Kasson, Oct. 17, 1884. Reeves, p. 32.

[2] Protocols : Protocol II, Annex 6, Annex 3. A. and P , LV, 1884–5 : C. 4739, pp. 22–5. Hertslet, pp. 45–7. S.E.D. 196. No. 83, Alvensleben to Bayard, March 13, 1886. No 85, Bayard to Alvensleben, April 16, 1885. No. 86, Alvensleven to Bayard, May 11, 1886. E. M. Satow, *Guide to Diplomatic Practice*, II, p. 144. Yarnall, p. 78. Banning, *Mémoires*, p. 12. Keltie, p. 207. Evans Lewin, p. 151. Keith, pp. 58, 65.

[3] Protocol III. J. A. Crowe, Private Correspondence, J.A.C. to Granville, Dec. 13, 1884. Stanley, II, p. 395.

[4] cf. below, p. 133.

[5] Protocols of the Conference.

[6] Protocol III.

THE CONFERENCE 99

Turkey's interests in East Africa[1] considerably complicated the delimitation of the Congo basin. But the difficulties raised were not insuperable, and only took time to surmount. They did not touch any of the main political issues of the conference, with which Turkey herself was not concerned.

Space does not permit enumeration of the personnel of all the delegations present. It must be sufficient to give those of the most important.

The British delegation consisted of the British Ambassador[2] at Berlin, Sir Edward Malet ; Percy Anderson[3] of the African department of the Foreign Office ; the Hon. Robert Meade,[4] Assistant Under-Secretary at the Colonial Office ; A. W. L. Hemming,[5] Principal Clerk of the Colonial Office ; and Joseph Archer Crowe,[6] who had sat on the Danube Commission and was attached to the British Embassy at Paris, and whose official title was at that time " Commercial Attaché for Europe." In addition to this the aged jurisconsult, Sir Travers Twiss,[7] was sent out in an unofficial capacity to lend his services to the British Embassy, as was also a geographer called Bolton,[8] from the cartographic firm of Stanford's in Whitehall. Four British

[1] Protocols III, IV : General Act, Chapter i, Art. I, par. 6. F.O./84/1818/ Malet to Granville, Dec. 23, 1884, Africa, 272. (A. and P., IV, 1884-5 : C. 4284, Malet to Granville, Dec. 23, 1884) (full text). Yarnall, pp. 73-4.
[2] F.O./84/1814/ Granville to Malet, Oct. 24, 1884, Africa, 48a. (Also in A. and P., LV, 1884-5. : C. 4205, No. 27.) Protocol I : General Act. J. A. Crowe, Private Correspondence, Oct. 28, 1884. Fitzmaurice, II, pp. 374-5. Banning, *Mémoires*, p. 11. Keith, p. 57. Stanley, II, p. 392. F.O. List, 1885.
[3] F.O./84/1814/ Malet to Granville, Nov. 8, 1884, Africa, 45 : (Also in A. and P., LV, 1884-5 : C. 4360, No. 2.) Granville to Malet, Nov. 12, 1884, Africa, 64. J. A. Crowe, Private Correspondence, Oct. 25, 1884. F.O. List, 1885. Stanley, II, p. 392. Fitzmaurice, II, pp. 37-45. Banning, *Mémoires*, p. 11.
[4] Ibid. C.O. List, 1885.
[5] F.O./84/1814/ Granville to Malet, Nov. 12, 1884, Africa, 64. C.O. List, 1885.
[6] F.O./84/1814/ Malet to Granville, Nov. 8, 1884, Africa, 45. (C. 4360, No. 2.) Granville to Malet, Nov. 12, 1884, Africa, 64. J. A. Crowe, Private Correspondence, Oct. 25, 1884. *Dilke Papers*, Vol. LVII : *Memoir*, Chapter xxv, pp. 71-2. F.O. List, 1885. Stanley, II, p. 392. Fitzmaurice, ii, p. 375. Banning, *Mémoires*, p. 12.
[7] F.O./84/1814/ Malet to Granville, Nov. 12, 1884, Tel. 36 : Granville to Malet, Nov. 12, 1884, Africa, 64. Fitzmaurice, II, p. 375. Banning, *Mémoires*, p. 12. D.N.B.
[8] F.O./84/1814/ Anderson to Hertslet (no date) : Hertslet to Anderson, Oct. 30, 1884 : Memo., Hertslet, Nov. 1, 1884 : Malet to Granville, Nov. 12. 1884, Tel. 36 : Granville to Malet, Nov. 12, 1884, Africa, 64. Fitzmaurice, II, p. 375.

merchants,[1] E. W. Bond, A. L. Jones, E. H. Cookson, and John Holt, of the Congo District Association, also represented British trading interests in an unofficial capacity at the conference, and gave much valuable assistance to the delegation proper. The mysterious Taubmann-Goldie[2] was likewise there unofficially, such evidence as exists concerning his activities, tending to show that he played an important, and at times a vital part in defending British interests.

France sent to Berlin her ambassador, Baron de Courcel,[3] an able and brilliant man, whose large part in the negotiations leading up to the Franco-German entente has already been noticed. He was assisted by Édouard Engelhardt,[4] an expert on fluvial navigation, and by Dr. Ballay, a lieutenant of De Brazza's in Africa, imbued with a bitter animosity to Stanley and the International Association. The French like the British delegation also made use of the services of a geographer, who was called Desbuissons.

Germany, as has been pointed out, inevitably occupied a special position at the conference. Bismarck was nominally president of it,[5] but actually he presided over only two of its meetings, the first and the last. His control over German policy was close and constant, but this for the most part was exercised through the intermediary of his subordinates at Berlin from the seclusion of his country retreat at Varzin. The other meetings of the conference were conducted[6] either by Count Hatzfeldt, the Minister for Foreign Affairs, or by Busch, Bismarck's confidential adviser, who was at that time Under-Secretary of State at the German Foreign Office.[7] These two men, together with the very able von Küsserow, one of the

---

[1] F.O./84/1814/ Minute. Anderson, Nov. 8, 1884 : Bright to Fitzmaurice, Nov. 11, 1884 : Granville to Malet, Nov. 12, 1884, Africa, 64.

[2] cf. *National Review*, Vol. XXXIII, March–August, 1899, Leonard Darwin, *British Expansion in Africa*, p. 972. Encyclopedia Britannica (11th edition), Article on Goldie, Dorothy Wellesley, *Sir George Goldie—Founder of Nigeria*, pp. 96–7, 146–7.

[3] L.J., Congo, 1885, No. 4, Ferry to Courcel, Nov. 8, 1884. Protocol I: General Act. Banning, *Mémoires*, pp. 10–11. Keith, p. 57. Stanley, II, p. 392.

[4] L.J., Congo, 1885, No. 4, Ferry to Courcel, Nov. 8, 1884. Banning, *Mémoires*, p. 11. Stanley, II, p. 392.

[5] Protocols, cf. I and X.

[6] Protocols, cf. II–IX, General Act. Banning, *Mémoires*, p. 10. Stanley, II, p. 391.

[7] Banning, *Mémoires*, p. 10.

THE CONFERENCE

initiators of the German colonial movement, who was attached to the commercial section of the Foreign Office, formed the permanent staff of Germany's delegation.[1] To this from time to time was added the presence of the Hamburg merchant, Adolf Woermann, who gave valuable advice in many of the technical, commercial, and economic questions discussed in connection with the first basis. The explorer and adventurer, Joseph Flegel,[2] also appears to have played some part in advising the German delegation behind the scenes, but the exact extent of his influence remains still to be revealed.

Portugal was represented not only by her minister at Berlin, the Marquis de Penafiel,[3] but also by the famous ex-cabinet minister, Serpa de Pimentel, whose presence there was in itself an indication of the pro-French and anti-British policy, which she was likely to pursue. She also made use of the services of a geographer and publicist, Luciano Cordeiro.[4] The Belgian delegation,[5] as has been seen, was composed of Count van der Straten Ponthoz,[6] Baron Lambermont, and Émile Banning[7] ; the American of Kasson[8] Sanford,[9] and Stanley.[10]

There were in all ten full sessions of the conference,[11] the first being held on November 15th, 1884, the last on February 26th, 1885, a date which (quite fortuitously) was the anniversary of the signature of the Anglo-Portuguese treaty. All its main work, however, was done by committees and sub-committees set up between these full sittings, which then submitted the results of their labours to final revision by them. The decisions of

---

[1] Ibid., pp. 10. 21–2. cf. also, Protocol XV, Annex I, Report of the Commission : and Protocol V. F.O./84/1816/ Malet to Granville, Dec. 1, 1884, Africa, 164a. L.J., Congo, 1885, Report of Engelhardt, p. 7. Thomson, p. 227. Stanley, II, p. 392.
[2] F.O./84/1814/ Anderson to Hertslet, Oct.—(no date)—1884. cf. also, J. A. Crowe, Private Correspondence, Nov. 19, 1884. (Reference to Lecture of Flegel's at meeting of " Kolonialverein ".) G.D./29/269/, F.O./146/ C.P. 5021, No. 93, Malet to Granville, Oct. 17, 1884 (Report of Lecture given by Flegel, Oct. 4, to German Geographical Society).
[3] Protocol I, General Act. Banning, *Mémoires*, pp. 12–13. Stanley, II, p. 392.
[4] Banning, *Mémoires*, p. 13. Stanley, II, p. 393.
[5] cf. above, p. 96.
[6] cf. also, Protocol I, General Act. Stanley, II, p. 391.
[7] Ibid.
[8] cf. above, pp. 96–7.
[9] cf. also, Protocol I, General Act.
[10] Ibid.
[11] Protocols.

the powers were embodied in a "General Act" signed and ratified by all those present at Berlin except the United States. The first fortnight of the conference,[1] from November 15th to December 1st, 1884, passed in consideration of the first basis, the question of the establishment of freedom of commerce in the basin and mouths of the Congo : most of December in that of the second,[2] concerning freedom of navigation on the Congo and the Niger. After this the conference adjourned over Christmas, resuming its labours again on January 7th, 1885. It was now the turn of the third basis concerning effective occupation to be discussed. This took only another three weeks.

The conference, however, continued to sit for almost another month.[3] The reason for this delay must be sought in that attending the negotiations for a territorial settlement of the Congo,[4] which had been proceeding, in one form or another, between France, Portugal, and the International Association, ever since it first met. These negotiations did not form part of the conference proper. Territorial questions had, it will be remembered, been expressly excluded by France from its programme.[5] Nevertheless, largely on account of Bismarck's insistence they were discussed whilst the conference was still sitting, and their results form an important contribution to its work. They were not embodied in the General Act, but took the form of separate treaties[6] appended to it, signed between France and the International Association, and Portugal and the International Association respectively.

Complementary to them were the formal treaties[7] by which all the powers at the conference, who had not already done so, beginning with Great Britain on December 16th, 1884, and ending with Belgium on February 23rd, 1885, recognised the International Association of the Congo as a sovereign state. These treaties were likewise not included in the General Act drawn up

[1] Protocols I–IV. cf. Part II, Chapter ii, pp. 105–18.
[2] Protocols IV–VI. cf. Part II, Chapter iii, pp. 119–41.
[3] Protocols IX, X.
[4] cf. Part II, Chapter v, pp. 152–75.
[5] cf. above, p. 56.
[6] cf. C. 4361. L.J., Congo, 1885. Hertslet, I, pp. 409–11, 232–3 : Convention, France and International Association of Congo, Feb 5, 1885 : Convention, Portugal and International Association of Congo, Feb. 14, 1885.
[7] cf. Protocol IX, Annex I. C. 4361. Hertslet, I, pp. 221–6 (Great Britain), 227–8 (Italy), 19, 21–5 (Austria), 230–1 (Netherlands), 240–1 (Spain), 239 (Russia), 242–3 (Sweden and Norway), 205–6 (Denmark), 196–7 (Belgium).

at Berlin, but simply appended to its protocols. They were vital to its proceedings, however, for it was thanks to them as well as to the territorial settlements made by the Association with France and Portugal, that the former was given adequate authority with which to sign the General Act, and that Bismarck, at the last meeting of the conference, was able to refer to it as " The Congo Free State ", a title which remained with it until Belgium annexed the Congo in 1908.[1]

Humanitarian questions occupied a small place at the conference. The possibility of completely wiping out the internal slave trade in Africa was indeed discussed,[2] but resulted only in the insertion of a vague and ineffective clause in the final act. That of abolishing the liquor traffic[3] was broached by Great Britain, but turned down by the conference without ever being discussed there, chiefly on account of the vested interests, principally German, which were involved. Neither

[1] cf. Keith, pp. 143-4.
[2] Protocols I, II, III, V, VI, VII. General Act, Chapter ii, Article IX. S.E.D. 196, No. 46, Kasson to Frelinghuysen, Dec. 22, 1884, Jan. 12, 1885. F.O./84/1814/ Nov. 7, 1884, Malet's Instructions, Africa, 59 : (cf. also C. 4241—full text.) Granville to Malet, Nov. 12, 1884 : (Also C. 4360, No. 3—full text.) Pauncefote to Granville, Nov. 14, 1884 : Granville to Malet, Nov. 15, 1884, Africa, 82 : F.O./84/1815/ Malet to Granville, Nov. 17, 1884, Africa, 68 : Granville to Malet, Nov. 18, Africa, 85 : Minute, Kennedy—on Protocol II, Nov. 22, 1884 : Malet to Granville, Nov. 24, 1884, Tel. 16 : Granville to Malet, Nov. 25, 1884, Africa, 101 : Malet to Granville, Nov. 26, 1884, Tel. 27 : Granville to Malet, Nov. 27, 1884, Africa, 114 : F.O./84/1816/ Rumbold to Granville, Dec. 2, 1884 : Twiss to Pauncefote, Dec. 3, 1884 : Malet to Granville, Dec. 6, 1884, Tel. 51 : Pauncefote to Selborne, Dec. 8, 1884 : Selborne to Pauncefote, Dec. 10. Malet to Granville, Dec. 9, Tel. 56. Granville to Malet, Dec. 9, Tel. 24 : F.O./84/1817/ Malet to Granville, Dec. 16, Africa, 230. : F.O./84/1818/ Malet to Granville, Dec. 22, 23 : Africa, 273. (Also in C. 4284, No. 1—full text.), Granville to Malet, Dec. 31, Africa, 192 : F.O./84/1819/ Malet to Granville, Jan. 3, 1885, Africa, 3 : Jan. 5, 1885, Tel. 1 : Jan 7, Tel. 6, 1885 : Feb. 21, 1885 : F.O./84/1822/ Malet to Granville, Feb. 21, 1885, Africa, 136 : (C. 4284, No. 2.) L.J., Congo, 1885, Engelhardt's Report pp. 28-30. D.D.F., V, Nos. 503, 512. Banning, *Mémoires*, pp. 22-3. Keith, p. 60. Reeves, pp. 42-3. Yarnall, pp. 73-4.
[3] Protocols : Protocol V, Annex 16. Protocol V. Protocol VI. S.E.D. 196, No. 46, Kasson to Frelinghuysen, Dec. 22, 1884 : Feb. 9, 1885. F.O./84/1815/ Granville to Malet, Nov. 12, 1884 : (Also C. 4360, No. 3—full text.) F.O./84/1816/ Malet to Granville, Dec. 6, 1884, Tel. 50 : F.O./84/1817/ Granville to Malet, Dec. 10, 1884, Tel. 26 : Malet to Granville, Dec. 10, 1884, Africa, 207 : C.O. to F.O., Dec. 10, 1884 : Memo., Hertslet, Dec. 10, 1884 : Pauncefote to Malet, Dec. 11. 1884 : Malet to Granville, Dec. 12, 1884, Tel. 60 : Dec. 13, 1884, Africa, 219 : Memo., Kennedy, Dec. 18. 1884 : F.O./84/1818/ Malet to Granville, Dec. 22, 1884, Africa, 263 : Memo., C. Hill, Dec. 22, 1884 : Malet to Granville, Dec. 23, 1884, Africa, 272 : (Also in C. 4284, No. 1—full text.) F.O./84/1819/ Malet to Granville, Feb. 21, 1885, Africa, 130 : (Also in C. 4284, No. 2.) Banning, *Mémoires*, pp. 22-3. D. Wellesley, *Taubmann-Goldie*, p. 33. Stanley, II, p. 397.

question had any bearing on the main political issues of the conference, and will therefore not be considered here. The succeeding chapters will now deal with the main subjects of discussion at the conference in so far as they were related to these issues, taking them in the following order:

    I.   The First Basis.
   II.   The Second Basis.
  III.   The Recognition by the Powers of the International Association.
  IV.   The Territorial Negotiations over the Congo.
   V.   The Third Basis.

It will be found that the first four questions are closely interconnected, whilst the fifth and last forms a chapter somewhat apart in the history of the conference, related only generally to those which precede it.

CHAPTER II

THE FIRST BASIS
FREEDOM OF COMMERCE IN THE BASIN AND MOUTHS OF THE CONGO

THE avowed object of the first basis of the conference was to secure free trade in the basin and mouths of the Congo.[1] Actually, however, the conference succeeded in establishing it in a far wider area, and the discussions which arose concerning it revealed an underlying unity in the views of England, Germany, and the Association towards the problems of free trade *as a whole* in Central Africa, in contrast to those of France and Portugal, which were radically different. The first group of powers aimed at extending,[2] the second at restricting the free trade principle as far as possible.

Differences between France and Germany were given peculiar emphasis, owing to the fact that neither country had yet fully realised the extent to which their opinions clashed, and did not hesitate, therefore, to give, at first both strong and public expression to them. The result was that there were open breaches between the French and German delegates, both in conference and in committee. As the discussions proceeded, however, Bismarck learned to adopt a more conciliatory tone, and even to make minor concessions to France, in the interests of the entente. But this did not prevent him from remaining fundamentally in sympathy with England and the Association, and from obtaining with their help a substantial victory for the principles of free trade.

England was as anxious as Germany to extend these principles, but at first tended to play a less conspicuous part in

[1] cf. above, p. 67.
[2] On paper only as it proved. But Germany and Great Britain were undoubtedly sincere at the time, whereas Leopold was undoubtedly not. cf. above pp. 80–1.

the debates, owing to her less advantageous diplomatic position. She warmed to the fray, however, and just at the moment when the German delegates were beginning to cool off in their opposition to the French, she came to the fore, partly no doubt for this very reason, as a major champion of free trade interests.

A constant feature in the situation was the close collaboration between Bismarck and the agents of the Association, whose dependence upon him for the direction and control of their policy became increasingly evident as the conference went on.

Portugal's attitude was at first indeterminate. She had made advances[1] to, and had been rebuffed, by England, France, and Germany in turn, before the conference opened. When it did so, therefore, she had the confidence of none of these powers, and was not certain what direction their policies would take. Impelled by a natural similarity of interest, however, she very soon gravitated towards France, with whom she collaborated more and more closely as the discussions proceeded.

Of these, it may be said in general, that they crystallised the latent tendencies of the five powers under review, to form themselves into two opposing blocs, which constituted the natural framework of their policies. In this way, they not only played the introductory act in, they also set the stage for, the main drama of the conference.

Before any rules could be laid down concerning free trade, it was clear that the area in which they were to operate must be exactly defined. Delimitation of the Congo basin, therefore, was the first problem which confronted the delegates. This at once caused difficulties with France,[2] who was the only

[1] F.O./84/1812/ Petre to Granville, July 11, 1884, Africa, 78: July 13, Tel. 78: Lyons to Granville, July 16, 1884, Africa, 70: Granville to Ampthill July 19, Africa, 16: Granville to Petre, July 19, Africa, 79: Lyons to Granville, July 23, Africa, 75: Memo., Anderson, July 25: Ampthill to Granville, July 25, Africa, 8: July 31, Africa, 9: Petre to Granville, Aug. 2, Africa, 83: Granville to Petre, Aug. 6, Africa, 81a: Granville to Ampthill, Aug. 7, Africa, 14a: Ampthill to Granville, Aug. 8, Africa 10: Pauncefote to Granville, Aug. 11: Granville to Pauncefote, Aug. 12: Memo., Pauncefote, Aug. 23: Petre to Granville, Aug. 29, Africa, 91: Scott to Granville, Aug. 30, Africa, 13: Granville to Petre, Sept. 3, Africa, 90c: Scott to Granville, Sept. 26, Africa, 17: F.O./84/1813/ Petre to Granville, Oct. 2, Africa, 93: Lister to Petre, Oct. 13, Africa, 96: Lister to Granville, Oct. 13: Petre to Granville, Oct. 14, Africa, 95: Oct. 16, Africa 96: Oct. 17, Africa, 97: F.O./84/1814/ Petre to Granville, Oct. 24, Africa, 102: Oct. 29, Africa, 103: Oct. 30, Africa, 105: Granville, to Petre, Nov. 5, Africa, 113: Petre to Granville, Nov. 14, Africa, 108.

[2] D.D.F., V, No. 455, Courcel to Ferry, Nov. 19, 1884: Footnote, Ferry to Courcel, Nov. 17, 1884. cf. Yarnall, p. 67.

THE FIRST BASIS

power opposed to the idea *in toto*. Portugal,[1] who might otherwise have objected, felt herself in too weak a position to assert her claims unaided to the disputed territories lying between 5° 12' and 8° South Latitude to which she aspired. She had therefore committed herself beforehand to the principle of delimitation by promising the powers free trade in these areas if, in return, her claims to them were recognised as valid. France[2] had also, in theory, committed herself beforehand to the principle, by consenting to draw up with Bismarck, before the conference opened, a joint project of declaration on free trade in the Congo basin, based almost textually on the clauses of the Franco-German entente, whose articles presupposed and stated the necessity for delimitation. But this did not prevent her from making violent efforts to oppose it, as soon as Bismarck submitted the project to the powers.

These efforts are of some interest, since they afford a first, as well as striking example, of a certain stiffening in her attitude towards the problem of international control in Central Africa, which had quite clearly taken place *since* the conclusion of the Franco-German entente as the result of her increased sense of Germany's need of her, following Bismarck's overtures in August and September.[3] They were destined to meet with bitter disappointment, however, because of the contradictory elements in the chancellor's policy which tended to throw him more and more, as the conference proceeded, into the arms of the Association, in direct opposition to French interests.

Bismarck was furious[4] when Courcel told him of Ferry's disinclination for any exact definition of the Congo basin, and of his desire to see the *status quo* undisturbed. If such were really the attitude of France, he told the French Ambassador, it would be better if the two countries had never undertaken to do anything together. This was strong language, and Courcel, evidently realising that the matter was serious and that France might indeed wreck the conference if she persisted, wisely took

[1] Protocol II, Speech of Penafiel, Nov. 19, 1884. Thomson, p. 226.
[2] cf. Protocol I, Bismarck's Speech and Annex I (text of project). L.J., Congo, 1885, Report, Engelhardt, pp.5–6. D.D.F., V, No. 452, Courcel to Ferry, Nov. 15, 1884. Banning, p. 20. cf. also, L.J., Congo, 1884, Nos. 25 and 26, Bismarck to Courcel, Sept. 13 ; Courcel to Bismarck, Sept. 29, 1884.
[3] cf. above, Chapter vi, pp. 62–71.
[4] D.D.F., V, No. 455, Courcel to Ferry, Nov. 19, 1884.

it upon himself, after this, to calm the chancellor down and to declare, on his own initiative, that France was ready for delimitation at least of the geographical basin of the Congo, though with reserves regarding her province of Gaboon.

Once he had conceded this point, no difficulty was found by the powers at the second meeting of the conference[1] in appointing a commission to deal with the whole question. Its first task was easy. This was to delimit the actual geographical basin of the Congo,[2] which was defined, without much discussion,[3] as being bounded by the watersheds or mountain-ridges of the adjacent basins of the Niari, the Ogowé, the Schari, and the Nile, on the north; the eastern watershed line of Lake Tanganyika on the east; and the watersheds of the basins of the Zambesi and the Logé on the south. Portugal[4] made some difficulties about the inclusion of Lake Tanganyika in the eastern boundary, but they were not pressed and were afterwards quietly overruled.

After this, however, the much more difficult question presented itself of giving the basin a wider extension, for the purposes of free trade, than geography itself permitted. From the first it was clear that the majority of the commission were in favour of some such extension.[5] But the opposition of France proved a severe stumbling-block to any easy solution of the problem. The so-called "Conventional Basin" eventually agreed upon represented, as is well known, an almost fantastic enlargement on the area of the geographical basin proper. On the West Coast[6] this was extended north and south to cover the territory lying between 2° 30′ South Latitude and 8° South Latitude. This coastal extension was then prolonged inland, until it met the original eastern boundary of the basin. This

---

[1] Protocol II, Nov. 19, 1884. Protocol III, Annex. L.J., Congo, 1885 p. 6. S.E.D. 196, No. 26, Kasson to Frelinghuysen, Nov. 24, 1884. D.D.F. V, No. 455, Courcel to Ferry, Nov. 19, 1884: No. 456, Courcel to Ferry, Nov. 20 F.O./84/1815/ Malet to Granville, Nov. 19, 1884, Africa, 6. Thomson, p. 225 Reeves, p. 38. Yarnall, p. 73.
[2] cf. Protocol III, Annex, Report of Commission on Delimitation of Congo Basin. S.E.D. 196, No. 26, Kasson to Freylinghuysen, Nov. 24, 1884.
[3] Protocol III, Annex, Report of Commission. General Act, Chapter i Article I. cf. Keith, p. 58.
[4] Protocol III, Annex, Report of Commission.
[5] L.J., Congo, 1885, Engelhardt's Report, p. 6. D.D.F., V, No. 456, Courcel to Ferry, Nov. 20, 1884. No. 459, Courcel to Ferry, Nov. 23, 1884.
[6] Protocol III, Annex, Report of Commission. General Act, Chapter i Article I.

was then itself extended between the parallels of 5° North Latitude in the north, and the mouth of the Zambesi in the south, until it touched the shores of the Indian Ocean. But these boundaries were not reached without considerable discussion. The West Coast extension[1] was the first to be considered. Here Portugal,[2] true to her previous understanding with the powers, made no difficulties about the southern limit being placed at the mouth of the Logé in Angola. But France[3] proved both fractious and obstinate about the line of the northern frontier, in spite of the fact that she found herself in a position of complete isolation in the commission in pressing her claims. There is no doubt that she would have liked to exclude the Gaboon altogether from the free trade area, fixing its northern limit on the coast at Massabé (5° 12'), which she considered the frontier of her possessions. But all the powers were in favour of *some* extension of it northwards into French territory, and she was forced therefore to confine her efforts to trying to bring it down as far south *within* these territories, as the attitude of the powers would permit.

The prime obstacle in her path[4] was the determined opposition of England, Germany, and the International Association to any large exclusion of the Gaboon coast from the free trade area, Germany, as the event proved, being prepared to go even further than England in her desire to see the frontier pushed up northwards as far as possible. When Stanley, at the second meeting of the commission, proposed that it should be placed at Fernan Vaz, England supported his proposal. Germany declared that it should be placed still further north. France objected strongly. Finally a compromise was reached, Courcel agreeing to accept Sette Camma, slightly to the south of Fernan Vaz, as the limit of the free zone. He also succeeded in exclud-

---

[1] Protocol III, Annex, Report of Commission. L.J., Congo, Engelhardt's Report, p. 7. F.O./84/1815/ Malet to Granville, Nov. 21, 1884.
[2] Protocol III, Annex, Report of Commission. D.D.F., V, No. 458, Courcel to Ferry, Nov. 22, 1884. cf. also, Banning, *Mémoires*, p. 19. Thomson, p. 226.
[3] Protocol III, Annex. Report of Commission. L.J., Congo, 1885, Engelhardt's Report, pp. 7-8. D.D.F., V, No. 455, Courcel to Ferry, Nov. 19, 1884: 458, Ibid., Nov. 22, 1884: No. 450, Ibid., Nov. 23, 1884: No. 460, Ibid., Nov. 23, 1884. F.O./84/1815/ Malet to Granville, Nov. 24, 1884, Tel. 17. cf. also, Thomson, pp. 225-6.
[4] Protocol III, Annex, Report of Commission.

ing the Ogowé from its inland boundary. Stanley's proposal[1] actually originated in the British delegation, and there was even some talk, at one time, of Great Britain bringing it forward herself. But finally it was decided to let Stanley do so, because it was thought that it would in this way have a better chance of success. In view of the circumstances in which they had been called to the conference, the British delegates not unnaturally preferred to play as inconspicuous a part as possible in advancing their opinions, in contrast to the Germans, who still did not hesitate at this juncture to express themselves as strongly as they felt inclined. Once this is known, of course, it but serves to emphasise still further the fundamental measure of agreement which existed between them.

It was a position that was not to last long, however, for it was after this committee meeting[2] that Courcel first began to make representations to Bismarck about the attitude of the German delegates. He was seriously alarmed at the open differences which he had had with them in commission, was afraid that further ones might arise over the Sette Camma line, and urgently pressed the chancellor, therefore, to come to some sort of an understanding with him, before the commission should meet again. This was not an easy matter, for Bismarck was by no means in a conciliatory mood. He objected strongly to the French claims,[3] complained bitterly of France's "territorial appetite in Africa", and was at first not disposed to listen to Courcel's demands. Eventually,[4] however, he consented to a working agreement, declaring himself willing to support French claims on the West Coast, if in return France would agree to support the proposal for an eastern extension of the Congo basin which had already been put forward in commission.

His suggestion was accepted by Courcel,[5] who encountered no further opposition from the German delegates therefore over the northern frontier of the West Coast extension. The Sette Camma boundary[6] was confirmed at the next meeting

[1] F.O./84/1815/ Malet to Granville, Nov. 22, 1884, Africa, 92.
[2] D.D.F., V, 458, Courcel to Ferry, Nov. 22, 1884 : No. 460, Ibid., Nov. 23, 1884.
[3] Ibid., No. 460, Courcel to Ferry, Nov. 23, 1884.
[4] Ibid.
[5] Ibid., No. 461, Ferry to Courcel, Nov. 24, 1884.
[6] Protocol III, Annex, Report of Commission. F.O./84/1815/ Malet to Granville, Nov. 24, 1884, Tel. 17.

THE FIRST BASIS

of the committee, and formally voted by the powers at the third meeting of the conference on November 27th.[1] But it is interesting to notice that their decision did not pass without an energetic protest from Malet, on behalf of the majority of the commission, together with the expression of a "wish", which was supported by Germany as well as by the United States, that France would see her way later on to recognising Fernan Vaz as the northern limit of the free zone. This wish was not fulfilled, but a slight rectification of the frontier, pushing it up a little higher beyond Sette Camma, had, in fact, to be made before it was finally inserted in the General Act.

The delimitation commission[2] had originally stated that the boundary should be drawn where the river flowed into the sea at Sette Camma. But when its decisions were being re-drafted,[3] after the third meeting of the conference, the British and German delegates found that there was actually *no* river flowing into the sea at this point. There was, however, a river Sette, whose mouth was some five miles to the north of it, which was also sometimes called the Sette Camma. They therefore suggested that this river should be the boundary. But the French refused to consider it; raised strong objections; and finally ended by declaring that if the matter were further pursued, they would retaliate by pushing the boundary right down to the mouth of the Nyanza, some forty miles below Sette Camma.

The point of the controversy[4] was that there were British and German factories at Sette Camma itself, which the French were as anxious to *exclude*, as the English and Germans were to *include* in the free area. The dispute dragged on,[5] and was not

---

[1] Protocol III, Nov. 27, 1884. F.O./84/1815/ Malet to Granville, Nov. 27, 1884, Tel. 31.
[2] Protocol III, Annex. F.O./84/1817/ Malet to Granville, Dec. 14, 1884, Africa, 225. L.J., Congo, 1885, p. 7, Engelhardt's Report.
[3] F.O./84/1817/ Malet to Granville, Dec. 14, 1884, Africa, 225.
[4] Ibid. cf. also F.O./84/1818/ Granville to Malet, Dec. 29, 1884, Africa, 187. F.O./84/1822/ Malet to Granville, Feb. 21, 1885, Africa, 130a. (C. 4284, No. 2.)
[5] Ibid. F.O./84/1817/ Granville to Lyons, Dec. 17, 1884. F.O./84/1818/ Granville to Malet, Dec. 29, 1884, Africa, 187: Malet to Granville, Dec. 23, 1884, Africa, 273: (Also C. 4284, No. 1.) F.O./84/1819/ Malet to Granville, Jan. 10, 1885, Africa, 28. Lister to Malet, Jan. 16, 1885: F.O./84/1822/ Malet to Granville, Feb. 21, 1885, Africa, 130a (C. 4284, No. 2). cf. also, Protocol V, Dec. 18, 1884.

112 THE BERLIN WEST AFRICAN CONFERENCE

finally settled till the middle of January 1885,[1] when the French at last consented to include the factories in the free zone by accepting the line of 2° 30′ as its boundary. Though of minor importance in itself, the point is of some interest, since it once more placed the British and German delegates in joint opposition to those of France, epitomising their relations, in this way, throughout the discussions over the West Coast extension.

The orientation of the powers over the East Coast extension was a little different. France,[2] having pledged herself to Germany, was unable to oppose it, as she would undoubtedly otherwise have done, owing to her interest[3] in the territories of the Sultan of Zanzibar, all of which lay within the free zone. England was also interested in these territories, over which she had helped, with France, to guarantee the sovereignty of the Sultan in 1862. Her commercial and political liabilites[4] were actually greater than those of France, and in addition to this,[5] she had important commercial establishments in the undefined country lying to the west of the Sultan's possessions, near the Great Lakes, which likewise fell within the free area. For this reason her attitude was at first more reserved than it had been over the West Coast extension.[6] But she was fundamentally in favour of as wide an extension as possible of the free trade principle,[7] and this consideration came in the end to weigh more with her than that of her particular interests.[8] Portu-

[1] Ibid. F.O./84/1819/ Malet to Granville, Jan. 10, 1885, Africa, 28, Lister to Malet, Jan. 6, 1885. F.O./84/1822/ Malet to Granville, Feb. 21. 1884, Africa, 130a. (C. 4284, No. 2.) cf. also, L.J., Congo, Engelhardt's Report, p. 8. Thomson, p. 226, Banning, *Mémoires*, pp. 19–20.
[2] cf. above, p. 110.
[3] Protocol III, Nov. 27, 1884. cf. Banning, *Mémoires*, p. 19.
[4] cf. Banning, *Mémoires*, p. 19. F.O./84/1813/ Memo., Clement Hill, Oct. 20, 1884. F.O./84/1821/ Report of Consul Holmwood, Feb. 2, 1885. Evans Lewin, pp. 155, 157–60, 165–7. Keltie, pp. 109, 225.
[5] cf. F.O./84/1815/ Malet to Granville, Nov. 23, 1884, Africa, 102. Johnston, *Colonisation*, pp. 276–7.
[6] Protocol III, Annex, Report of Commission. F.O./84/1815/ Malet to Granville, Nov. 22, 1884, Tel. 13 : Memo., Lister, Nov. 23 : Granville to Malet, Nov. 22, 1884, Africa, 96 : Malet to Granville, Nov. 23, 1884, Africa, 102: Granville to Malet, Nov. 24, 1884, Africa, 99 : Granville to Malet, Nov. 25, Africa, 103 : S.E.D. 196, No. 36, Kasson to Frelinghuysen, Nov. 24, 1884. D.D.F., V, No. 459, Courcel to Ferry, Nov. 23, 1884.
[7] cf. F.O./84/1814/ Granville to Malet (Instructions), Nov. 7, 1884, Africa, 59 (C. 4241). F.O./84/1815/ Malet to Granville, Nov. 25, 1884, Tel. 15 (C. 4241).
[8] cf. F.O./84/1815/ Malet to Granville, Nov. 15, 1884, Tel. 19, Tel. 23 : Granville to Malet, Nov. 25, 1884, Africa, 102 : Granville to Malet, Nov. 26, 1884, Africa, 111 ; Granville to Malet, Nov. 27, 1884, Africa, 115.

THE FIRST BASIS

gal,[1] though she insisted on reserving her sovereign rights in Mozambique, which was also included in the free zone, was not opposed to the East Coast extension as a whole. Germany[2] and the Association,[3] neither of whom had recognised interests in East Africa, were unreservedly in favour of it.

None of the other powers had any objections to offer, and there were thus no serious objections of any kind to the proposed scheme. That in these circumstances it took so long to settle was due almost entirely to the curious and unexpected manner in which it was suddenly forced upon the attention of the delegates by Stanley,[4] acting openly with the collaboration of Kasson and secretly with that of Bismarck.[5] As a result of Stanley's action[6] the American and German plenipotentiaries were the only ones able to acquiesce at once in the proposals made, first by him, then by Kasson, in commission on the 20th and 22nd November. All the others had to write home for instructions, and this caused considerable delay.

On November 24th, Courcel, who had meanwhile come to terms with Bismarck about the West Coast Extension,[7] was

---

[1] Protocol III, Annex, Report of Commission. Protocol IV. Protocol VI.
[2] Protocol I, Bismarck's Speech. Protocol III, Annex, Report of Commission. F.O./84/1815/ Malet to Granville, Nov. 23, 1884, Africa, 102 : Nov. 25, 1884, Tel. 25. D.D.F., V, No. 459, Courcel to Ferry, Nov. 23, 1884 : No. 460, Ibid. S.E.D. 196, No. 36, Kasson to Frelinghuysen, Nov. 24, 1884. Yarnall, p. 73.
[3] Remembering that in this question its interests were represented by Stanley, acting in collaboration with Kasson who was responsible for suggesting E.C. extension in beginning. cf. Stanley, II, p. 394. Protocol III, Annex, Report of Commission. Ibid., Kasson's Proposition. S.E.D. 196, No. 36. Kasson to Frelinghuysen, Nov. 24, 1884 : Nov. 26, 1884 : Dec. 1, 1884 : D.D.F., V, No. 458, Courcel to Ferry, Nov. 22, 1884 ; No. 459, Ibid., Nov. 23, 1884 : F.O./84/1815/ Malet to Granville, Nov. 21, 1884, Africa, 90. Ibid., Nov. 22, Tel. 13. Banning, *Mémoires*, p. 19. Thomson, p. 225. Reeves, p. 39. Yarnall, p. 73.
[4] Protocol III, Annex, Report of the Commission. Ibid., Kasson's Proposition. S.E.D. 196, No. 36. Kasson to Frelinghuysen, Nov. 24, 1884. F.O./84/1815/ Malet to Granville, Nov. 21, 1884, Tel. 12 : Nov. 22, 1884, Tel. 13 : Nov. 23, Africa, 102. D.D.F., V, No. 458, Courcel to Ferry, Nov. 22, 1884 : No. 459, Ibid., Nov. 23. Stanley, II, p. 394. Thomson, p. 225. Reeves, p. 39. Yarnall, p. 73. Banning, *Mémoires*, p. 19.
[5] cf. D.D.F., V, No. 460, Courcel to Ferry, Nov. 24, 1884.
[6] Protocol III, Annex, Report of Commission. S.E.D. 196, No. 36, Kasson to Frelinghuysen, Nov. 24. F.O./84/1815/ Malet to Granville, Nov. 21, 1884, Tel. 12 ; Nov. 22, Tel. 13 : Nov. 23, Africa, 102 : Nov. 24, Tel. 17. D.D.F., V, Nos. 458, 459, Courcel to Ferry, Nov. 22, 23 : No. 461, Ferry to Courcel, Nov. 24, 1884.
[7] D.D.F., V, No. 460, Courcel to Ferry, Nov. 24, 1884 : No. 461, Ferry to Courcel, Nov. 24, 1884. cf. above, p. 110.

able to come forward,[1] together with the German plenipotentiaries, in support of the so-called " American proposition "[2]; but the other powers, being still without instructions, were still unable to give an opinion. These instructions finally arrived in time for the third meeting of the conference on November 27th,[3] when, by general agreement, the Eastern extension was then voted by the powers, together with a special provision, added to it by Courcel, guaranteeing the sovereign rights of all existing kingdoms on the East coast. The provision also recommended that the powers should use their good offices with the governments concerned to secure free transit of goods across their territories. This was satisfactory to all parties, since it allowed for Portuguese susceptibilities over Mozambique, as well as for French and British ones over Zanzibar, and at the same time, provided a visible token of the goodwill of France and Great Britain, if not of Portugal, towards the cause of free trade in East Africa.

The Congo Basin, " Geographical " and " Conventional ", was now defined. It remained to discuss the application of free trade principles within it. The delimitation clauses[4] of the German project were merely the introduction to a whole series of detailed and complicated provisions, drawn up for this purpose. These were now considered by the powers one by one.[5] There was no wholesale opposition to them from France. Having been rebuffed in her initial attempt to veto delimitation completely, she evidently thought twice about pursuing the same tactics over the free trade proposals, much and heartily as she disliked them, confining her attention instead to raising difficulties over each point as it came up. In this she was throughout supported by Portugal, who now began, for the first time, to co-operate closely with her. England, Germany, and the Association were of course unanimous in

---

[1] Protocol III, Annex, Report of Commission. F.O./84/1815/ Malet to Granville, Nov. 24, 1884, Tel. 17. S.E.D. 196, No. 36, Kasson to Frelinghuysen, Nov. 24, 1884.
[2] cf. S.E.D. 196, Kasson to Frelinghuysen, Dec. 1, 1884.
[3] Protocol III. F.O./84/1815/ Malet to Granville, Nov. 27, 1884, Tel. 31. S.E.D. 196, No. 38, Kasson to Frelinghuysen, Dec. 1, 1884.
[4] cf. text, Protocol I, Annex I.
[5] Protocol III. Protocol IV, Annex I, 2, Report of Commission on Project of Declaration relating to Freedom of Commerce in the Basin of the Congo and its Affluents. Protocol V, Annex II, 2, Declaration of Commission.

THE FIRST BASIS

their desire to give as wide a scope as possible to the free trade clauses of the act, and between them did, in effect, manage to score a substantial victory for the cause of free trade, in spite of the fact that Germany was forced to make certain concessions to France in the interests of the entente.

The first question to be discussed[1] was that raised in the second paragraph of the German project, stipulating that the flags of all nations should have free access to the *littorals* of the Congo territories as well as to the river itself and its affluents. This was not considered by the British delegates to give sufficient assurances[2] regarding the coasting trade, and a special provision was therefore inserted, at their request, guaranteeing complete freedom to all nations carrying on this trade, by sea or by river, in the neighbourhood of the Congo. The provision[3] did not pass without a protest from Courcel, but Malet insisted on his point, and backed by Busch succeeded in carrying it in face of French opposition.

After this the powers passed to the consideration of " compensatory taxes ",[4] of taxes, that is to say, which they were prepared to see levied in the Congo basin as compensation for useful expenditure in trade. The German project specially made allowance for these,[5] no doubt as an initial concession to France, though it was qualified by the express exclusion of import duties,[6] which were the subject of further provisions in the next clause. England would have liked to have abolished compensatory taxes altogether,[7] but was unable to do so, owing to the attitude of compromise[8] assumed from the beginning by Germany. She did, however, succeed in carrying a

---

[1] Protocol III.
[2] Ibid. cf. also, Protocol IV, Annex I, 1, Declaration of Commission. Par. 2. General Act, Article II. F.O./84/1815/ Granville to Malet, Nov. 7, 1884, Africa, 59 : (Instructions). (C. 4241.) Malet to Granville, Nov. 26, Tel. 26. Memo., Kennedy, Nov. 29. F.O./84/1817/ Malet to Granville, Dec. 10, 1884, Africa, 207. F.O./84/1818/ Malet to Granville, Dec. 23, 1884, Africa, 273. (C. 4284, No. 1.)
[3] Protocol III.
[4] Ibid. cf. also, Protocol IV, Annex I, 2, Report of Commission.
[5] cf. text, Protocol I, Annex I, Par. 3.
[6] Ibid. Par. 4.
[7] F.O./84/1815/ Granville to Malet (Instructions), Nov. 7, 1884, Africa, 59 (C. 4241). F.O./84/1818/ Malet to Granville, Dec. 23, 1884, Africa, 273 (C. 4284, No. 1).
[8] cf. Protocol I, Bismarck's Speech. Protocol I, Annex I, par. 3, German Project.

special amendment,[1] to the effect that there should be no differential treatment of any kind, a form of commercial discrimination which her traders particularly disliked.

The most heated discussions arose over the question of import duties. These were expressly prohibited by the German project.[2] No mention was made in it of export duties,[3] however, and there is no doubt that Germany hoped, by this omission, which implied the right to levy them, as well as by the latitude which had already been conceded over compensatory taxes, to give full satisfaction to French susceptibilities. This did not prove to be the case, however, France,[4] backed by Portugal, showing herself violently opposed to any absolute veto on import duties. Consequently Germany was forced to modify her attitude during the course of the discussions,[5] and to suggest that a twenty years' limit should be set on their restriction, at the end of which time the powers should be free to reconsider the whole question. This compromise[6] was finally accepted by the conference.

The change in Germany's attitude was very sudden, and was clearly made *in extremis* only, in order to avoid an unpleasant rupture with France. When Courcel, at the third meeting of the conference,[7] began to indicate the line which would be taken by his government, urging that the fiscal powers of the conference should be limited, and its activities confined to the exclusion of most-favoured-nation treatment, he was met with vigorous arguments from Küsserow, who declared that one of the main objects of the German Government in drawing up their project had been not only the removal of differential treat-

---

[1] Protocol III. Protocol IV, Annex I, 2. Report of Commission. 1, Declaration of Commission, Par. 3. General Act, Article III, F.O./84/1815/ Malet to Granville, Nov. 25, 1884, Tel. 24: Memo., Anderson, Nov. 25: Granville to Malet, Nov. 26, Africa, 110: Malet to Granville, Nov. 26, Tel. 26: Memo., Kennedy, Nov. 29.
[2] cf. text, Protocol I, Annex I, 1, par. 3.
[3] cf. D.D.F., V, No. 455, Courcel to Ferry, Nov. 19, 1884.
[4] Protocol III. Protocol IV, Annex I, 2, Report of Commission. F.O./84/1816/, Malet to Granville, Dec. 1, 1884, Africa, 164a. J. A. Crowe, Private Letters, Nov. 19, 1884. Reeves, p. 40 Banning, *Mémoires*, p. 21. Thomson, p. 227.
[5] Protocol IV, Annex I, 2, Report of Commission, Protocol IV. F.O./84/1816/ Malet to Granville, Nov. 29, 1884, Tel. 36. Ibid., Dec. 1, 1884, Africa, 164a. L.J., Congo, 1885, pp. 10–11.
[6] Protocol IV. F.O./84/1816/ Malet to Granville, Dec. 1, 1884, Africa, 164a. D.D.F., V, No. 472, Courcel to Ferry, Nov. 29, 1884.
[7] Protocol III.

THE FIRST BASIS

ment, but also the exclusion of import and transit dues. No conclusion was reached at this meeting, and the matter was then referred to commission,[1] where Courcel, backed by the Portuguese, pressed with even greater violence and insistence than before for the abolition of absolute restrictions on import duties, urging, as a solution of the problem, that they should be included in the category of " compensatory taxes ". In so doing, however, he found himself in opposition to the majority of the commission, and in particular to the German and Belgian delegates, who argued strenuously against his proposal. It seemed as if a deadlock had been reached. But at the next meeting of the commission the situation suddenly brightened.[2] The French Ambassador withdrew his proposal, accepting in its place a German one for a twenty years' limit on the restriction put forward by Herr Woermann,[3] which was then adopted by the whole commission, and finally ratified by the conference on December 1st.

Germany had of course reached an agreement with France between the two sittings of the commission, and also apparently with the Association, since Lambermont,[4] who had hitherto been such an ardent opponent of Courcel's, declared himself satisfied with Woermann's proposition as soon as it was made. Equally clearly England had *not* been approached beforehand by the German Government,[5] since her first reaction to it was a vigorous protest. She did not go so far as to oppose it, however, evidently realising that to do so would be impractical in view of Germany's attitude. The clause was never popular in England,[6] where it aroused a good deal of opposition in commercial circles as soon as it became known.

[1] Ibid. Protocol IV, Annex I, 2, Report of Commission. F.O./84/1816/ Malet to Granville, Dec 1, 1884, Africa, 164a. (Enclosure, Memo., J. A. Crowe, on Debates in Commission, Nov. 27 and Nov. 28, 1884, on Import and Transit Dues.)
[2] F.O./84/1816/ Malet to Granville, Nov. 29, 1884, Tel. 36 : Dec. 1,1884, Africa, 164a (as above).
[3] Ibid. cf. also, Protocol IV, Annex I, 2., Report of Commission. L.J., Congo, 1885, pp. 10–11.
[4] F.O./84/1816/ Malet to Granville, Dec. 1, 1884, Africa, 164a.
[5] Ibid.
[6] F.O./84/1817/ Hutton to Granville, Dec. 12, 1884. F.O./84/1818/ Memo., Clement Hill, Dec. 23, 1884 : Oldham Chambers of Commerce to Granville, Dec. 26, 1884 : Hutton to Granville, Dec. 30, 1884. F.O./84/1819/ Hutton to Granville, Jan. 3, 1885 : Hutton to Fitzmaurice, Jan. 3, 1885. F.O./84/1820/ Granville to Malet, Jan. 17, 1885, Africa, 22. Anderson to Pauncefote, Jan. 17, 1885.

But from the beginning it was clear to the British delegates at the conference that it was the best arrangement possible in the circumstances, and they therefore made no attempts to antagonise Bismarck by an official veto.

One other question remained to be considered in connection with the first basis. This was the proposal[1] for a complete interdiction of monopolies and privileges contained in the fifth paragraph of the German project. There was little discussion on it, however, the general feeling of the powers being strongly in its favour.[2] The terms of the paragraph were interpreted in a wide sense, therefore, and adopted as they stood by the conference, with a few amplifications.

It was now the beginning of December. The problems arising out of the first basis had all been dealt with, and the thoughts of the delegates were already beginning to turn to those which next confronted them in the second basis, problems which, at least as far as the Congo was concerned, were the logical complement of those which they had just been discussing.

[1] cf. text, Protocol I, Annex I, par. 5.
[2] Protocol IV, Annex I, 2, Report of Commission. Protocol V. cf. Banning, *Mémoires*, pp. 20–1. Thomson, pp. 226–7.

CHAPTER III

THE SECOND BASIS
FREE NAVIGATION OF THE CONGO AND THE NIGER

THE second basis of the conference aimed at securing the free navigation of the Congo and the Niger.[1] As had been the case with the first basis France collaborated beforehand with Germany in drawing up a joint project of declaration,[2] which was then submitted by Germany to the rest of the powers. But this collaboration did not prevent serious differences from arising between the French and German delegates as soon as its clauses came actually to be considered.

Owing to the technical nature of the subject[3] it was at once referred to commission, where all the most important discussions concerning it took place, and where all its major problems were thrashed out during the first half of December. These discussions tended, on the whole, to bring out in even stronger relief than before the same fundamental features of the situation which had already manifested themselves over the first basis. There was the same underlying tension between France and Germany: the same convergence of opinion between Germany and England: the same close collaboration between Germany and the Association: the same solidarity of France and Portugal—all emphasised to an increasing degree.

As the discussions proceeded, a similar phenomenon also presented itself of minor concessions made by Germany in the interests of the entente, to France, whose small value however was from the beginning offset and given a peculiar emphasis

---

[1] cf. above, p. 67.
[2] Protocol V, Annex IV, Project of Act of Navigation of Congo/Niger, presented by the German Plenipotentiaries. cf. also, Protocol I, Bismarck's Speech. L.J., Congo, 1885, Engelhardt's Report, p. 22.
[3] Protocol IV. Protocol V, Annex, Report of Commission Charged to Examine Project of Act of Navigation for Congo/Niger.

120 THE BERLIN WEST AFRICAN CONFERENCE

by one of the first magnitude made by Bismarck to *British* interests, in defiance of those of France. This was his acceptance of Great Britain's demand for separate treatment of the Niger and the Congo,[1] which meant, in effect, her refusal to recognise international control there, and the assertion of the right herself to control the navigation of the lower river which she claimed as her own.

It was France,[2] it may be remembered, who had originally asked for, and later insisted on, the inclusion of the Niger question in the programme of the conference, Bismarck conceding the point, as he did so many others, at the height of his quarrel with England, without fully realising its implications. The reason for the French demand was that of late years there had been acute commercial rivalry between France and England on the lower Niger as well as considerable friction all along the Guinea coast. By bringing the matter up at the conference, therefore, France hoped with Germany's aid to secure the triumph of her interests, and to inflict a severe defeat on those of Great Britain.

Great Britain,[3] however, had from the first shown herself tenacious of her rights there, a fact which in view of the circumstances was hardly surprising. For over three hundred years[4] she had played an active part on the West African coast between Dahomey and the Cameroons, first as a slave-trader,[5] then as the policeman[6] restricting the slave-traffic, and finally as a legitimate trader. During the eighteenth century[7] she had

---

[1] Protocol IV. Protocol V. Protocol V, Annex, Report of Commission. Annex 5, Draft of Declaration Presented by H.E., the Plenipotentiary of Great Britain for Securing Freedom of Navigation on Niger: Annex 15, Revised Project Proposed by Great Britain: Annex 7, Project of Niger Act Proposed by Commission: Annex 17, Memo., Anderson. F.O./84/1816/ Malet to Granville, Dec. 1, 1884, Tels. 38, 39, Africa, 160a, Tel. 42: Granville to Malet, Dec. 1, Tels. 14, 15: Malet to Granville, Dec. 2, Tel. 44: Dec. 8, Tel. 54. F.O./84/1817/ Malet to Granville, Dec. 12, Tel. 59: Dec. 13, Africa, 215. L.J., Congo, 1885, pp. 13–16. S.E.D. 196, Kasson to Frelinghuysen, Dec. 8, 1884: Dec. 13, 1884. Banning, *Mémoires*, pp. 33–5.
[2] cf. above, pp. 61, 65.
[3] F.O./84/1813/ Memo., Lister, Oct. 14, 1884. Memo.: Anderson, Oct. 14, 1884. Granville to Malet, Oct. 17, 1884, Africa, 37: (C. 4205, No. 18): Oct. 22, Africa, 46: (C. 4205, No. 26). F.O./84/1814/ Granville to Malet, Instructions, Nov. 7, 1884, Africa, 59 (C. 4241). cf. above, pp. 75–6.
[4] cf. A. C. Burns, *History of Nigeria*, pp. 72–145.
[5] Ibid., pp. 72–4.
[6] Ibid., pp. 110–21.
[7] Ibid., pp. 70, 83.

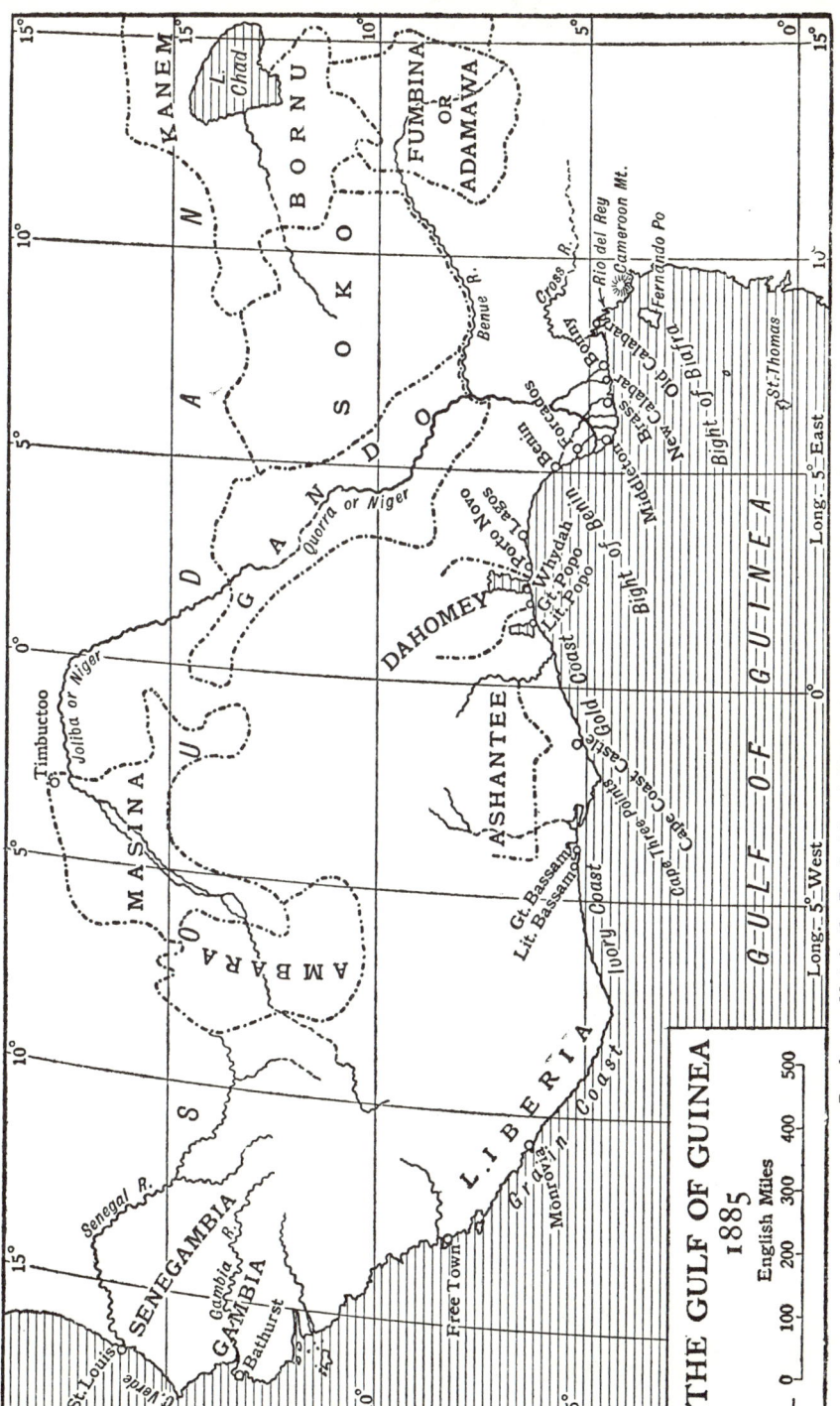

Based on a Map in the Royal Atlas of Modern Geography by Keith Johnston, Edinburgh, 1885.

THE SECOND BASIS

managed to secure an almost complete monopoly of the traffic in slaves. Hence, when it was publicly condemned at the beginning of the nineteenth century,[1] it devolved upon her, and upon her alone, to suppress the activities of illegal slavers in this part of the world.[2] There was no question of the interference of any other power, nor of the establishment of any joint system of control with France, such as at first existed on the Congo. The area was simply regarded as a British preserve, which indeed it was destined to remain for another three-quarters of a century.

Side by side with the suppression of the slave trade by British ships,[3] a small legitimate commerce soon began to grow up, also exclusively British in character, the merchants trading in palm-oil, palm-kernels, ivory, and benniseed, in exchange for cheap manufactured wares, particularly cotton goods from Manchester. This trade increased steadily, but was at first confined entirely to the coast.

The very existence of the Niger was hardly suspected in the eighteenth century,[4] and its course was still at this time a baffling mystery. The discovery of the mouth of the river,[5] and the exploration of practically the whole of its eastern bend, which took place between 1800 and 1860, was due entirely to British energy and initiative, which was for the most part organised and subsidised by the government. This led to the gradual expansion of British trade up the Niger itself.[6] The difficulties encountered by the merchants,[7] however, were even greater than those which they had met with on the coast, owing to the particular hostility felt by the natives to any spread of their influence inland, since it deprived them of the lucrative profits which they had for years been accustomed to make as middlemen.

In spite of the frequent visits of British warships,[8] it soon

---

[1] Ibid., p. 84.
[2] Ibid., pp. 110–21.
[3] Ibid., pp. 110, 114, 115, 119, 148, 154.
[4] Ibid., pp. 85, 87.
[5] Protocol I, Malet's Speech. cf. Protocol V, Annex 17, Memo., Anderson on the Niger Question. Johnston, p. 188. Keltie, pp. 101, 196, 259. Burns, pp. 90–109.
[6] Burns, pp. 148–50.
[7] Ibid., pp. 148–52. Johnston, p. 185. Keltie, p. 266.
[8] Ibid., p. 120.

became evident that more adequate and continuous supervision was needed, if order was to be maintained. In 1849,[1] therefore, the government appointed a consul for the Bights of Benin and Biafra, whose headquarters were placed at Fernando Po, and whose jurisdiction extended from Dahomey to Cameroons. The appointment of a separate consul for Lagos in 1853[2] relieved this official of an important section of the coast, and gave him more time for the supervision of the Niger and Oil Rivers. After the annexation of Lagos in 1861,[3] the Governor of Lagos was also made consul for the Bight of Benin. But the arrangement was discontinued in 1867, when the consul at Fernando Po again took charge of all the territory lying between the eastern boundary of Lagos and the Cameroons. Between 1866 and 1869,[4] there was also a consulate at Lokoja, at the junction of the Niger and the Benue, but it was found so difficult to protect it that it had to be abandoned at the end of this time.

During the next decade[5] various efforts were made to strengthen the power of the consul, but unfortunately they were more efficient on paper than in actual fact, and it was not until after 1880, with the sudden emergence of the French upon the scene, that really effective steps were taken for strengthening his position. Since the conquest of Senegal in 1860[6] France had been steadily pushing southwards towards the Gulf of Guinea, and eastwards, in the interior, towards the upper reaches of the Niger. By 1865 her occupation extended inland as far as the upper Senegal,[7] whilst on the coast her influence was recognised by treaty from Cape Blanco to British Gambia. The immediate effect of the Franco-Prussian War[8] was to damp the colonial ardour of the French. But once their country was on its feet again, they began to show renewed and increasing zest for colonial adventure. Their drive towards the upper Niger began in consequence to assume serious dimen-

---

[1] Ibid., pp. 120–1, 146.
[2] Ibid., p. 146.
[3] Ibid., p. 138.
[4] Johnston, p. 188. Burns, pp. 150–1.
[5] Burns, pp. 151–3.
[6] Johnston, pp. 188–9. D. Wellesley, pp. 13–14.
[7] Keltie, p. 97.
[8] Johnston, p. 262. D. Wellesley, pp. 14–15.

THE SECOND BASIS

sions. A vast series of military campaigns,[1] launched in 1880, in the interior of Senegambia, had as one of its main objectives to reach the Niger, and to tap its trade, by connecting it with a railway to the navigable portion of the Senegal. Gallieni,[2] for this purpose, traversed the difficult country between Medina and the upper Niger in that year, and in 1881 succeeded in making a treaty, which gave to France the protectorate of the left bank of the river. At the same time an even more daring attempt was made by the French to secure complete control of the Niger trade, by entering into state-subsidised competition with the long-established, but insecure and ill-supported settlements of British traders at its mouth.

British trade on the Niger was at this time suffering badly from lack of adequate protection.[3] In addition to this the traders had of late years been doing their best to cut their own throats, through their lack of unity, and their suicidal competition amongst themselves. This not only reduced their profits considerably ; it also rendered their struggle with the native middlemen even harder than was necessary. That in these circumstances they were not completely wiped off the map by the French was due entirely to the energy and foresight of one man. Sir George (then Captain) Taubmann-Goldie,[4] a little-known Rhodes of Nigeria, first visited the Niger in 1877. It at once became clear to him that unity was essential if the British companies were to hold their own, and he therefore spent the next two years amalgamating them. In 1879[5] he formed the " United African Company " out of the four remaining British firms on the river, and in 1881[6] he applied to the

[1] Keltie, pp. 147, 259, 261.
[2] Johnston, p. 202.
[3] G.D. 29/269, F O./146/Correspondence Respecting Affairs in the Oil River Districts on the West Coast of Africa and the Question of the British Protectorates, Confidential Print, No. 4824. No. 27, Remarks Clement Hill on Memorial of Liverpool African Association describing Disturbed Conditions and Attacking Consul Hewett, History of Oil Rivers Disputes which are Caused by Trade Jealousies and Monopolies. cf. also, Keltie, pp. 146, 267-8. Johnston, p. 189. Burns, pp. 152-4.
[4] Burns, p. 154. Johnston, *Colonisation*, p. 189. *Encyclopedia Britannica* (11th ed.), Vol. XII, Taubmann-Goldie, pp. 211-12. D. Wellesley, *Goldie*, pp. 16-22. Keltie, p. 266.
[5] Burns, p. 154. *Encyclopedia Britannica*, p. 212. Johnston, p. 189. D. Wellesley, p. 19. N. M. Geary, *Nigeria under British Rule*, pp. 177-8. Keltie, p. 268.
[6] Burns, p. 163. D. Wellesley, p. 19. Keltie, pp. 268-9. *Encyclopedia Britannica*, p. 212.

government for a charter in its name. But his demand was refused on the ground that the capital of the company was too small. He thereupon set out to increase it, raising it within a year from £125,000 to £1,000,000. At the same time he changed its name to that of the " National African Company ", preparatory to a second demand for a charter. Meanwhile,[1] however, the establishment of two powerful French companies at the mouth of the river, one with a capital of £160,000, the other of £600,000, had unfortunately rendered this an impossibility, since it was clear that in these circumstances France could justly and effectually have protested against it. There was nothing for Goldie to do but to try and buy the French firms out.[2] This he at once set about, but it was not until the end of October 1884, after two years' hard struggle, that he at last succeeded in doing so.

Meanwhile the British Government had itself been stirred into action through fear of France. During the year 1883,[3] French activities all up and down the Guinea Gulf increased to such an alarming extent, that they were at last spurred into a decision[4] to assume more effective control in this part of Africa. It took them another whole year, however, to give effect to their decision, and it was not until May 16th, 1884,[5] that Hewett, the British consul for the Bights of Benin and Biafra, who was then home on leave, and who had been entrusted with the task, was at last given the instructions for which he had been waiting for months. These charged him to secure a protectorate over the whole of the Oil River district from the northernmost part of the Niger delta down to Calabar, and also

---

[1] Burns, p. 155. D. Wellesley, pp. 19–21. *Encyclopedia Britannica*, p. 212. Keltie, p. 269.

[2] Keltie, pp. 269–70. Burns, p. 155. Geary, pp. 177–8. F.O./84/1814/ Taubmann-Goldie to Anderson, Nov. 1, 1884.

[3] G.D./29/269. F.O./146/ C.P. 4825, Nos. 1, 3, 4, 5, 10, 14, 18, 39. C.P. 4869, Nos. 1, 4,* 11, 31, 37, 42,* 43, 52. C.P. 4955, Nos. 27, 33. C.P. 5004. No 11 * *(Also in A. and P., LV, 1884–5, C. 4279, Nos. 7 and 9. No. 4, A. and P., LV, 1884–5, C. 4279, No. 7. No. 42, C. 4279, No. 9.)

[4] C.P. 4825, Nos. 2, 14, 18. C.P. 4869, Nos. 18, 38, 42, 45,* 48, 58,* 61, 62, C.P. 4955, Nos. 4, 14, 17. C.P. 5004, Nos. 1, 3, 8, 15, 22, 23, 39, 43, 46, 58, 70, *(Also in C. 4279, Nos. 10 and 11, but with important omissions. No. 45. C. 4279, No. 10—important omissions. No. 58, C. 4279, No. 11—important omissions.)

[5] C.P. 5004, No. 88, Granville to Hewett, May 26, 1884. (C. 4279) (full text) : No. 22. cf. also, Keltie, p. 198.

THE SECOND BASIS

over the Cameroons down to the British Baptist settlement at Victoria, which was itself to be annexed.

Thanks to the delay in their issue, however, Hewett found himself forestalled at the Cameroons by Bismarck's agent, Dr. Nachtigal,[1] who, arriving a few days before him, annexed the whole district in the name of the German Government. This was an unexpected as well as irritating development in British plans for a Niger Protectorate, plans which had long been known at the Foreign Office as the " scheme for keeping the French away from the Niger,"[2] and which had been put into execution solely out of fear of France, and of possible French annexation. That Germany would annex any part of this coast, however small, had not even been contemplated, when these plans had been sketched out. Nevertheless it was the manner, rather than the mere fact of Germany's seizure of the Cameroons, which was resented by Great Britain, since this district was of comparatively small value in itself, and its loss did not interfere seriously with the main part of Hewett's programme, which he now proceeded with great speed and efficiency to put into execution.

On July 14th,[3] the very day on which he interviewed Nachtigal at the mouth of the Cameroons River, he annexed the British settlement at Victoria. During the months of July and August[4] he succeeded in making treaties of protectorate with native chiefs over the whole coast-line between Lagos and the Rio del Rey (the northern boundary of the Cameroons), and by the end of September he was up the Niger,[5] where, in October and November, he concluded further treaties with the chiefs of the Niger and Benue, bringing all the lower portion of the Niger up to its confluence with the Benue, as well as a large western reach of the Benue itself, under British protection.

---

[1] C.P. 5021 (C. 4279, No. 25), Admiralty to F.O., Aug. 26, 1884 : No. 31, Hewett to Granville, July 30, 1884. cf. also Evans Lewin, p. 140. Keltie, p. 202. Johnston, p. 408. Adams, p. 157.
[2] C.P. 5004, No. 22, Granville to Aberdare, Feb. 6, 1884. cf. Appendix XIII.
[3] C.P. 5021 (C. 4279, No. 25), Evans Lewin, pp. 140-1. Keltie, p. 202. cf. Appendix XIII.
[4] C.P. 5021, Nos. 31, 39, 52, 74. cf. Keltie, p. 202 (short reference). C.P. 5063, Nos. 15-28. cf. Appendix XIII.
[5] G.D./29/270/ Enclosures in No. 28/Hewett's 37 Treaties on Niger and Benue. Burns, p. 156 (short reference). E.B., p. 212, Ibid. cf. Appendix XIII.

Thanks to his efforts, and to those of Goldie, therefore, the British delegates were able to come forward at the conference with the claim,[1] essential to their case in pressing for the exclusion of the Niger from international control, that Great Britain was in possession not only of its mouth, but of the whole of its lower course, and that no other nation had any commercial interests there.

This claim was substantially correct. But it is important to realise how very recently indeed steps had been taken to make it effective, whilst in some cases it was not yet even wholly so. Otherwise the French attitude and French hopes are somewhat inexplicable. Hewett's treaties[2] on the coast had only been concluded a few weeks, those on the Niger itself only a few days,[3] before the conference opened, the last being signed on November 14th.[4] Many of these treaties were only of a temporary and provisional nature, although Hewett declared himself confident of being able to turn them, and did in fact succeed in turning them, into permanent ones later on. As for commercial supremacy on the river, it was only on November 1st that Goldie was able to write to Granville that the last French firm had been bought out there.[5] That Great Britain in these circumstances would be able to win her case at the conference table was by no means a foregone conclusion. Indeed, if Bismarck had not supported her, it seems more than likely that she would not have succeeded in doing so—or at any rate only partially—in spite of her long-standing associations with this part of Africa.

Bismarck's motives in giving her his support are not hard to explain. It has been seen how, even before the conference opened,[6] he had begun to show himself more conciliatory towards British aims on the Niger, which he had hitherto opposed violently, and how this change in his attitude had been related to his growing dissatisfaction with the entente, as well as to his increased sense of the need for backing the claims of the Association on the Congo against those of France.

[1] Protocol I, Malet's Speech. Protocol V, Annex 17, Memo., Anderson. cf. also, Burns, p. 156. Keltie, p. 270.
[2] C.P. 5021, Nos. 31, 39, 52, 74.
[3] C.P. 5063, Nos. 15, 28. G.D./29/270/ Enclosures in 28.
[4] Ibid.
[5] F.O./84/1814/ Goldie-Taubmann to Anderson, Nov. 1, 1884.
[6] cf. above, pp. 76-7.

THE SECOND BASIS

The policy now pursued by him at the conference was only the logical development of these sentiments. Growing evidence of France's "territorial appetite in Africa",[1] of which he was only now beginning to be fully aware, made him more anxious than ever to help the Association. Great Britain's non-committal attitude towards it,[2] on entering the conference, has already been seen. The connection with the Niger question becomes clear, when it is realised that just at the moment[3] when the second basis was coming up for discussion, Bismarck was deliberately putting pressure on Great Britain in order to induce her to recognise the Association as a sovereign power. There is no doubt that his desire to succeed in doing so was the decisive factor in the situation, which at the same time determined him to throw the whole weight of his opinion into the scale, in supporting British claims on the Niger against those of France.

So well did he succeed in doing this, that the British proposal for separate treatment of the two rivers was in fact carried in conference,[4] without any public opposition of any kind from the French. The original German project,[5] drawn up with France, advocating a joint system of international control for both rivers, was actually submitted by Bismarck to the powers[6] at the first meeting of the conference on November 15th. But he appears very soon to have made clear his changed attitude to the French, for Courcel wrote home[7] the next day to his government saying he feared that a less active form of interference would be possible on the Niger than on the Congo. The project was not circulated until November 25th,[8] and did not come up again for discussion until the fourth meeting of the conference on December 1st.[9] Meanwhile Bismarck evidently brought strong pressure to bear on the French Ambassador, for when Malet now pleaded with great force and insistence[10] that there should be no International Commission on the Niger and

---

[1] cf. above, p. 110. [2] cf. above, pp. 90–1.
[3] cf. below, pp. 143–7. [4] Protocol II.
[5] Protocol V, Annex 4. [6] Protocol I.
[7] D.D.F., V, No. 453, Courcel to Ferry, Nov. 16, 1884.
[8] L.J., Congo, 1885, Engelhardt's Report, pp. 23–4.
[9] Protocol IV.
[10] Ibid. cf. also, F.O./84/1816/ Malet to Granville, Dec. 1, 1884, Tels. 38, 39, 42. L.J., Congo, 1885, Engelhardt's Report, pp. 24–5. S.E.D. 196, No. 40, Kasson to Frelinghuysen, Dec. 8, 1884. Banning, *Mémoires*, pp. 34–5.

that the whole question should be treated separately, Courcel at once concurred in his demands, with the reserve only that the problems of the Congo should not finally be settled until those of the Niger had been fully discussed. Malet agreed to this. None of the other powers had any objections to offer, and the British proposal was therefore carried unanimously by the conference, which then appointed a commission to examine the German project, but with instructions to study the two rivers separately.

There can be no doubt that this decision was a severe blow to France. She had hoped for German support on the Niger, because of that which had originally been promised her by Germany on the Congo. Actually she lost it on the Niger, largely as a result of Bismarck's efforts to disentangle himself from his earlier commitments with her on the Congo. It was indeed a bitter irony of fate that she should thus have suffered a double defeat of her interests, each intimately connected with the other, and both with what was really a substantial victory for Great Britain, since international control of the Congo was what the latter had always asked for, whilst on the Niger, where it would have meant the defeat, not the triumph of British interests, she both asked for, and obtained, the recognition of her own right to control the navigation of the lower river.

It was probably not unconnected with this initial humiliation that France now managed to score a number of minor victories in the controversies which arose over the navigation of the Congo, carrying her point, in nearly every case where there was any serious disagreement. Germany, in the first place, had every reason to placate her ; whilst England, having gained what she wanted on the Niger, was also inclined to be more conciliatory over the Congo. But there were other factors in the situation too. Not only were French victories of small value when compared to the diplomatic defeat which France had just suffered on the Niger, they were also in themselves less important than they actually appeared to be, and there is no doubt that this was largely the reason why she was allowed to secure them. Bismarck, all this time, was doing his utmost, *outside* the official bases of the conference,[1] to further the inter-

[1] cf. below, Part II, Chapters iv and v, pp. 142-75.

THE SECOND BASIS

ests of the Association. So successful were his efforts in this direction, that in the end they were responsible for nullifying most of the triumphs scored by France in the Congo Navigation Act, triumphs which were nearly all potentially political in character, and aimed directly against the Association.

This can be clearly illustrated by a careful investigation of the clauses of the Act,[1] and the debates which arose concerning them. These covered three main questions[2]: the question of the rules to be laid down for the free navigation of the river; the question of the powers and functions of the International Commission which was to be entrusted with their application; and the question of the neutralisation of the river in time of war.

Discussion only arose over a minor point in connection with the first. The fundamental principle of the German project,[3] about which all the powers were agreed, was that there should be full and complete freedom of navigation on the Congo, no taxes being levied, except "compensatory" ones, such as harbour, pilot, lighthouse and buoy dues, called for by the requirements of navigation itself. This was ensured by Articles XIII and XIV of the General Act.

Great Britain,[4] who was herself ready to apply these rules to the Niger, would have liked to have seen them extended to all the other rivers of Africa as well. But Bismarck, though in principle in favour of such an extension,[5] had from the beginning made it clear that he considered it the business of the conference to discuss the Congo and the Niger only, since he was not going to risk offending the susceptibilities of France in this matter.[6] Malet therefore himself approached the dele-

---

[1] cf. Protocol V, Annex 6, Project for Act of Navigation of Congo Proposed by Commission. General Act, Chapter iv, Articles XIII-XXV.
[2] Protocol V, Annex, Report of Commission Charged to Examine Projects of Act of Navigation for Congo and Niger. Protocol V. F.O./84/1817/ Malet to Granville, Dec. 13, 1884, Africa, 22 : Dec. 16, 1884, Africa, 233. Banning, *Mémoires*, pp. 28–33.
[3] Protocol V, Annex, Report of Commission. F.O./84/1817/ Malet to Granville, Dec. 13, 1884, Africa, 222. (Enclosure, Memo. : J. A. Crowe, Sub-Commission on Act of Navigation of Congo and Niger.)
[4] F.O./84/1814/ Granville to Malet, Nov. 7, 1884 (Instructions), Africa, 59. (C. 4241.) F.O./84/1818/ Malet to Granville, Dec. 23, 1884, Africa, 273. (C. 4284, No. 1.)
[5] Protocol I, Bismarck's Speech.
[6] cf. L.J., Congo, 1885, Engelhardt's Report, p. 22.

gates of France and Portugal about it.[1] But he found them so strongly opposed to the whole idea that he refrained from bringing it forward in commission, where it was consequently never discussed.

There was, however, general agreement there[2] that the affluents of the Congo should in all respects be subject to the same rules as the Congo itself; whilst by Article XVI[3] of the General Act, not only these affluents, but also all roads, railways or laterals which might at any future date be constructed alongside it, were similarly included in the system of free transit. This article[4] actually owed its origin to Belgian initiative, which had been responsible for inserting a proposal to the effect in the German project. It was regarded as an innovation in international law, but provoked no opposition, on account of the essentially reasonable nature of the claim on which it was based, the necessity, namely, for some such assimilation of terrestrial routes, owing to the innavigability of the Lower Congo.

A suggestion for still further developing this clause,[5] however, which was also due to Belgian initiative, but which was *not* inserted in the German project, but only raised later in commission, was *not* accepted by it, and was responsible for some very acrimonious discussion. This was a proposal brought forward by Colonel Sanford, for giving permission to the state eventually in control of the greatest part of the Congo, to construct a railway, or to grant a monopoly to a company for this purpose, round the cataracts of the river connecting Stanley Pool with the sea. First brought up by Sanford under the heading of " monopolies "[6] during the course of the debates which arose on free trade, at the third meeting of the conference on November 27th, this proposal was then adjourned for further consideration, until the second basis

[1] F.O./84/1816/Malet to Granville, Dec. 2, 1884, Africa, 171 : Dec. 5, 1884, Tel. 47 : Granville to Malet, Dec. 9, 1884, Tel. 25. F.O./84/1818/ Malet to Granville, Dec. 23, 1884 (C. 4284, No. 1).
[2] Protocol V, Annex, Report of Commission. F.O./84/1817/ Malet to Granville, Dec. 13, 1884, Africa, 222. (Enclosure, Memo.: J. A. Crowe, Sub-Commission.)
[3] Ibid. Also Banning, *Mémoires*, p. 28. Thomson, p. 228.
[4] Banning, p. 28. Thomson, p. 228.
[5] cf. Banning, pp. 24–7. Thomson, pp. 228–9.
[6] Protocol III. Reeves, pp. 41–2. Thomson, p. 229.

should come up for discussion, when Sanford, on December 1st,[1] made another long speech in its defence. After this it was referred to commission,[2] together with the German navigation project. Here England and Germany at once showed themselves strongly in favour of it,[3] and it was of course hotly upheld by the Belgian delegates, Baron Lambermont and Émile Banning, who had originally been responsible for its formulation. But they found it impossible to overcome the determined opposition of France and Portugal, both of whom feared that the proposed concession might go to the Association, and who therefore refused to have anything to do with it. No settlement of the question was reached, and it was then referred back again to the conference on December 18th.[4] But deadlock having again been reached here, Sanford finally withdrew his proposal, in order to allow for amendments, on the understanding that he would bring it up again at a later meeting. He never did so, however, but instead withdrew it completely at the ninth meeting of the conference on February 23rd.[5] The reason for this[6] was that meanwhile a treaty had been drawn up, after long and laborious negotiations of a territorial nature, between Portugal and the Association, which in effect guaranteed to the Association the right to build the proposed railway. Sanford's proposal was therefore superfluous.

Such an eventuality was of course not foreseen by Courcel when he argued in commission that all consideration of the question should be postponed until a territorial settlement of some kind had been effected between France, Portugal, and the Association on the Congo.[7] Nothing indeed could afford a better illustration of how little he suspected its final nature, nor how favourable it would be to the Association.

A similar disillusionment was destined to attend the success of his efforts, as well as those of the Portuguese delegates, to reduce the International Commission of the Congo to a position

[1] Protocol IV. Thomson, pp. 229-30. Yarnall, p. 68.
[2] Protocol IV. Thomson, p. 230.
[3] Protocol V, Annex, Report of Commission. F.O./84/1817/ Malet to Granville, Dec. 13, 1884, Africa, 222. F.O./84/1818/ Memo., Clement Hill, Dec. 20, 1884. Thomson, p. 230.
[4] Protocol V. Thomson, pp. 230-1.
[5] Protocol IX. Banning, p. 26.
[6] cf. below, pp. 173-4. Also Thomson, p. 231. Banning, p. 26.
[7] Protocol V, Annex, Report of Commission.

of complete practical impotence. Their aim, of course, was to minimise any form of international control on the river which might be damaging to French or Portuguese sovereignty there. But already in December 1884, the International Commission, which had been given a name[1] though hardly a form, by Leopold, eight years before, and had therefore justly been associated with him ever since, meant less to him for the realisation of his ambitions than did the International Association, which was itself shortly about to be transformed into the Congo Free State.[2] It was of little avail, therefore, to work against the Commission, when the Association, thanks to his efforts, was very soon to take control of large stretches of the Congo, and at the same time to acquire full sovereign rights there.

Like some happier Io, the projects of the Belgian King were indeed passing at this moment through a series of strange forms, unwatched by comprehending Argus eyes, and relatively untormented by the gadflies of his opponents, who for the most part seemed not intelligent enough to attack any but the corpses left behind them from their various transmutations.

In justice to Leopold's opponents, however, it is only fair to add that his own adherents had themselves not all fully grasped the implications of the situation, and that for this reason, both Lambermont and Banning hotly contested with France every debated privilege of the International Commission,[3] regarding each failure to carry their point, not only as a humiliating, but as a vital defeat for the interests of the Association—which of course it was not.

They were supported in their efforts by both England and Germany,[4] but less wholeheartedly by Germany than by England,[5] the more lukewarm attitude of the German delegates being due less probably to consideration for French interests, than to Bismarck's own more accurate estimate of the situation. It was he who was helping Leopold to realise his plans,[6] and he must therefore have been fully aware of the small

[1] cf. above, p. 13.
[2] cf. below, Part II, Chapter iv, pp. 142–51.
[3] Protocol V, Annex, Report of Commission. Banning, pp. 28–9. Thomson, pp. 231–2.
[4] Protocol V, Annex, Report of Commission. Banning, p. 28.
[5] Protocol V, Annex, Report of Commission.
[6] cf. below, Part II, Chapter iv, pp. 142–51.

THE SECOND BASIS

importance which now attached to the International Commission. England probably proved a stauncher supporter of it, precisely because she was unaware of the true extent of either Bismarck's or Leopold's ambitions for the Association.

France as usual found a firm supporter in Portugal,[1] whose interests were identical with hers, and whose knowledge of the situation similar. She also discovered a new ally[2] in this question in Russia. The most important precedent for the river commission on the Congo, was that which had been instituted in 1815 on the Danube. Russia objected and had always objected to this strongly, and for traditional reasons, therefore, now showed herself opposed to any wide extension of the powers of that which it was proposed to set up on the Congo.

The vital points of controversy which arose over the whole question concerned the sovereignty of the commission on the river, and its financial powers. Little difficulty was found in outlining its main functions,[3] which were, in general, to secure free navigation on the Congo, and, in particular, to draw up rules for this purpose, to police it, and to assess the compensatory dues permitted by the earlier clauses of the Act. But when it came to giving it the unqualified right to exercise these functions, there was less unanimity of opinion.

The provisions of the Act[4] specially stipulated that the Commission should not be able to assess dues where other powers exercised authority on the river. Any infringement of the rules laid down by it[5] was also to be checked by its agents, but only where they exercised direct authority. Elsewhere this was to be done by the riverain powers. This meant that wherever they clashed the authority of the International Commission was in every case to be subordinate to that of these powers. That it had not yet been decided where the latter were

---

[1] Protocol III. Protocol V, Annex, Report of Commission. Banning, p. 28; Thomson, p. 232.
[2] Protocol V, Annex, Report of Commission. Protocol V. Banning pp. 28-9, 30-1.
[3] Protocol V, Annex, Report of Commission, Article IX. General Act, Articles XIX, XX. Protocol V, Annex 6, Project of Commission, Articles V–VIII. F.O./84/1818/ Memo., Clement Hill, Dec. 20, 1884.
[4] General Act, Article XX (Project of Commission, Article VIII). Thomson, p. 31.
[5] General Act, Article XX (Project of Commission, Article VII).

134 THE BERLIN WEST AFRICAN CONFERENCE

going to be established on the river did not alter the fundamental nature of the principle at stake, which constituted in effect a denial of the sovereign rights of the Commission. Precedent could actually be cited against it,[1] for the Danube Commission itself was sovereign on the lower part of the river, where it enjoyed complete immunity from the authority of the riverain powers established there.

Banning, taking his stand upon this,[2] had from the beginning urged Bismarck to grant similiar privileges to the International Commission of the Congo in the navigation project which he drew up with France before the conference met. But Bismarck refused to do this. Banning therefore himself brought forward a proposal to this effect in commission.[3] But France, Portugal, and Russia all argued that the Danubian régime was an exception which could not be applied to other rivers. Germany took no decisive stand, and England followed suit. Banning found himself isolated therefore, and failed to carry his point. On the motion of Courcel, the discussion of the most important part of his proposal was postponed until after the conclusion of the territorial negotiations, and in fact never resumed again ; on that of the English jurisconsult, Sir Travers Twiss, the rest was whittled down to a mere guarantee of the personal inviolability of the members of the Commission in fulfilling their functions.

If the administrative powers of the Commission were in this way severely curtailed, so also were its financial ones. It was clear that the meagre navigation dues allowed by the Act would not be sufficient for its purposes. Loans from the powers were a necessity if it was ever to come to life at all. Permission to raise these loans[4] was indeed given it by the clauses of the Act, but at the same time the governments making them were expressly exempted from any obligation to guarantee them. This meant, in effect, that the money could never be raised, since the risks involved in a barbarous and undeveloped coun-

---

[1] Protocol V, Annex, Report of Commission. Banning, pp. 28–9.
[2] Banning, p. 31.
[3] Protocol V, Annex, Report of Commission. Banning, pp. 28–9. Thomson, pp. 231–2.
[4] General Act, Article XXIII. Protocol V, Annex 6, Project of Commission, Article XI. Protocol V, Annex, Report of Commission. Banning, pp. 29–30. Thomson, p. 232.

THE SECOND BASIS 135

try were clearly too great to be undertaken without adequate backing. Before it was even constituted, therefore, the Commission was deprived of the very means of functioning at all. For this it had chiefly France and Portugal to thank, but also Germany, whose indeterminate attitude was undoubtedly the decisive factor in the situation. There is no doubt, too, that Germany actually *changed* her attitude in favour of France as the discussions proceeded. The German project[1] had originally suggested that loans to the International Commission should be guaranteed, but, in point of fact, England was the only power in commission, besides Belgium, who showed herself ready to guarantee them.[2] Consequently France scored what appeared to be a substantial victory for autonomous interests on the Congo—though mainly no doubt because Bismarck knew that it was worse than Pyrrhic.

The third question to occupy the attention of the navigation commission was that of the neutralisation of the Congo and its affluents in time of war.[3] Three projects, an English, a German, and a Belgian, were submitted to it for consideration on this subject. Though differing in certain details these projects were all agreed on essentials. Each advocated that the Congo should be neutralised, and not only its affluents with it, but also all the land routes assimilated to it in the Conventional Basin. France, who presented no project, thereby implying her virtual agreement with that of Germany, would undoubtedly have liked to veto this extension to land routes,[4] but in view of the strong line taken by Germany, and the marked solidarity of opinion which showed itself between Germany, England, and Beligum, she was forced to waive her objections, and made no public protest in commission.

There was thus no serious difference of opinion amongst the powers over the neutralisation question, as originally presented to it. But trouble arose when Kasson introduced a proposal for neutralising not only the Congo River, and its

[1] Protocol V, Annex 4, Article IV. Thomson, p. 231.
[2] Protocol V, Annex, Report of Commission. Banning, pp. 29–30.
[3] Protocol V, Annex, Report of Commission: Annex 8, German Neutrality Proposal: Annex 9, Belgian Neutrality Proposal: Annex 10, British Neutrality Proposal.
[4] Banning, p. 32. F.O./84/1817/ Malet to Granville, Dec. 13, 1884, Africa, 218. (Enclosure Memo., Anderson on Kasson's Proposition.) cf. D.D.F., V, No. 482, Ferry to Courcel, Dec. 12, 1884.

136 THE BERLIN WEST AFRICAN CONFERENCE

assimilated routes, but also the whole Conventional Basin, as defined in the first basis.[1] His aim, of course, was to help the Association by freeing it from the danger of attacks from stronger powers. As had been the case with the East Coast extension, he was in reality acting, not only on behalf of the Association, but also with the secret co-operation of Bismarck, whose approval he had obtained before submitting his proposal to the powers.[2] Consequently the German delegates were at once able to support it,[3] just as they had done his earlier demands—freely and unconditionally. The Belgian delegates, who had apparently *not* been told about it beforehand, were at first somewhat taken aback, but gave it their unreserved support as soon as its meaning became clear to them. As for Great Britain, she too, after some initial hesitation, came round to the same point of view. Anxiety over her interests in the neighbourhood of the Great Lakes[4] at first led her to ask for the exclusion of the eastern half of the Conventional Basin from the proposed neutrality clauses. But later she withdrew this demand,[5] and gave unreserved support to Kasson's proposition.

It was found impossible to carry it,[6] however, owing to the insurmountable opposition of France and Portugal, who both having possessions that were affected by it, both declared that

[1] Protocol V, Annex, Report of Commission: Annex 12, U.S. Neutrality Proposal: Annex 13, Kasson's Speech in Defence of Dec. 10, 1884, in Commission. S.E.D. 196, No. 36, Kasson to Frelinghuysen, Nov. 24, 1884, Dec. 13, 1884. F.O./84/1817/ Malet to Granville, Dec. 10, 1884, Tel. 58: Granville to Malet, Dec. 11, 1884, Tel. 27: Malet to Granville, Dec. 13, 1884, Africa, 218. Banning, pp. 32-3. Thomson, pp. 232-4. G. L. Beer, *African Questions at the Peace Conference*, pp. 259-60. Reeves, p. 47.

[2] S.E.D. 196. No. 36, Kasson to Frelinghuysen, Nov. 24, 1884. Thomson, p. 233. cf. also, Banning, p. 47 (but he is wrong in stating that Kasson introduced his proposition with connivance and support of G.B. also).

[3] Protocol V, Annex, Report of Commission. F.O./84/1817/ Malet to Granville, Dec. 10, 1884, Tel. 58. D.D.F., V, No. 483, Courcel to Ferry, Dec. 12, 1884.

[4] F.O./84/1816/ Dec. 4, 1884, Opinion of Lord Chancellor on Neutrality Proposal of Sir Travers Twiss. Granville to Malet, Dec. 4, 1884, Tel. 20. F.O./84/1817/ Malet to Granville, Dec. 13, 1884, Africa, 218 (Enclosure Memo., Anderson, Dec. 13, On Kasson's Proposition).

[5] F.O./84/1817/ Granville to Malet, Dec. 11, 1884, Tel. 27: Malet to Granville, Dec. 13, 1884, Africa, 218: (Enclosure Memo., Anderson, Dec. 13, On Kasson's Proposition). F.O. to Malet, Dec. 16, 1884, Africa, 161. Protocol V, Annex, Report of Commission.

[6] Protocol V, Annex, Report of Commission. S.E.D. 196, No, 43, Kasson to Frelinghuysen, Dec. 13, 1884. F.O./84/1817/ Malet to Granville, Dec. 10, 1884, Tel. 58: Malet to Granville, Dec. 13, 1884, Africa, 218: (Enclosure Memo., Anderson, Dec. 13). D.D.F., V, No. 483, Courcel to Ferry, Dec. 12, 1884. Banning, p. 33. Thomson, p. 233. Beer, pp. 259-60.

it represented an inadmissible infringement of their sovereign rights. A belligerent state,[1] Courcel declared, could not be expected to deprive itself of part of its own means of action in time of war. The proposal,[2] added the Portuguese delegate, would moreover have the effect of submitting the territories of any one power to two different systems, according to whether their territories lay inside or outside the Conventional Basin. This was an impossible state of affairs. There were angry scenes in commission, Courcel, on one occasion,[3] so far forgetting his usual urbanity as to cry out angrily to Malet and Küsserow, " Pour quoi nous prenez-vous, des brigands ? "

Even angrier scenes took place in private. Courcel, in a long conversation with Busch and Hatzfeldt,[4] complained bitterly of the aggravating effect of the "two American propositions", by which he meant Sanford's railway proposal and Kasson's present proposal, upon Franco-German relations. Recriminations on the German side were no less bitter. Hatzfeldt reproached Courcel roundly with the "retrograde" tendencies of French policy, tendencies, he declared, which constituted a regrettable betrayal of the terms and the spirit of the entente which had been concluded between the two countries at Varzin. For some time, he added, it was clear that there had been complete lack of understanding between them. Bismarck had supported Sanford's and Kasson's propositions merely because he was anxious to establish as wide a free area as possible in the centre of Africa. Why could not France help him in this ? Courcel replied that both these questions lay outside the official programme of the conference. Moreover, Bismarck had not even approached France about them. France had already made important concessions over the Eastern extension and the twenty years' prohibition of import dues. It was unreasonable to expect her to make others, for which she was apparently to receive no compensation. The way the entente had already turned, he concluded, did not encourage the French ever to consider again the formation of another.

[1] Protocol V, Annex, Report of Commission. Thomson, p. 233.
[2] Protocol V, Annex, Report of Commission.
[3] Banning, p. 33.
[4] D.D.F., V, No. 483, Courcel to Ferry, Dec. 12, 1884. cf. also, Thomson, pp. 234–5. (Short reference.) (Thomson uses German documents for report of Courcel's interview with Hatzfeldt.)

It was impossible to beat down French opposition. Deadlock having been reached in commission,[1] a sub-committee was at Kasson's own suggestion appointed to examine the question.[2] But Courcel refused to sit on this committee. At last, however, probably urged on by Bismarck,[3] he himself approached Kasson, with the result that a provisional settlement was at last reached. On the demand of the French ambassador,[4] a division was now admitted between the original proposal laid before the commission for neutralising the river alone and Kasson's more comprehensive one. To the first,[5] Courcel declared he had objection. But Kasson's proposition more properly concerned the declaration on free trade which had already been drawn up in connection with the first basis, and could with advantage form a supplementary article to it, final discussion of it being reserved until a later date. The commission agreed to this, and their decision was then endorsed by the conference.

France scored a substantial, though still an indecisive, victory therefore over the neutrality question in the second basis. She was destined to follow it up, however, for the final settlement of the whole question was also undoubtedly more favourable to her views than to those of either Bismarck or Kasson. By the neutrality clauses of the General Act,[6] which, by common agreement, were in the end formed into a separate chapter of their own, the Conventional Basin was *not* in fact neutralised, French and Portuguese sovereignty were *not* in any way impaired there, and Kasson's proposition was whittled down to a mere promise, on the part of the powers signatory to the Act, to use their good offices with the countries established in the Conventional Basin, to try and induce them to neutralise their territories in event of war. Neutralisation,

---

[1] S.E.D. 196. No. 43, Kasson to Frelinghuysen, Dec. 13, 1884. F.O./84/1817/ Malet to Granville, Dec. 13, 1884, Africa, 213 (Enclosure, Memo., Anderson, Dec., 13, On Kasson's Proposition). Thomson, p. 234.
[2] F.O./84/1817/ Malet to Granville, Dec. 13, 1884, Africa, 218 (Enclosure, Memo., Anderson, Dec. 13).
[3] cf. D.D.F., V, No. 486, Courcel to Ferry, Dec. 14, 1884.
[4] Protocol V, Annex, Report of Commission: Annex II, Text of French " Transactional Proposal " (Anon., in Protocols). F.O./84/1817/ Malet to Granville, Dec. 13, 1884, Africa, 218 (Enclosure, Memo., Anderson, Dec. 13). Banning, p. 33. Thomson, p. 234.
[5] Protocol V, Annex, Report of Commission.
[6] General Act, Chapter iii, Articles X–XII.

that is to say, was not made obligatory, these countries being left to neutralise or not to neutralise their territories, according as they felt inclined. Recourse to the mediation of other powers, in the case of a dispute, was indeed made obligatory on them, before any appeal to arms, but at the same time they were expressly exempted from any further obligation to accept the arbitration of these powers in the dispute in question. It is clear, therefore, that the fundamental principles of Kasson's proposition were *not* incorporated in the terms of the Final Act, and that the vast neutral area in Central Africa, which both he and Bismarck,[1] as well as Leopold, had hoped and worked for, did *not* therefore come into existence.

On the other hand,[2] the insertion of an entirely new clause in the Act, for which Émile Banning was responsible, allowing any state in possession of territory in the Conventional Basin, to declare itself permanently neutral, should it wish to do so, did in effect give to the Association what was most essential to it, namely the right, of which it, alone of all the powers concerned, was at once quick to avail itself, to declare its own territories neutral. If Bismarck's *international* ambitions for the Congo Basin, therefore, came to nothing, so far as neutrality was concerned, Leopold's more national ones for the Association, which were at first a part of these, did in fact emerge considerably strengthened by the safeguards which he succeeded in obtaining from the powers, snatched, as it were, from the very jaws of what would otherwise have been an unbroken triumph for France and Portugal.

That this was possible was due principally to the efforts made by Bismarck on his behalf,[3] *outside* the official bases of the conference, efforts thanks to which the Association was able to attain at its conclusion to a position of territorial power and prestige which enabled it finally to be recognised as a sovereign

---

[1] cf. especially D.D.F., V, No. 486, Courcel to Ferry, Dec. 14, 1884.
[2] General Act, Chapter iii, Article X. Proctocol IX, Annex III, Report of Commission, 3. Project of Declaration on Neutrality, Article B. Protocol IX. S.E.D. 196, No. 59, Kasson to Frelinghuysen, Feb. 16, 1885. F.O./84/1821/ Malet to Granville, Feb. 14, 1885, Africa, 104, 105, Tel. 33 : Feb. 15, 1885, Tel. 33. F.O./84/1822/ Malet to Granville, Feb. 17, Tel. 36, Africa, 117 : Granville to Malet, Feb. 17, Tel. 25 : Malet to Granville, Feb. 19, 1885, Tel. 38. L.J., Congo, 1885, Engelhardt's Report, pp. 36-7. Banning, pp. 48-9. Thomson, pp. 236-7. Beer, pp. 260-1.
[3] cf. below, Part II, Chapters iv, v, pp. 142-75.

state. Once again, therefore, the *ex officio* policy of the chancellor proved to be a powerful force in the background, working against the interests of France.

The original neutrality clause[1] of the Congo Act concerning the river and its affluents only was taken over verbatim[2] in that which was simultaneously drawn up in commission for the Niger, an Act[3] which in every way resembled that of the Congo, except with regard to the International Commission. Instead of this[4] Great Britain and France both engaged themselves in identical terms, to apply the clauses of the act wherever they were sovereign on the river, together with any other regulations, which they might at any future date think fit to pass in the interests of free navigation. The other powers signatory[5] to the Act also gave a provisional engagement to do the same in the event of their ever exercising sovereignty over any part of it.

In this way, the refusal to recognise French interests on the lower Niger was softened by the recognition of their claims to the upper Niger—which had never been disputed—the whole being respectably concealed behind a façade of international interest which in fact never materialised, for the simple reason that it was not allowed to either by France or by Great Britain.

It seems clear in conclusion that the second basis not only helped to crystallise to an increasing degree the already growing solidarity of England, Germany, and the Association as opposed to that of France and Portugal; it also resulted in a heavy defeat of French interests on the Niger, and at the same time increased Franco-German tension on the Congo almost to breaking-point of the entente. It likewise witnessed significant developments in one of the openly-admitted sources of this tension, namely, Bismarck's growing sponsorship, it might almost be said, his adoption, of the cause of the International

---

[1] cf. above, pp. 127–8. General Act, Chapter iv, Article XXV.
[2] General Act, Chapter v, Article XXXIII. cf. Protocol V, Annex, Report of Commission. Protocol V.
[3] General Act, Chapter v, Articles XXVI–XXXIII. Protocol V, Annex, Report of Commission. Protocol V. F.O./84/1813/Malet to Granville, Dec. 13, 1884, Africa, 222 (Enclosure, Memo., J. A. Crowe, Sub-Commission). L.J., Congo, 1885, Engelhardt's Report, p. 16. D.D.F., V, No. 478, Courcel to Ferry, Dec. 8, 1884. Banning, p. 35.
[4] General Act, Chapter v, Articles XXX and XXXI.
[5] Ibid. Article XXXII.

Association, an adoption which was probably the most important single feature of the situation, since it was the pivot on which German policy, and with it the fate of the whole conference now turned.

Bismarck's championship of the Association owed its origin, as has been seen, to the contradictory position in which the chancellor found himself at the very time of the formation of the Franco-German entente (in a moment of anger against England), owing to his ignorance of local politics in Africa, and the large part played in them by the French. But if his efforts to strengthen the position of the Association were noticeable even *within* the official framework of the conference, more striking still were the effects of those which he was all the time making *outside* it upon the course of its discussions. They formed the background to the Niger question. They figured constantly, if only by implication, in the debates concerning the Congo. No understanding of the situation would be complete without them, and it is these, therefore, that will form the subject of the next chapters.

CHAPTER IV

THE CONFERENCE RECOGNISES THE ASSOCIATION

BISMARCK'S first efforts to further the cause of the Association were directed towards an improvement in its legal status. This was curiously undefined when the conference opened. Its flag had then been recognised by the United States as that of a "friendly government";[1] by Germany as that of a "friendly state".[2] France, in the pre-emption treaty, had undertaken "to respect the stations and free territories of the Association and to place no further obstacle to the exercise of its rights";[3] but she had gone no further than this, and had in no way, according to her own interpretation, acceded to the Association the rights of a sovereign body.[4] In the view of all the other governments of Europe these rights were even more undeniably not possessed by it, since they had made no attempt to recognise the Association in any form. For them it still remained a private body therefore, without any of the privileges of a state.

Consequently, as has been seen, it had no official representation of any kind at Berlin, its adherents figuring somewhat indiscriminately in both the American and Belgian delegations Legally it did not exist at all at the conference, and it was only once mentioned by name during its discussions.[5] Nevertheless the terms of its existence had a vital bearing on every issue of

---

[1] cf. above, p. 79. Text, Protocol IX, Annex I. Hertslet, I, *Map of Africa by Treaty*, pp. 244–6.
[2] cf. above, pp. 77, 80. W.B., Congo, 1885, No. 43. Protocol IX, Annex I. Hertslet, I, pp. 219–20.
[3] Pp. 79–80. Protocol IX, Annex I. Hertslet, II, p. 562.
[4] D.D.F., V, No. 485, Ferry to Laboulaye, Dec. 13, 1884; No, 489, Ferry to Courcel, Dec. 16, 1884. Yarnall, p. 69. Thomson, pp. 259–60. Banning, pp. 6–7.
[5] Protocol II, Kasson's Speech. S.E.D. 196, No. 34, Kasson to Frelinghuysen, Nov. 20, 1884. Thomson, pp. 237–8.

importance raised there, and for this reason it figured constantly in the thoughts of the delegates, even, as Courcel declared on one occasion,[1] " comme la dame de leurs pensées ", forming for them an object of perpetual, if not always conscious preoccupation.

Inevitably, as the discussions proceeded, it assumed in most of their minds the form of a state, if at first only a phantom state,[2] nameless, nationless, and penniless, for the simple reason that its adhesion to the Final Act was implicit in practically every one of its clauses, most of which could quite clearly not be made valid without the consent of every power established in the Conventional Basin of the Congo. Equally clearly, however, this consent could not be given a legal form, unless all the powers concerned had a recognised legal status.

No one realised this better than Bismarck. There is no doubt that he must have been fully alive to the implications of the situation when he recognised the Association on November 8th, and that he became increasingly so as time went on. The very success of his efforts in securing, with the help of England and the agents of the Association, such a widespread and substantial triumph for the principles of free trade in the first basis, made it imperative that the Association itself should at the same time be placed in a position strong enough to guarantee them. Otherwise they risked being negated at the outset. Added to his general desire, therefore, to further Leopold's interests, was the close bearing which they had in this connection on the main issues of the conference, rendering the matter one of peculiar urgency and importance.

Clearly the first power to be approached was Great Britain. Not only did she pursue a policy which was generally friendly to the Association, her example was also one likely to react with most force on the opinion of other powers at the conference. Already, before it opened, Bismarck had begun to make advances to the British Government. At the beginning of November he sent instructions to Münster,[3] telling him to inform Granville that the German Government considered it

[1] Banning, p. 16. Quoted by Thomson, p. 238. Königk, p. 121.
[2] cf. Thomson, p. 238.
[3] F.O./84/1814/ Münster to Granville, Nov. 2, 1884. (A. and P., LV, 1884-5: C. 4205, No. 30, Ibid.—full text). cf. Thomson, pp. 238-9.

desirable in the interests of commerce and civilisation that the Association should be recognised by all the powers at the conference, just as it had been by the United States.

Great Britain was at this moment considering the attitude which she should adopt towards the Association. This was eventually defined,[1] as has been seen, in the highly non-committal sense of Granville's note to Malet of November 15th, telling him that the Association was not yet in British eyes considered to be a state. Its efforts to become one would be watched with sympathy and interest, and recognition would follow if it succeeded. But meanwhile its authority was not to be regarded as sovere gn in its own territories, and consular jurisdiction should for the present be maintained there. Bismarck's suggestions therefore appear to have had at most but an indirect effect upon Great Britain's attitude towards the Association when the conference opened.

On November 19th[2] the chancellor once more approached the Foreign Office on the subject. Germany, he told Malet, holding it of advantage for the future of free trade in the basin of the Congo to assist the Association in its endeavours to become a state, intended shortly to recognise it in the same terms as the American Government. He would be very glad if Great Britain would do the same. Somewhat unfortunately for the chancellor Malet learnt the same day,[3] from a private source, that Germany had in reality recognised the Association a week before. The reason for the treaty being kept secret[4] was actually a misunderstanding, of a perfectly " bona fide " nature, which had arisen between Bismarck and Leopold, after it had been signed. Bismarck would have liked to publish it before the conference opened. But he refrained from doing so, because he thought that Leopold would not be pleased if the open references to him in the preamble were made known so soon. Leopold, on the other hand, refrained from doing anything, because he thought that Bismarck was simply waiting

---

[1] cf. above, p. 190. F.O./84/1814/ Granville to Malet, Nov. 15, 1884, Africa, 78.
[2] F.O./84/1815/ Malet to Granville, Nov. 19, 1884, Tel. 4.
[3] F.O./84/1815/Malet to Granville. Nov. 19, 1884, Tel. 4. (The informant appears to have been Sir Travers Twiss. cf. Malet to Granville, Nov. 21, 1884, Tel. 11.)
[4] Banning, pp. 36–7.

CONFERENCE RECOGNISES ASSOCIATION

for the earliest favourable opportunity to publish it. When Malet, on November 22nd,[1] came to see Bismarck, and to complain to him about this, the latter at once explained to him what he still sincerely believed to be Leopold's responsibility in the matter, and at the same time read out in confidence to the British ambassador the text of the treaty. Nevertheless, the impression made on the British Government by Malet's discovery was naturally not a favourable one, and did not do anything to encourage speedy acquiescence in Bismarck's demands.

The reception of these demands in London was in fact somewhat cool. Lister,[2] at the Foreign Office, declared that it was one thing to assist the Association in its endeavours to become a state, it was another to recognise it as being one. It was usual in such cases to have a clearer idea of its boundaries than seemed actually to be possessed of those of the Association, as well as some proof of the validity of its territorial claims. The proper mode of procedure would, in his opinion, be for the Association to explain its constitution, to give assurances to the powers about personal, religious, and commercial freedom, and then to petition the conference to recognise its sovereignty.

Sir Julian Pauncefote,[3] the Permanent Under-Secretary of the Foreign Office, agreed with Lister about the necessity for obtaining more adequate information about the Association, but doubted the expediency of bringing up the question of its status before the conference. Instead he advocated that Malet should give Bismarck a copy of Granville's note of November 15th, defining Great Britain's attitude, and at the same time ask the chancellor whether some means could not be devised of recognising the Association *outside* the conference, not as an actual state, but as a state " in course of formation ", proper reserves being insisted upon regarding religious liberty and freedom of trade. The Lord Chancellor, who was the next to be consulted,[4] was all in favour of these reserves, and agreed in substance

---

[1] F.O./84/1815/ Malet to Granville, Nov. 23, 1884, Africa, 98.
[2] F.O./84/1815/ Malet to Granville, Nov. 19, 1884, Tel. 4, Minute, Lister.
[3] F.O./84/1815/ Malet to Granville, Nov. 19, 1884, Tel. 4, Minute, Pauncefote.
[4] F.O./84/1815/ Note, Selborne, Nov. 28, 1884, on Draft Dispatch, Granville to Malet, Africa, 44.

with what Pauncefote said. But he did not approve of the proposal to recognise the Association as a "state in course of formation", on the ground that it was too vague. Sufficient safeguards would in his opinion be obtained by adhering strictly to the wording of the agreement made by the United States with the Association in April, which, when closely studied, offered a useful medium for reservations. By recognising the flag of the Association as that of a "friendly government", this agreement did not, he maintained, really recognise it as a sovereign state. The view so stated was also logically developed throughout the rest of its clauses, which never once referred to the Association as a state, but merely as the representative of certain "free states of the Congo", which had temporarily placed the administration of their affairs in its hands. Great Britain could with advantage therefore avail herself of this phraseology in order to accord a less definite form of recognition to the Association than that which Bismarck seemed to contemplate.

On November 24th[1] Granville, who had evidently taken his advice,[2] wrote to Malet in this sense, at the same time insisting on the need for fuller information regarding the boundaries and resources of the Association, as well as for further consultation with the powers. He also reiterated his statements of the 15th, emphasising in particular the view held by the British Government that consular jurisdiction should for the present be maintained in the territories of the Association, and should continue to be maintained there until the states under its supervision had developed sufficiently to acquire a proper claim to sovereignty.

Meanwhile, however, Bismarck was growing more and more impatient. When Malet gave him a copy of this note on December 1st,[3] he declared that he was willing to concur in the maintenance of consular jurisdiction, but urgently besought the British Ambassador to do his utmost to induce Granville to abandon his other reserves, and to recognise the Association without any further delay. The work of the conference, he

[1] F.O./84/1815/ Granville to Malet, Nov. 24, 1884, Africa, 98.
[2] Selborne's written commentary was actually made after the dispatch had been drafted, but it seems clear from this that the views expressed there on this point must have been his.
[3] F.O./84/1816/ Malet to Granville, Dec. 1, 1884, Tel. 40.

said, would be more than incomplete if the Association were not given the vitality which it would alone receive from recognition. This was particularly necessary at the moment, because there was imminent danger of the whole of its territories passing into the hands of France. Recognition and recognition only could save the situation, and enable it successfully to combat French claims. The chancellor spoke with great earnestness, and in addition managed to convey to Malet the impression that if Great Britain did not grant his request, he would contrive to make things very unpleasant for her on the Niger. The fear which he thus succeeded in instilling into the British ambassador was in fact instantaneous in its effects, for there can be no doubt that it was responsible for the immediate change which now took place in Great Britain's attitude.

On the very day on which this conversation took place,[1] Malet wired home a report of it, together with his own impressions. The next morning he received a wire back from Granville, authorising him to negotiate a treaty with the Association for the recognition of its flag as that of a friendly government,[2] with due reserves regarding most-favoured-nation treatment and consular jurisdiction. Malet at once set about his task,[3] at the same time announcing his satisfaction at this timely concession on the part of Granville, which had been responsible for immediately assuring to him the co-operation of the German, Belgian, and American representatives over the Niger question.

The treaty was now drafted at his request by Sir Travers Twiss,[4] revised by Pauncefote[5] and Selborne,[6] and finally signed on December 16th.[7] Its exact wording is of some interest, since it formed the model, with one exception,[8] for all the subsequent

[1] cf. above, F.O./84/1816/ Malet to Granville, Dec. 1, 1884, Tel. 40.
[2] F.O./84/1816/ Granville to Malet, Dec. 2, 1884, Tel. 16.
[3] G.D./29/156/ Malet to Granville, Dec. 5, 1884. cf. also, Leopold to Granville, Dec. 7, 1884.
[4] F.O./84/1816/ Twiss to Pauncefote, Dec. 5, 1884.
[5] F.O./84/1816/ Draft, Pauncefote, Dec. 10, 1884, of British Treaty with International Association. Pauncefote to Selborne, Dec. 10, 1884.
[6] F.O./84/1816/ Selborne to Pauncefote, Dec. 11, 1884. Pauncefote to Hill, Dec. 12, 1884.
[7] For text cf. Protocol IX, Annex I. Hertslet, I, pp. 221-6. cf. also, Banning, *Mémoires*, p. 37. Keith, p. 63. Thomson, p. 240.
[8] The Belgian Agreement. cf. below, p. 149.

recognitions of the Association at the conference.[1] Like the American treaty it recognised the flag of the Association as that of a friendly government.[2] Like the German as well as the American treaty it forbade the levy of import or transit duties on the merchandise of its nationals in the territories of the Free States administered by the Association;[3] stipulated that these nationals should have full rights of entry and establishment;[4] and that they should be accorded most-favoured-nation treatment.[5] Like the German treaty it also added a special provision[6] that these privileges should continue to be in force in the event of any future cession to another power. In addition to this it added clauses[7] which did not figure at all in either the American or the German treaties providing for the continued maintenance of consular jurisdiction in the territories administered by the Association. The German definition[8] of the boundaries of the Association, however, was *not* accepted in the British treaty, which throughout avoided any express mention of them. By a special declaration also,[9] the Association was particularly called upon to state that it was lawfully invested with the administration of the " Free States established, or being established, in the basins of the Congo and the Niari Kwilu "; whilst special emphasis was laid, in the wording of the treaty itself, in an even more marked manner than in the American agreement upon the importance of these " Free States ", as opposed to that of the Association, which was carefully distinguished from them, as the body merely administering the districts where they were established.

The idea behind this was of course to grant a less definite

[1] cf. below, p. 149 for other agreements.
[2] Convention G.B. and I.A. of Congo, Declaration of British Government. Declaration, U.S.A. and I.A. of Congo. Declaration, Frelinghuysen.
[3] Convention G.B. and I.A., Article I. Convention, Germany and I.A., Article I, Declaration, Sanford.
[4] Convention, G.B. and I.A., Article II. Convention, Germany and I.A., Article II. Declaration, Sanford.
[5] Convention, G.B. and I.A., Article III. Convention, Germany and I.A., Article III. Declaration, Sanford.
[6] Convention, G.B. and I.A., Article X. Convention, Germany and I.A., Article IV.
[7] Convention, G.B. and I.A., Articles V–IX. cf. Banning, p. 37.
[8] Convention, Germany and I.A., Article VI. In the British Convention there is only an allusion in Article II to " the territories which are or shall be under the government of the said Association."
[9] Convention, G.B. and I.A. Declaration of the Association.

CONFERENCE RECOGNISES ASSOCIATION 149

political status, as well as a less definite form of recognition to the Association, than that which had been given it in the German treaty. The point was a juridical nicety[1] insisted on by Pauncefote and Selborne, in accordance with the views which they had already expressed on this subject. But since the " Free States " in question never came into existence except on paper[2] it never acquired any practical importance, except perhaps later on in actually *facilitating* the transformation of the Association itself into the Congo Free State.

Great Britain's recognition of the Association was followed in identical terms by that of Italy on December 19th,[3] of Austria-Hungary on December 24th,[4] and of Holland on December 27th, 1884[5]; of Spain on January 7th,[6] of Russia on February 5th,[7] of Norway and Sweden on February 10th,[8] and of Denmark on February 23rd, 1885.[9] Belgium was the last power at the conference to recognise the Association on this same date February 23rd, 1885,[10] and then not by treaty, but by a special declaration. In this declaration, however, she acknowledged its sovereignty in much fuller terms than any other country, and also made no reserves about consular jurisdiction. On the 5th[11] and 14th[12] February respectively, France and Portugal had meanwhile concluded territorial settlements with the Association,

[1] F.O./84/1815/ Malet to Granville, Nov. 19, Tel. 4, Minute, Pauncefote: Note, Selborne, Nov. 28, 1884, On Draft Dispatch, Granville to Malet, Nov. 24, 1884. F.O./84/1816/ Twiss to Pauncefote, Dec. 5, 1884: Draft of Treaty, Pauncefote, Dec. 10, 1884: Selborne to Pauncefote, Dec. 11, 1884: Pauncefote to Hill, Dec. 11, 1884: Pauncefote to Selborne, Dec. 12, 1884.
[2] cf. Keltie, p. 211.
[3] Protocol IX, Annex I. Hertslet, I, pp. 227–8. Keith, p. 63. Reeves, p. 54.
[4] Protocol IX, Annex I. Hertslet, I, pp. 194–5. Keith, p. 63. Reeves, p. 54.
[5] Protocol, IX, Annex I. Hertslet, I, pp. 230–1. Keith, p. 63. Reeves, p. 54.
[6] Protocol IX, Annex I. Hertslet, I, pp. 240–1. Keith, p. 63. Reeves, p. 54.
[7] Protocol IX, Annex I. Hertslet, I, p. 239. Banning, p. 61. Keith, p. 63. Reeves, p. 56.
[8] Protocol IX, Annex I. Hertslet, I, pp. 242–3. Keith, p. 63. Reeves, p. 56.
[9] Protocol IX, Annex I. Hertslet, I, pp. 205–6. Keith, p. 63. Reeves, p. 57.
[10] Protocol IX, Annex I. Hertslet, I, pp. 196–7. cf. Thomson, p. 240. Banning, pp. 61–2. Keith, p. 63. Reeves, p. 57.
[11] Protocol IX, Annex I. General Act (Appendix). Hertslet, I, pp. 409–11. Banning, p. 58. Reeves, pp. 54–5.
[12] Protocol IX, Annex I. General Act (Appendix). Hertslet, I, pp. 232–3. Banning, p. 61.

150 THE BERLIN WEST AFRICAN CONFERENCE

which also comprised recognitions of its flag, in return for the same privileges conceded by it to the other powers. Thanks to these agreements the recognition of the Association by the individual governments represented at the conference was now followed by its recognition by the conference as a whole.

At its ninth meeting, on February 23rd,[1] a letter was read to the delegates from Colonel Strauch, announcing that the Association had now, with one exception, been recognised by all the powers at the conference. The exception alluded to was Turkey, who actually did not accord her recognition until June 25th, 1885.[2] But the omission was clearly not important, and at the last meeting of the conference on February 26th,[3] Bismarck, who presided over it, was therefore able without dissent to announce the adhesion of the Association to the Final Act, and in so doing to transform it officially into a sovereign power, since in no other capacity would it have been able to exercise this right. In this way he also justified a further reference to it in his speech as the " Congo State ", although this title was not formally assumed by it until a later date.

The chancellor's initial purpose in securing the recognition of the powers had thus been fulfilled. The Association had been enabled to sign the Act, and thereby to give indubitable validity to the Berlin decisions, which might otherwise have been of questionable value from the point of view of international law. Besides this the recognitions of the powers undoubtedly gave substantial assistance to it in the territorial negotiations which it had all this time been carrying on *outside* the official bases of the conference, with France and Portugal. Bismarck was of course aware of this. It had not been his prime consideration in working for the recognition of the powers.[4] But as events proceeded it assumed equal, if not greater importance in his mind, one, as has been seen, which he did not hesitate to emphasise in strong terms to Malet.[5]

[1] Protocol IX. Yarnall, p. 71. Thomson, p. 240. Reeves, pp. 57–8. Keith, p. 62. Banning, *Partage*, pp. 124–6.
[2] Hertslet. Keith, p. 62.
[3] Protocol X. Thomson, p. 240. Keltie, p. 211. Banning, *Mémoires*, p. 62. Yarnall, p. 7. Reeves, pp. 58–60. Keith, pp. 62–3. Banning, *Partage*, pp. 126–7.
[4] cf. above, pp. 143–4.
[5] cf. above, pp. 144 146–7.

The reason for this was largely the turn taken by the territorial negotiations themselves. In trying to help the Association here, Bismarck discovered that his hands were to a great extent tied by his commitments with France. Unless he wished to break completely with the French he found that it was difficult to give in a *direct* form to the Association the full measure of support which he desired. The question of recognition therefore assumed a new and peculiar significance, by providing him with a means of *indirect* assistance to the Association which was all the more valuable, on account of the limitations set to his action in other ways. As it was even this surreptitious form of support did not pass unnoticed or uncriticised by the French and Portuguese, from whom it provoked lively recriminations.[1] But the history of these belongs more properly to that of the territorial negotiations themselves, which will now be considered in the next chapter.

[1] cf. D.D.F., V, No. 475, Courcel to Ferry, Dec. 3, 1884: No. 477, Courcel to Ferry, Dec. 5, 1884: No. 483, Courcel to Ferry, Dec. 12, 1884. Thomson, pp. 234–5. Banning, *Mémoires*, p. 38. Yarnall, pp. 68–9. cf. below, pp. 162–3.

CHAPTER V

THE TERRITORIAL NEGOTIATIONS

FRANCE had only consented to collaborate with Bismarck in summoning the West African Conference[1] on condition that all territorial questions should be excluded from its programme. She did this, not because she was unaware of the importance of these questions,[2] nor of their relevance to the general issues at stake, but because she considered that she would, in this way, have a better chance of substantiating her own claims in West Africa, which she could then negotiate direct with her rivals, undisturbed by any outside interference. Bismarck acquiesced in her demands, because they seemed to him the necessary price to pay for French co-operation. In their original form they referred only to the Congo,[3] since, at the request of France herself, the projected discussions on free trade and free navigation had, at first, been rigorously limited to this area. When later, however, the Niger was also, at her request, included in the official bases for discussion,[4] it was tacitly understood that the provision should apply here, too, owing to its general character. There is no doubt that by this means France hoped, with the assistance of Germany, to secure for herself a predominant position in both the Niger and Congo basins. Germany did not proffer the expected assistance, however, and her hopes were therefore doomed to disappointment.

It has already been seen how, even before the conference opened,[5] Bismarck had begun to realise the necessity for some solution of the territorial problem being reached before it

[1] cf. above, p. 68.
[2] cf. Thomson, p. 243.
[3] cf. above, p. 69.
[4] cf. above, p. 70.
[5] cf. above, pp. 76–7.

THE TERRITORIAL NEGOTIATIONS 153

closed, and to discuss it with the British ambassador. This necessity became more and more apparent as it proceeded, since, in spite of every effort to exclude them, territorial considerations inevitably intruded themselves into its discussions. Their importance in the Niger question,[1] and the manner in which they were dealt with there, by the recognition of the conference first of British claims on the lower then of French on the upper river, before handing over its control to these two powers respectively, has already been seen. The effect of honestly facing the territorial question in this instance had, in fact, been to destroy the hopes originally entertained by France of setting up an international régime, under cover of which she undoubtedly expected to advance her own interests later on, against those of Great Britain.

Luckily for her no such wholesale frustration of them was possible by such means on the Congo, where the situation was in every way more favourable to her. In the first place her commercial interests were greater, her territorial claims in consequence sounder; secondly, her political rivals, Portugal and the Association, were both weak powers, one of which, the Association, was not even possessed of sovereign rights; thirdly, the very extent of international interest in the basin served up to a point to further her ends by diverting attention from the vital question of territorial partition to that of the international system of free trade and free navigation which it was hoped to set up there. Nevertheless France did not succeed even here in obtaining anything like what she had hoped for. Interest could not be side-tracked indefinitely from the territorial aspect of the question, and though she managed to exclude any express mention of it from the official debates of the conference, she was not successful, as she had hoped, in postponing all consideration of it until after the conference was over.

Negotiations for a territorial settlement of the Congo were in fact set on foot, and conducted side by side with its official work, with which they were co-terminous. This meant that France did not secure the free hand with Portugal and the Association which she had been expecting. Although the territorial negotiations took place outside the official discus-

[1] cf. above, pp. 120-8, 140.

sions of the conference they could not escape their influence. The attitude of Germany and England, in particular, were factors in the situation which had constantly to be taken into account. Both these powers were anxious to support the claims of the Association against those of France and Portugal, and from time to time both played an active part in the negotiations. The situation was complicated by the fact that both, for different reasons, found it difficult to bring any direct pressure to bear on France: Bismarck, on account of the Franco-German entente, which he did not wish to strain to breaking-point; England, on account of her bad relations with France, which were so largely a result of the entente. Nevertheless they managed between them to do a good deal for the Association.

The final solution of the territorial question was a compromise, but a compromise, when every consideration is taken into account, particularly the precarious legal and financial position of the Association, which was undoubtedly more of a triumph for its interests than for those of either of its rivals. It was sufficiently so, in the first instance, to nullify, as has been seen, many of the advantages accruing to France in the official discussions of the conference,[1] advantages of which the illusory nature, therefore, can itself be taken as a gauge of the extent to which the French misjudged the situation, as well as of that to which the successes of the Association were gained at their expense. Secondly, whatever the Association may have had to cede to Portugal and France, it did after all emerge from the conference as a sovereign state, established in a key position at the mouth of the Congo, in possession of its most important harbour, as well as of the greatest part of its course, and with guaranteed rights of access to the interior. These rights were sufficient, as history was to show, for Leopold to exploit, later on, and to annex in its name, the whole vast hinterland of the Congo Basin, undisturbed by either France or Portugal. The rights of these two countries on the river, and their territorial acquisitions at the conference, helped them to expand, and also to develop their already existing possessions to the north and to the south of it. But they did not seriously interfere with the development of Leopold's more extensive

[1] cf. above, pp. 128–39.

THE TERRITORIAL NEGOTIATIONS 155

ambitions in Central Africa. This was undoubtedly a triumph for the Association, a triumph which, as Leopold himself was the first to recognise,[1] was due chiefly to the efforts made by Bismarck on his behalf during the years 1884-5, the part played by Great Britain at the conference being necessarily subordinate to that of Germany.

It is important to realise this, because otherwise the impression may very easily be gained from a superficial reading of the negotiations that, at a certain stage in the proceedings, Bismarck completely abandoned the Association and reversed his whole policy in favour of France.[2] This was not really the case, however. It is true that he refused to mediate directly between France and the Association. But this did not prevent him from being anxious, and from remaining anxious, to further the cause of the Association, and from doing everything in his power to help it in other ways. It was he, in the first place, who was originally responsible for inaugurating the territorial negotiations, at the express request of the agents of the Association, as well as for insisting on their conclusion before the end of the conference—an important, in fact a vital point in their favour. Secondly, it was he, as has been seen, who succeeded in obtaining for it the successive recognition of the powers at the conference, bringing it into existence in this way, as a sovereign state.[3] The importance assumed by this question of recognition in the territorial negotiations has also been seen. That it could in fact have such importance serves of course only to show what a very precarious position the Association was in, and to give all the more value therefore to the large measure of success attending Bismarck's efforts to assist it. There is in fact no doubt that incalculable moral support was given to the Association by these recognitions, largely because they provided such an unmistakable barometer of the state of Bismarck's feelings towards it, as well as of the extent to which he was prepared to make them prevail over those of others. It was thus made clear, both to France and to Portugal, that the Association must be taken seriously, and that its claims must not be overridden, as there is no doubt that they might

[1] cf. Thomson, p. 140.
[2] cf. Banning, p. 38.
[3] cf. above, Chapter iv, pp. 142-51.

otherwise have been, by the partition of the Congo between these two powers.

If it be true, therefore, that but for the Franco-German entente, the Association might, with Germany's help, have obtained a good deal more at the conference than it actually did, it is even more certain that without the assistance which was in fact afforded it by Germany, it would, in all probability, have been crushed out of existence altogether, like a nut between the jaws of a nutcracker, by the rival pretensions of France, on the one hand, and Portugal on the other. This assistance, moreover, was not all of an indirect nature. Though he refused to interfere between France and the Association, Bismarck was quite willing to exert, and did in effect combine finally with England and France to exert, pressure of a highly efficacious kind upon Portugal in order to induce her to come to reasonable terms with the Association. In spite of the limitations set to his action by the entente, therefore, it seems a fair estimate of the situation that the Association owed most of what it gained at the conference to *him*, and that what it gained was in fact the lion's share of the spoils.

Portugal, though she profited handsomely by the Berlin settlement, received a good deal less from it than she would have done from the Anglo-Portuguese Treaty, her losses representing entirely gains made by the Association at her expense, with the help of Bismarck. France, in spite of the fact that she obtained at the conference a greater proportion of the demands which she actually put forward than either Portugal or the Association, probably owed less to Bismarck than she had the right to grudge him. The reason for this was that these demands undoubtedly represented only a small part of much vaster ambitions, which were never even voiced by her at Berlin, owing to the hostile attitude of the chancellor, who by dragging the whole question into the limelight there made their realisation impossible. It is more than probable, therefore, that she would have fared better if there had been *no* conference, and *no* entente, at least not of the kind which actually existed between her and Germany, and, if alone, she had been left to fight out her claims with Portugal and the Association, in the favourable atmosphere created by the unpopularity of the Anglo-Portuguese Treaty.

THE TERRITORIAL NEGOTIATIONS

It now remains to trace the course of the negotiations which actually took place between her, Portugal, and the Association. These passed through three phases. Opening at Berlin, under the auspices of Bismarck, at the beginning of December 1884, they broke down at the end of the month, owing to the reluctance of either England or Germany to make approaches to France, and were then transferred to Paris at the beginning of January 1885. Here France and the Association managed to come to an agreement on February 5th. But neither party could cope with Portugal, and the negotiations were therefore once more transferred to Berlin, in the middle of February, where, with the help of England and Germany, Portugal was finally induced to sign a convention with the Association on February 14th.

The first phase opened with joint approaches made by the agents of the Association to England and Germany, upon whom the necessity was urged of some solution being reached of the territorial problems of the Congo, before the close of the conference. On December 9th[1] Stanley paid a special flying visit to London for this purpose, whilst Strauch and Lambermont meanwhile consulted Hatzfeldt.[2] The growing solidarity of France and Portugal at the conference,[3] uneasy rumours as to their intentions after it had broken up, the prevalent fear that they in fact were planning to partition the Congo between them, were at this moment causing grave anxiety to Leopold's adherents.[4] For this reason they considered it imperative that the entente, of which they suspected the existence between these two countries, should be destroyed, and its plans frustrated, by means of proposals put forward separately, on behalf of the Association (backed if necessary by strong pressure), which should enable it to come to reasonable terms with them.[5] Portugal, being the weaker power, they argued, should be the

[1] F.O./84/1817/ Memo., Clement Hill, Dec. 10, 1884: Stanley to Hutton, Dec. 10, 1884.
[2] Thomson, p. 252. Banning, p. 37.
[3] Thomson, pp. 248–9, 252.
[4] Ibid., pp. 253–4. F.O./84/1817/ Private letters to Granville (Danger of Franco-Portuguese Territorial Claims. Need for Supporting Germany and Backing I.A.): Nov. 27, 1884, Conversations Dutch Minister, General Sanford, and American Ambassador: Nov. 28, 1884, Conversation with American Minister: Nov. 29, 1884, From a Member of Conference: Dec. 9, 1884, Extract from Berlin
[5] Thomson, pp 252–3.

first to be approached. Once she had been isolated, and an agreement forced upon her, it would then be possible to come to terms with France.

Of the nature of Portugal's claims, beyond the general knowledge that she desired to possess the territories lying between 8° and 5° 12′ south latitude, they had at the moment no precise indication. But of those of France, with whom they had been fruitlessly negotiating for over eight months, they were only too well aware.

Ever since the rival expeditions of Stanley and de Brazza to the Congo, France and the Association had not ceased to put forward conflicting and apparently irreconcilable claims, which had been a source of constant and increasing friction between them.[1] De Brazza, it will be remembered, had first stolen a march on Stanley, in 1880, by annexing the right bank of Stanley Pool, by means of treaties with King Makoko, whilst Stanley was occupied in trying to create a route between Vivi and Isanghila.[2] Stanley had then in turn outwitted de Brazza, whilst the latter went home to report on his treaties, by annexing not only the left bank of the pool, but also the whole of the rich districts watered by the Niari Kwilu, on the right bank of the Congo.[3] This was a bitter blow to the French, who had hoped to incorporate these territories in their province of Gaboon, to which they were contiguous. The *fait accompli* had nevertheless to be faced, and the rights of the Association to the Niari Kwilu, were in fact recognised by France in the Pre-emption Treaty of April 23rd.[4] This did not mean, however, that she thereby renounced all hopes of ever acquiring it, or even of doing so, before what she considered the inevitable financial collapse of the Association in any case forced it to sell this district to her later on, together with its other possessions.

After the treaty had been signed, negotiations were set on foot for a delimitation agreement between her and the Association,[5] and in order to gain her objective, she now advanced a

---

[1] cf. above, p. 15.
[2] Keith, pp. 42–3. Stanley, I, pp. 231–4. Keltie, pp. 135–7. Yarnall, p. 10. Thomson, pp. 80, 82–4. Reeves, p. 23. Banning, p. 39.
[3] Keith, pp. 44–7, 48. Stanley, I. Keltie, p. 137. Yarnall, p. 10. Thomson, pp. 85–6, 94–100. Reeves, p. 24. Banning, p. 39.
[4] Thomson, p. 245. cf. text, Hertslet, II, p. 562.
[5] Thomson, pp. 245–7.

THE TERRITORIAL NEGOTIATIONS 159

new claim, whose express aim was to win back the Niari Kwilu.[1] Stanley's annexation of the left bank of Stanley Pool was not valid, she argued, because the chief with whom he had made his treaties was not really sovereign there at all, but was only a vassal of King Makoko, on the *other* side of the Pool, whose territories had been legitimately annexed by de Brazza, in the name of France. France did not wish to keep the left bank, but was willing to renounce it, if in return the Association abandoned its claim to the Niari Kwilu, and the stations which it had founded there.

The elastic dimensions assumed by Makoko's empire, in the interests of French diplomacy, were naturally not appreciated by the Association, which refused to treat on such a basis.[2] Consequently a deadlock was reached in the negotiations. Since neither party seemed able to produce a working compromise it was finally agreed that the matter should be referred to arbitration. This was in July 1884, when preparations were set on foot for the sittings of the arbitration commission. But these were interrupted by the summoning of the conference, and never resumed, because meanwhile the attitude of France had undergone a radical change. In July Ferry insisted that the commission should hold its sittings in Europe.[3] Now he declared it essential that it should adjudicate " on the spot ", that is to say in Africa. This was held by the representatives of the Association to be equivalent to a refusal to accept arbitration at all, since in their eyes France counted, in this way, on the confused relations existing between sovereign and vassal in Africa, in order to carry her own claims uncontested.[4] They therefore refused the French offer outright in the middle of December.[5] Once more deadlock had been reached, and this time apparently hopeless deadlock ; and no doubt the despair now felt by Leopold and his adherents, of ever reaching a reasonable settlement with France, was one of the immediate causes of their demand for British and German mediation.

---

[1] Banning, p. 39. Thomson, p. 245. Keith, pp. 48–9. D.D.F., V, No. 464, Ferry to Courcel, Nov. 25, 1884.
[2] Thomson, pp. 245–6.
[3] Thomson, p. 246.
[4] Ibid., p. 247.
[5] Thomson, p. 247. cf. also, F.O./84/1818/ Malet to Granville, Dec. 20, Africa, 261.

The identical proposals made by them to the British and German governments were—that Portugal should receive the whole of the territories lying between the mouth of the Logé and the south bank of the Congo, with the right to expand inland as far as 14° east latitude, and along the Congo itself as far as Nokki.[1] France, if she were prepared to pay an indemnity for it, should have both banks of the Niari Kwilu, together with the territory situated to the south of it, up to 1° 12′ south latitude, the interior delimitation of her possessions, in this case, giving her access to the upper Congo, running in a diagonal line from the point of this latitude on the coast (at Massabé), to the junction of the River Juo with the Congo (near Brazzaville). If she were *not* prepared to pay an indemnity the Association was at any rate ready to recognise the right bank of the Niari Kwilu as the frontier of her possessions. No faith was placed in French pretensions to the right bank of Stanley Pool, " peopled by the migratory subjects of King Makoko,"[2] and the Association therefore itself claimed the whole right bank of the Congo, up to and including the right bank of Stanley Pool, as well as the left bank of the river from Nokki, up to and including the left bank of the pool. In addition to this it also demanded the territory north of the Congo, to the south of the French boundary line, along the latitude of 5° 12′ south latitude.

These proposals were favourably received both in London and Berlin, but since neither the British nor the German Government was aware that the other had been approached, their first step was to communicate with each other. On December 11th,[3] Granville wired to Malet, telling him to consult Bismarck, and to try and secure his support for the scheme; whilst on the same day Hatzfeldt received instructions from Bismarck, to suggest joint action to England for the purpose of bringing pressure to bear upon Portugal.[4] The next afternoon Hatzfeldt took the initiative,[5] by drawing the British ambassador aside before a committee meeting, in order to repeat to him the arguments of Strauch and Lambermont for

[1] F.O./84/1817/ Memo., Clement Hill, Dec. 10, 1884 : Malet to Granville, Dec. 13, 1884, Tel. 61. cf. Thomson, pp. 254–5. Banning, p. 39.
[2] Thomson, p. 255.
[3] F.O./84/1817/ Granville to Malet, Dec. 11, 1884, Tel. 28.
[4] Thomson, p. 254.
[5] F.O./84/1818/ Malet to Granville, Dec. 20, Africa, 261.

THE TERRITORIAL NEGOTIATIONS 161

a speedy settlement of the territorial question before the close of the conference. He then showed Malet their proposals, and asked him whether he thought the British Government would approve of them. On investigating them Malet found that they were exactly the same as those which had been submitted by Stanley to Granville, and was therefore able at once to intimate the acquiescence of his government. The same evening Malet, Anderson, Hatzfeldt, and Küsserow all met to discuss in detail the execution of their plans.[1] Malet declared that the proposals affecting France and the Association would come best from Germany. Hatzfeldt then suggested that Malet should undertake first to approach Portugal. To this Malet finally agreed, on the understanding that Hatzfeldt would approach France later. In this way birth was given to what was unofficially known amongst the German and Belgian delegates as the " Combinaison ".[2]

Though so devoutly worked and wished for, however, it was destined to meet with little practical success. When Malet went to see Serpa the next day,[3] the latter consented to telegraph his proposals to Lisbon, but at the same time foreshadowed the refusal of his government, by expressing the view that they would probably not even be considered there. The demands of the Association were in fact refused outright by Portugal, who declared that she must have not only the whole south bank of the Congo, but also the whole of the Congo territories up to 5° 12′ south latitude. This meant, with France claiming down to the same line on the coast, that even if the Association obtained the left bank of Stanley Pool, it would in any case be cut off from all access to the sea, and in this way inevitably run to ruin and disaster. It was in vain that Malet threatened and fulminated. Portugal stood firm, backed possibly by the secret support of France.[4] Be this as it may, the terms of Serpa's refusal in any case made Strauch and Lambermont more suspicious than ever of the existence of a " Franco-Portuguese Entente ",[5] whose object was to partition the Congo

[1] Ibid. Thomson, p. 84.
[2] Thomson, p. 84.
[3] F.O./84/1817/ Malet to Granville, Dec. 13, 1884, Tel. 61. G.D./29/179/ Malet to Granville, Dec. 13, 1884 (Private letter). cf. Thomson, pp. 87-8.
[4] cf. Thomson, p. 87.
[5] Ibid., p. 88. F.O./84/1817/ Malet to Granville, Dec. 13, 1884, Tel. 61.

between France and Portugal, without regard for the interests of the Association. Alarmed by their representations,[1] Malet now tried to make Germany play her part in the negotiations by presenting the proposals of the " Combinaison " to France without further delay. But whether " from malice prepense ", or otherwise, Hatzfeldt had fallen ill on December 13th, the day of Malet's own interview with Serpa, and remained ill for the next few days. Küsserow refused to take any responsibility; and the British ambassador did not succeed in getting near Bismarck himself, until December 17th,[2] when to his intense surprise he discovered that the chancellor had in reality no intention at all of approaching France. When Malet urged this course upon him, pointing out that he had already made advances to Portugal on such an understanding, Bismarck hummed and hawed; said that the claims of the Association were more extravagant than he thought; that substantial support had already been given to it by British and German recognition; and finally that it would now be best to let it fight its claims out alone with France.

The truth of the matter was that the chancellor had lately been the recipient of bitter reproaches from France,[3] regarding his support of the Association at the conference, reproaches which had been coupled with threats as to the consequences of such a policy, if it were still further developed into support of its territorial claims against her own. These threats had caused him to modify his attitude. Germany's recognition[4] of the Association, as well as Bismarck's efforts to secure that of Great Britain and other powers at the conference; his attitude over the extension of the geographical basin; over Sanford's railway proposal, over neutrality; and over the International Commission, had all been singled out as special objects of attack. Ever since November 8th,[5] Courcel told Hatzfeldt at the beginning of December, the attitude of the Association had endangered the entente, by giving the French public the idea that

[1] F.O./84/1818/ Malet to Granville, Dec. 20, 1884, Africa, 261.
[2] F.O./84/1817/ Malet to Granville, Dec. 17, 1884, Tel. 70. F.O./84/1818/ Malet to Granville, Dec. 20, 1884, Africa, 261.
[3] D.D.F., V, No. 475, Courcel to Ferry, Dec. 3, 1884: No. 477, Courcel to Ferry, Dec. 5, 1884. Thomson, pp. 234–5. Banning, p. 38. Yarnall, pp. 68–9.
[4] D.D.F., V, No. 483, Courcel to Ferry, Dec. 12, 1884. Banning, p. 38. Thomson, pp. 234–8. Yarnall, pp. 68–9.
[5] D.D.F., V, No. 477, Courcel to Ferry, Dec. 5, 1884.

THE TERRITORIAL NEGOTIATIONS 163

Leopold was upheld by Germany in his territorial claims. But if Bismarck really supported these claims it would mean the end of the entente, and the ruin of the conference. The French ambassador was rather fond of making these kind of remarks at the German Foreign Office, and similar threats had been made by him in other connections.[1] But it was impossible to ignore the fact that in this case they were of a much more serious nature, owing not only to the intrinsic importance of the issues at stake, but also to the effect already produced upon France by the cumulative series of disappointments which she had suffered at the conference.[2] In the interest of his " Friedenspolitik " with her, therefore, Bismarck now decided to acquiesce in her demands,[3] and to refrain from direct interference in the territorial questions at issue between her and the Association.

He did consent, however, at Malet's urgent request,[4] to report to Courcel the nature of the negotiations which had already taken place between Portugal and Great Britain, acting on behalf of the Association. He appears, even, to have done a little more than this, and to have dropped a broad hint to the French ambassador that the Portuguese should be made to adopt a more reasonable attitude towards the Association; for Courcel, in reply, declared, as if under protest,[5] that France had no special partiality for Portugal, and that she was quite ready for a triple partition of the Congo between herself, Portugal, and the Association.

Bismarck was very pleased with this note,[6] which he at once communicated to Malet and Lambermont. Whether or no France had ever contemplated the partition of the Congo between herself and Portugal it meant, in effect, that she now in any case renounced such a scheme, and was ready to admit the Association to a share of the spoils. Though it had no practical success,[7] therefore, the " Combinaison " could not be

---

[1] D.D.F., V, No. 483, Courcel to Ferry, Dec. 12, 1884. cf. above, p. 137.
[2] cf. Thomson, p. 243.
[3] cf. Thomson, pp. 257-8. Banning, p. 38. F.O./84/1818/ Malet to Granville, Dec. 22, Tel. 77.
[4] F.O./84/1817/ Malet to Granville, Dec. 17, 1884, Tel. 70. F.O./84/1818/ Malet to Granville, Dec. 20, 1884, Africa, 261. cf. Thomson, p. 257.
[5] Thomson, p. 257. cf. also, F.O./84/1818/ Malet to Granville, Dec. 20, 1884, Africa, 261.
[6] Thomson, p. 257.
[7] Ibid., p. 258.

said to have failed entirely of its object, since it had succeeded in eliciting such a statement from France. Thanks to it, as well as to the recognitions already secured to the Association by Bismarck, the former was now in a far stronger position for treating alone with France, if treat alone it must, than it would have been a few weeks before.

Ferry was anxious that this should be the case,[1] but Bismarck was equally anxious that the negotiations should be concluded before the end of the conference.[2] It was agreed, therefore, that the sittings of the conference should be adjourned till after Christmas,[3] whilst meanwhile territorial negotiations should be begun at Paris between France and the Association. In this way they entered upon their second phase at the end of December 1884.

The conference adjourned on the 22nd,[4] and on the 30th[5] Messrs. Eugène Pirmez, a member of the Belgian liberal party, and Émile Banning, arrived in Paris, as the official representatives of the Association. Lambermont was also sent out in an unofficial capacity by Leopold,[6] and arrived there two days earlier for this purpose, whilst Sanford appears likewise to have been sent out later by Leopold, in an unofficial rôle.[7]

The negotiations opened with a conversation on the morning of the 31st,[8] between Jules Ferry and a certain M. Billot, an official of the French Foreign Office, on the one hand, and Pirmez and Banning on the other. During the course of this conversation it became clear that French claims had not altered since the beginning of the conference. They still comprised, as Ferry now explained, a demand for the Niari Kwilu in exchange for the left bank of Stanley Pool. Pirmez and Banning refused to recognise French rights to the left bank of the pool, but declared themselves willing to cede the Niari Kwilu to France in return for an indemnity of five million francs. This offer was refused by Ferry, however, who declared

[1] Ibid., p. 243.
[2] F.O./84/1818/ Malet to Granville, Dec. 20, 1884, Africa, 261.
[3] Ibid.
[4] Protocol VI.
[5] Banning, p. 38. Thomson, p. 258. D.D.F., V, No. 497, Montebello to Billot, Dec. 26, 1884.
[6] Ibid.
[7] D.D.F., V, No. 497, Montebello to Billot, Dec. 26, 1884.
[8] Banning, pp. 40–1. Thomson, pp. 258–61.

THE TERRITORIAL NEGOTIATIONS 165

that it was impossible for him even to ask the French Chamber for such a sum. Compensation, he added somewhat illogically, in view of his earlier remarks, could be given by France in other ways, by her recognition of the Association, and by the assistance which she was willing to afford it in coming to an agreement with Portugal. No conclusion was reached and the discussion was then adjourned on this indeterminate note.

Two days later another was held, in which marked progress was made.[1] It was agreed, in the first place, that Manyanga, half-way between Brazzaville, the limit originally suggested by the " Combinaison ", and Vivi, that for which Ferry at first contended, should form the French boundary on the right bank of the Congo. Secondly, the Association consented in principle to the cession of the Niari Kwilu, although still without a definite promise of an indemnity from Ferry, who declined to offer anything more than a sum between 200,000 and 300,000 francs, as compensation for the stations built there by the Association. Pirmez then let fall a suggestion for a lottery, which, somewhat to Banning's surprise, was eagerly taken up by Ferry. But since Pirmez could not put the proposal forward officially, without the authority of Leopold, no definite agreement was reached, and the discussion was adjourned *sine die* until the Belgian King had been consulted.

After a couple of abortive visits paid that afternoon to Hohenlohe and Lord Lyons,[2] both of whom declared that they could do nothing to help him in the matter of the indemnity, Pirmez then sent Banning to Brussels that night.[3] The next morning Banning saw Leopold and explained the situation to him. Leopold agreed to accept the lottery, and Banning returned to Paris with this news on January 5th.[4] Pirmez then went to see Ferry to tell him the satisfactory results of Banning's mission. Ferry was delighted, and together they sketched out the details of the proposed plan, it being agreed that the lottery should be raised in France, in the name of the Association, and that it should aim at raising at least six million francs.

Nearly every difficulty with France had now been settled,

---

[1] Banning, p. 41. Thomson, pp. 261–2. F.O./84/1819/ Lyons to Granville, Jan. 3, 1884, Africa, 3.
[2] Banning, p. 42. F.O./84/1819/ Lyons to Granville, Jan. 3, 1884, Africa, 3.
[3] Banning, p. 42. Thomson, p. 262.
[4] F.O./84/1819/ Lyons to Granville, Jan. 5, 1885, Africa, 4.

166 THE BERLIN WEST AFRICAN CONFERENCE

and it seemed as if the conclusion of an agreement were but a matter of a few days.[1] It was destined, however, to take a very much longer time. Leopold had from the beginning made it a condition of his signing any convention with France,[2] that the latter should first use her good offices with Portugal, in order to induce her to recognise the claims of the Association to the whole right bank of the Congo, as well as to the left bank, up to a point situated in deep water, which could then be used as a terminus for a railway round the cataracts of the river. Ferry had promised to do this [3] but had meanwhile been intriguing with the Portuguese, behind Leopold's back, and giving *them* promises of help, in their dealings with the Association. The result of this double-dealing was not only a considerable delay, but also a temporary breakdown in the negotiations between France and the Association, which at one moment looked as though it might become final.

The Portuguese were just as anxious for French mediation in treating with the Association, as was the Association itself in treating with them.[4] Their suspicions had at once been aroused by the news of Pirmez's and Banning's mission to Paris in December,[5] and as soon as they heard of it they made arrangements to send an envoy of their own there, too. This envoy, a certain Senhor Carlos du Bocage, who was the Portuguese military attaché at Berlin, and a nephew of the Portuguese Foreign Minister, was given instructions to try and win the confidence of Ferry, and to impress upon him the need for Franco-Portuguese co-operation in dealing with the Association. He arrived in Paris on the same day as Leopold's representatives,[6] and had his first interview with Ferry on the afternoon of December 31st, immediately after the latter had seen the Belgian delegates. Ferry appears, from the first, to have received him favourably, but to begin with Du Bocage was careful to maintain a reserved attitude, and not to make known his country's claims, until he knew precisely the nature of those put forward by the Association.

---

[1] Banning, p. 42. Thomson, p. 262.
[2] Thomson, p. 264. Banning, p. 53.
[3] Banning, p. 54.
[4] cf. D.D.F., V, No. 492. Laboulaye to Ferry, Dec. 22, 1884.
[5] Thomson, pp. 264-5.
[6] Ibid., pp. 265-6. cf. Banning, p. 54.

When Ferry finally told him on January 9th that these comprised a demand for the whole right bank of the Congo up to Manyanga,[1] as well as to the territory north of the river, south of the French boundary line, and to the left bank down to a port in deep water, whence a railway could be constructed round the cataracts of the river, he declared that it was impossible for his government even to treat on such a basis.[2] Portugal, he said, must have the whole left bank, though she would be willing to cede to the Association the right to build a railway there, provided it were clearly understood that the sovereignty of the territory remained hers. On the right bank the frontier of the Association would be fixed at Boma, Portugal retaining the lower river. It was impossible to recognise the claims of the Association to the territories on the north bank of the Congo, south of the French boundary line, since Portugal herself claimed at least part of the coast-line, including the port of Banana.

These claims were very similar to those put forward by Serpa in December,[3] and if they had been recognised by Leopold, would of course similarly have had the effect, in combination with those put forward by France, of ruining the Association, by cutting it off from all access to the sea. That Ferry should not now have hesitated to present them officially to Pirmez,[4] declaring that he was *sous engagement* with Portugal and could offer him nothing better, seems to show, therefore, that he had gone *back* on his originally avowed intention in December,[5] of giving the Association a fair deal, and that whether he had intended to do so earlier or not, that now, at any rate, he was making an attempt to partition it between France and Portugal. It was an attempt, however, that was even more certainly doomed to failure than any earlier one would have been, owing to the increased power and prestige which had since been acquired by the Association.

Pirmez, who had been kept waiting a whole week for the

[1] Thomson, pp. 266, 270.
[2] Thomson, pp. 266-7, 270. Banning, p. 54. D.D.F., V, No. 517, Ferry to Courcel, Jan. 11, 1885.
[3] cf. above, pp. 161-2.
[4] Banning, pp. 54-5. Thomson, p. 267. F.O./84/1819/ Lyons to Granville, Jan. 14, 1885, Africa, 8.
[5] cf. above, pp. 163-4.

168 THE BERLIN WEST AFRICAN CONFERENCE

results of " French Mediation " with Portugal,[1] was naturally furious when they were presented to him in this form. A stormy scene ensued, at the end of which Ferry finally broke off the negotiations,[2] declaring that since Pirmez persisted in refusing his offers, he would write to Berlin to say that he had found it impossible to come to an understanding with the Association.

This he in fact did the same day,[3] taking care to blame the Association, not Portugal, for the deadlock which had occurred. Pirmez also communicated with Berlin the next day.[4] There is no doubt that both he and Ferry would now have liked Bismarck to intervene in their favour.[5] This the chancellor refused to do, however, true to his original decision not to interfere in territorial questions where France was concerned.[6] There was nothing for them to do, therefore, but to resume their efforts to try and reach an agreement.

After a week Ferry himself re-opened the negotiations.[7] Both parties were now chastened by their disappointments, and prepared to make some concessions. The Association declared itself ready to give Portugal the left bank of the Congo up to 13° east,[8] though itself retaining the whole of the right bank and the territories to the north of it up to the French boundary. Ferry in turn declared himself willing to submit these proposals to Portugal.[9] This he did, but only to have them turned down by the Portuguese.[10] They were willing, they declared, to renounce the right bank of the Congo, but they demanded the left up to Nokki, and also claimed the enclave of Cabinda, a strip of territory lying to the north of the Congo, which was of little value in itself, but to which they attached importance, for

---

[1] Banning, p. 54. Thomson, p. 267. F.O./84/1819/ Lyons to Granville, Jan. 14, 1885, Africa, 8.
[2] F.O./84/1819/ Lyons to Granville, Jan. 14, 1885, Africa, 8.
[3] D.D.F., V, No. 517, Ferry to Courcel, Jan. 11, 1885.
[4] Banning, p. 55. Thomson, p. 267. F.O./84/1819/ Malet to Granville, Jan. 12, 1885, Tel. 9.
[5] cf. Banning, pp. 55–6. Thomson, pp. 262–3, 268. F.O./84/1819/ Lyons to Granville, Jan. 14, 1885, Africa, 8. D.D.F., V, No. 517, Ferry to Courcel, Jan. 11, 1885.
[6] cf. D.D.F., V, No. 517, Courcel to Ferry, Jan. 12, 1885. F.O./84/1820/ Malet to Granville, Jan. 21, 1885, Tel. 16. Thomson, p. 262.
[7] Banning, p. 57. Thomson, p. 269.
[8] Banning, pp. 55–7. Thomson, pp. 268–9. D.D.F., V, No. 531, Ferry to Laboulaye, Jan. 21, 1885.
[9] D.D.F., V, No. 531, Ferry to Laboulaye, Jan. 21, 1885.
[10] D.D.F., V, No. 534, Laboulaye to Ferry, Jan. 22, 1885 : No. 574, Ferry to Courcel, Jan. 28, 1885. cf. Banning, p. 57. Thomson, pp. 269–70.

THE TERRITORIAL NEGOTIATIONS 169

traditional reasons, as it figured in the Portuguese constitution as an appanage of the Crown. These demands of Portugal were then in turn refused by the Association,[1] and deadlock having once again been reached, the whole question was once again referred back to Berlin.[2] Bismarck was still unwilling to interfere between France and the Association, however, and the problem was therefore difficult to solve.[3] Finally, after prolonged discussions between the French, British, and Belgian delegates at Berlin,[4] it was decided that the Association should continue to treat separately with France, so long as France bound herself, *d'honneur*, to assist it afterwards in its negotiations with Portugal, these taking place at Berlin; and on February 5th a convention was signed at Paris between France and the Association, on this understanding.[5]

By this convention France, as previously agreed,[6] received the whole of the rich province of the Niari Kwilu, whose southern boundary was defined as running from the mouth of the Chiloango to its source, and thence along the water-parting of the Niari Kwilu and the Congo to Manyanga. On the Congo itself she received the right bank from Manyanga as far as, and inclusive of, the basin of the Likona. The Association received the territories south of the Chiloango line, subject to arrangements to be made with Portugal, and also the whole right bank of the Congo up to Manyanga. Most-favoured-nation treatment was also accorded to it by France, who likewise recognised its flag as that of a friendly government, and promised to respect its neutrality, subject to the conditions respecting it, which should be laid down by the conference.

Nothing was said in the treaty itself about the French promise of mediation with Portugal, but a special letter from

---

[1] Banning, p. 57.
[2] D.D.F., V, No. 574, Ferry to Courcel, Jan. 28, 1885. Banning, p. 57. Thomson, pp. 271–2. Yarnall, p. 70. F.O./84/1820/ Lyons to Granville, Jan. 29, 1885, Africa, 15.
[3] D.D.F., V, No. 574, Ferry to Courcel, Jan. 28, 1885. cf. Marginal Comment of Bismarck's on Tel. of Courcel, Jan. 29—" M. de Bismarck ne se soucie pas d'intervenir entre les deux parties." cf. also, Banning, p. 57. Thomson, pp. 272–3.
[4] Banning, p. 58. Thomson, p. 373. cf. D.D.F., V, No. 563, Ferry to Borchgrave, Feb. 5, 1885.
[5] Ibid.
[6] cf. text, Protocol IX, Annex III. Hertslet, I, pp. 409–11. General Act, Appendix. Banning, p. 58. Thomson, p. 273.

the French Government was appended to it, confirming this promise.[1] Another convention was also added to it, dealing with the indemnity to be paid by France, for the stations founded by the Association in the Niari Kwilu[2]; whilst further declarations provided for the raising of a lottery in France, to the value of twenty million francs, in order to pay for the cession of the whole district.[3]

The negotiations having been concluded with the French, there remained for the Association what Leopold called the " grosse et terrible difficulté " of arriving at an understanding with Portugal.[4] It was not, however, quite so " grosse " and so " terrible " as he imagined. The transference of the negotiations to Berlin had been an admission of Ferry's failure, not only to mediate between Portugal and the Association, but also to back up Portuguese claims against those of Leopold. Portugal was now isolated and abandoned by France, who had formally pledged herself by treaty to use her influence on behalf of the Association, and had expressed her willingness to join with England and Germany to bring pressure to bear upon the Portuguese in its favour.[5] Though Courcel was officially the mediator between the Association and Portugal,[6] the full responsibilities of this rôle had in reality devolved upon Bismarck, who was once more in control of the situation.[7] This was in every way therefore more favourable to the Association than to Portugal.

Portugal herself was aware of the position in which she stood, and was anxious for a settlement.[8] This was made easy for her by the attitude of Leopold, who, as soon as he heard that the negotiations were going to be transferred to Berlin, and that he need fear no more, therefore, from the results of French double-

[1] D.D.F., V, No. 563, Ferry to Borchgrave, Feb. 5, 1885. Thomson, p. 273. Reeves, p. 55.
[2] General Act, Appendix, Additional Convention. D.D.F., V, No. 567, Ferry to Montebello, Feb. 6, 1885. Thomson, p. 273.
[3] D.D.F., V, No. 564, Ferry to Borchgrave, Feb. 5, 1885 : No. 567, Ferry to Montebello, Feb. 6, 1885. Thomson, p. 273.
[4] Thomson, p. 274.
[5] F.O./84/1820/ Lyons to Granville, Jan. 29, 1885, Africa, 15. D.D.F., V, No. 565, Ferry to Courcel, Feb. 6, 1885.
[6] Banning, p. 58. Thomson, p. 274. Yarnall, p. 71. L.J., Congo, 1885, Courcel to Ferry, Feb. 19, 1885 : Annex III, Penafiel to Courcel, Feb. 7, 1885 : Annex IV, Courcel to Penafiel, Feb. 9, 1885.
[7] cf. Thomson, pp. 280, 281.
[8] D.D.F., V, No. 557, Laboulaye to Ferry, Feb. 4, 1885. Yarnall, p. 70.

THE TERRITORIAL NEGOTIATIONS

dealing, announced that he was ready to concede the latest demands of the Portuguese delegates,[1] the right, that is to say, to the Cabinda enclave, and the left bank of the Congo up to Nokki.

That in these circumstances it took so long to negotiate a settlement was due to a somewhat unforeseen factor in the situation. This was the desire of the Portuguese delegates themselves, actually to *produce* pressure on the part of the powers, in order to clear themselves before public opinion in their own country, and particularly before the Lisbon Cortes, which was extremely sensitive on the subject of colonial concessions. For this reason they repeatedly put forward quite impossible demands, which they never expected to be granted, simply in order to provoke an ultimatum of some kind, which they could then show to their government. A somewhat artificial atmosphere of difficulty was in this way imparted to the whole situation, which was in reality of the simplest nature, since the back of the whole problem had been broken when France came to terms with the Association, and at the same time abandoned Portugal.

The new concessions offered by the Association were officially formulated on February 2nd,[2] and then transmitted by Courcel to Penafiel, the Portuguese ambassador at Berlin.[3] Though declaring his willingness to accept them in principle, Penafiel at once expressed a desire that they should be put in a stronger form, and also that they should have the official backing of France, Germany, and Great Britain.[4] It was impossible, he said, for his government to face the Cortes with a statement that they had made concessions of territory for the purpose of being agreeable to an Association which they had not even recognised as a sovereign body. Though the propositions had been formulated to him by the French ambassador, they had not been accompanied by the expression of any wish, on the part of the French Government, that they should be accepted. But if Great Britain, France, and Germany could come to an

[1] Thomson, p. 274. D.D.F., V, No. 567, Ferry to Montebello, Feb. 6, 1885.
[2] Ibid.
[3] Thomson, p. 276. Banning, p. 58. F.O./84/1821/ Malet to Granville, Feb. 5, 1885, Tel. 26.
[4] Thomson, pp. 276–7. F.O./ 84/1821/ Malet to Granville, Feb. 4, 1885, Tel. 23.

agreement as to what his government should yield, and officially put the proposal for it before him, together with the grounds on which they recommended it, then his government, which was sincerely desirous of coming to an agreement, would at least have something with which to go before the Cortes. Great Britain, France, and Germany, therefore, addressed identical triple notes to the Portuguese Government on February 7th, recommending an arrangement with the Association, by which the latter should have the north bank of the Congo, and the coast-line as far as the Chiloango line, with the exception of the Cabinda enclave.[1]

But there was no reply to these notes for several days, and the situation at Berlin, where the whole work of the conference was being held up by the delay in the territorial negotiations, became somewhat tense.[2] Bismarck, at a dinner given to the delegates on the 10th, impatiently declared that the Belgian and Portuguese plenipotentiaries ought to be locked up together in one room, like an English jury, until they had managed to come to a decision. Then the next day the Portuguese answer at last arrived.[3] To the surprise of the powers, however, it consisted in a refusal of their demands, Portugal declaring that she must have not only the Cabinda enclave, but also the port of Banana at the mouth of the Congo, and the left bank of the Congo up to Vivi, instead of Nokki.

The claim to Banana seemed to confirm the rumours which had been afloat at the conference since the beginning of February,[4] that Portugal had actually seized the mouths of the Congo, including the ports of Boma and Banana, at the end of January.[5] This was as a matter of fact not true, though she

[1] F.O./84/1821/ Malet to Granville, Feb. 7, 1885, Africa, 93: Malet to Granville, Feb. 8, 1885, Tel. 31. G.D./29/179/ Malet to Granville, Feb. 7, 1885 (Private letter). L.J., Congo, 1885, Courcel to Ferry, Feb. 19, 1885: Annex II, Courcel to Penafiel, Feb. 7, 1885. Thomson, pp. 276-7.
[2] Banning, p. 59.
[3] F.O./84/1821/ Malet to Granville, Feb. 14, 1885, Africa, 101. Thomson, p. 278.
[4] F.O./84/1821/ Granville to Petre, Feb. 3, 1885, Tel. 14: Hutton to Granville, Feb. 3, 1885: Malet to Granville, Feb. 4, 1885, Tel. 24: Admiralty to F.O., Feb. 7, 1885: Granville to Malet, Feb. 10, 1885, Tel. 22: Fitzmaurice to Lister, Feb. 12, 1885. F.O./84/1822/ Admiralty to F.O., Feb. 18, 1885. G.D./29/156/ Leopold to Victoria, Feb. 1, 1885: Leopold to Granville, Feb. 3, 1885. J. A. Crowe, Private Letters, Feb. 11, 1885. Banning, pp. 59-60. Thomson, p. 275.
[5] F.O./84/1822/ Admiralty to F.O., Feb. 18, 1885. Thomson, p. 275.

THE TERRITORIAL NEGOTIATIONS 173

had indeed attempted to do so. But she had been prevented by joint action on the part of French and British men-of-war, and had only succeeded in taking possession of the coast between 5° and 5° 12′ south latitude.[1] Whatever may have been her intentions earlier, there is no doubt that the demand now made by her for Banana, as well as for the limit of Vivi, on the left bank of the Congo, was not a serious one. Its object, as Penafiel carefully explained to Courcel and Malet the next day, was simply to elicit an even stronger form of remonstrance from the powers.[2] At the same time he indicated to them the terms of the answer they might make, assuring them of its favourable reception this time by the Portuguese Government. Bismarck was much irritated at having to join in such a farce, but eventually consented to do so.[3] An ultimatum was therefore addressed by the three powers to Portugal on February 13th, in which her claims to Banana and the left bank of the Congo up to Vivi were refuted, whilst at the same time she was told that if she persisted in these claims, recognition of the territorial rights already conceded to her on the Congo would be completely withdrawn.[4]

This at last had the desired effect, and on February 15th,[5] Portugal finally gave her assent to the demands originally formulated by the Association on the 2nd. A convention was signed that day at Berlin between her and the Association.[6] In this, as previously agreed, the Cabina enclave, which was defined as stretching from Cabo Lombo to Massabé on the coast, and inland for thirty-five miles, went to Portugal, as well as the left bank of the Congo up to, and including Nokki.[7] The Association was given the left bank from there upwards, the inland boundary of its possessions, and of those of Portugal, to the south of the Congo, running eastwards along the latitude of Nokki, to the intersection of this line with the River Kwango,

[1] F.O./84/1822/ Admiralty to F.O., Feb. 18, 1885.
[2] F.O./84/1821/ Malet to Granville, Feb. 14, 1885, Africa, 102.
[3] Ibid. cf. also, Banning, pp. 60–1.
[4] F.O./84/1821/ Malet to Granville, Feb. 14, 1885, Africa, 101. Thomson, pp. 278–9.
[5] F.O./84/1822/ Malet to Granville, Feb. 19, 1885, Africa, 124. Thomson, p. 279.
[6] Banning, p. 61. Thomson, p. 279. F.O./84/1822/ Malet to Granville, Feb. 16, 1885, Tel. 34.
[7] cf. text, Protocol IX, Annex III. General Act, Appendix. Hertslet, I, pp. 232–3. Also Banning, p. 61. Thomson, p. 279. Reeves, p. 56.

thence following the course of this river southwards. To the north of the Congo the Association retained all the territory ceded to it by its previous agreement with France, with the exception of course of that part of the Cabinda enclave which fell within it.

The railway question was, at the special request of Penafiel, not mentioned in the treaty, but formed the subject of a separate interchange of notes appended to it, in which it was agreed that the Association should have the right, in agreement with Portugal, to build the desired railway round the cataracts of the Congo.[1] As in the French treaty, most-favoured-nation treatment was granted to the Association, just as it had been by France, whilst Portugal, in return, recognised its flag, just as France had done, as that of a friendly government.[2]

By its conventions with France and Portugal, therefore, the Association gained the whole right bank of the Congo up to Manyanga; an important stretch of territory to the north of the river, including a strip of coast twenty-two miles long, above its mouth, which gave it command of the estuary, since it included the port and magnificent harbour of Banana, which had no parallel on the south bank; the south bank itself from Nokki upwards, with special permission to build a railway between Nokki and the sea; and lastly territory to the south of the Congo, extending eastwards for a considerable distance along the latitude of Nokki.[3]

France, by the treaty of February 5th, was completely cut off from the mouth of the Congo. But she obtained the much coveted valley of the Niari Kwilu, which she was free to incorporate in her province of Gaboon. She also obtained the right bank of the Congo from Manyanga upwards. This meant that although she did not herself have free access to the sea along the Congo, she could easily utilise its upper course for the exploitation of the interior of the Gaboon, by forming a connection between it and the Niari Kwilu whose source lay very near to Stanley Pool, and of whose mouth she had the undisputed control.

Portugal, by her treaty with the Association, obtained the

---

[1] Thomson, p. 279.
[2] Text, cf. p. 173, Note 7.
[3] cf. Stanley.

THE TERRITORIAL NEGOTIATIONS 175

whole of the Congo territories up to the left bank of the river, and the river itself up to Nokki, just as she had done in the Anglo-Portuguese Treaty.[1] But of the territory to the north of the Congo, which she had been given in this treaty, she retained only the Cabina enclave, which, cut off as it was from the mouth of the river, was of no value in itself. Her possession of the left bank of the river up to Nokki, however, and of Nokki itself, which was a port in deep water, afforded her valuable means of access to her (now) enlarged province of Angola.

What the Association undoubtedly lost as a result of Bismarck's refusal to mediate on its behalf with France, was the Niari Kwilu, and—possibly—though this is less certain—the Cabinda enclave.[2] Neither of these districts, however, was important to Leopold for his economic and strategic security on the Congo. This was the essential to him, and this was fully and firmly assured to him at the conference, under the ægis of Bismarck's diplomacy.

[1] cf. above, p. 20.
[2] cf. Thomson, p. 280.

CHAPTER VI

THE THIRD BASIS: EFFECTIVE OCCUPATION

THE preceding chapters will have made clear the close connection existing between the discussions arising out of the first and second bases of the conference, and those regarding the territorial negotiations over the Congo which were set on foot so soon afterwards. One main theme runs throughout their history. It is the breakdown of previously concerted co-operation between France and Germany; the discovery by Germany of the latent harmony between her views and those of England; the consequent collaboration of these two powers, and their joint championship of the interests of the Association, which (somewhat incorrectly) they considered to be synonymous with the principles of free trade, against those of France and Portugal, which (quite correctly) they considered to be particularly antagonistic to these principles.

No such grouping of the powers is apparent with regard to the third basis. This has been considered last in the study of the conference, not only because of the late place which it occupies there in point of time, but also because it does, in effect, from a distinct and isolated chapter in its history.

Its object was to define the political obligations towards the peoples under their control, which were to be imposed in future on any powers occupying any part of the coasts of Africa.[1] But of those five whose relations have hitherto been so closely studied, only three, England, France, and Germany, were at all closely concerned in this question, Portugal and the Association, in accordance with the true nature of their secondary rank in the European state system, sinking quietly into the background, when it came to such a discussion of the general principles of colonial occupation.

[1] cf. above, p. 67.

THE THIRD BASIS

As for the rest of the powers at the conference, they, as hitherto, continued to play an entirely subordinate rôle in framing its decisions. If it be true that (with the exception of the United States) they were all at heart in favour of *restricting* rather than of *expanding* the obligations of occupying powers in Africa, it is equally certain, as events were to show, that they were none of them prepared to take a firm stand in the matter, should England, France, and Germany, between them, decide to adopt the contrary course.[1] Their attitude as a positive factor in the situation, therefore, may at once be discounted. That of America was too Utopian to be of any practical importance.

The issue narrows itself, therefore, into a study of the relations of England, France, and Germany. These are at first sight somewhat puzzling, when viewed in connection with the previous history of the conference. Not Anglo-German collaboration, but Anglo-German tension is the keynote to their understanding, the only constant feature in the situation being the evident antagonism of interest still existing between France and Germany. This, however, was much less acute than heretofore, and throughout subordinate to the main conflict which arose between England and Germany over the whole question.

Germany's attitude was simply this: she was anxious to give as wide an application as possible to the principles of effective occupation in Africa, to see to it, that is to say, that in future powers occupying territory there should have no legal claim to it unless they exercised strong and effective political control. Great Britain, on the other hand, went further than any of those present at the conference in her desire to minimise the obligations of occupying powers. Her point of view, like that of Germany, can be explained by their relative positions in the colonial field. As the greatest colonial power in the world, with at that time no less than six gradated systems of administrative control, direct and indirect, in her various colonies and dependencies, Great Britain clearly stood to lose most by any extensive or rigid definition of what such control should be.[2] Germany, on the other hand, as the youngest colonial power in

---

[1] Protocol VIII: Report of Commission Charged with Examining the Project of Declaration Relative to New Occupations on the Coasts of Africa: Eighth Meeting of Conference, Jan. 31, 1885. Banning, p. 45.
[2] cf. L.J., Congo, 1885, Engelhardt's Report, p. 25.

Europe, clearly had most to gain by such a definition, which, by embarrassing other powers (notably Britain) in perhaps long-established but (in the new view) imperfectly maintained claims, would give her just the opportunity she was waiting for, herself to intrude upon them and invalidate them completely, by a swift assumption of political control. If the conflict which arose between the two countries, therefore, seems strange after the *rapprochement* which had already been effected between them at the conference, it is at once understandable when related to the particular question at issue. So is the somewhat non-committal attitude of France.

The whole idea of laying down rules for effective occupation was, it should be remembered, not only German, but anti-British in origin, springing, together with the formation of the Franco-German entente and the decision to summon a conference on West Africa, out of Bismarck's annoyance over Britain's attitude in the Angra Pequena question.[1] His interpretation of her motives in this question has been shown to have been mistaken. So were the deductions which he drew from it with regard to the Congo. Nevertheless, he was right in his *general* deduction which he made the basis for the formulation of his demands about effective occupation that her slow and gradual methods of colonial penetration, starting often from some well-established centre which gave her vague claims to the surrounding territory, unsubstantiated in detail, constituted in themselves a serious handicap to the activities of a young and vigorous nation like Germany, anxious to compete with her on equal terms, but lacking the same initial advantages.

Unfortunately, here as elsewhere, he forgot to calculate with the ambitions of France, who, as the second greatest colonial power in the world, occupied a position very similar to that of Britain in relation to Germany in these matters, and entertained views similar to the British.[2] The result was that he had considerably to modify his schemes, in deference to French wishes, before they even reached the conference. In the first place he was forced, as has been seen, to divorce the question of free trade from that of effective occupation[3]; secondly, he was

---

[1] cf. Bourgeois et Pagès, *Origines*, p. 208. D.D.F., V, No. 407, Courcel to Ferry, Sept. 21, 1884, p. 424. Above, pp. 65–6.
[2] cf. above, pp. 65–6.
[3] cf. above, pp. 64–5.

THE THIRD BASIS

obliged to confine the latter to the coasts of Africa alone, as well as to future occupations only[1]; thirdly, he had to give great prominence in the joint project finally submitted by France and Germany to the conference, to a purely formal clause regarding notification inserted by the French[2]; whilst the wording of the main part of the project concerning the jurisdiction and duties of occupying powers, was left more vague and non-committal than he would have wished. The considerable measure of success which thus attended France's efforts to whittle down the chancellor's proposals, before the conference even opened, probably accounts in part for the comparatively quiescent attitude adopted by her when it met. Principally, however, this must be ascribed to the vigorous policy pursued by Great Britain, who, by taking the main brunt of the opposition to Bismarck's schemes upon her own shoulders, undoubtedly deprived France of the unpleasant duty of doing so herself.

This of course was in the logic of the situation, since the third basis menaced British even more than French interests. That the British Government *did* so vigorously oppose Bismarck's schemes, however, and besides *succeeded* in its efforts, must be ascribed largely to the persistence of one man. This was the Lord Chancellor, Lord Selborne, who, in face of a hostile cabinet, and the opposition not only of influential opinion in the Foreign Office, but also of both Foreign Office and Colonial Office experts at Berlin, as well as of the British ambassador there himself, was ultimately responsible for carrying the most vital point at issue with the German Government. This was the proposal, formulated by him for a distinction between "annexations" and "protectorates", carrying with it the recognition of the latter as a perfectly legitimate, but much less complete form of government, exempt from any of the obligations imposed by the conference upon occupying powers. Bismarck was very averse to conceding the point, but finally he yielded, his concession marking a signal triumph for the principles of vague and loose definition for which Great Britain stood, since it clearly provided her with the means of evading all the regulations of the third basis, should she wish to do so.

His surrender was due to Selborne's insistence. That he was

[1] cf. above, pp. 65, 67.
[2] L.J., Congo, 1885, Engelhardt's Report, pp. 23-4.

180 THE BERLIN WEST AFRICAN CONFERENCE

in the last resort amenable to pressure, however, should probably in part be ascribed to other factors. In the first place his realisation of the hollowness of the Franco-German entente, in the first and second bases, must surely have inclined him to a course which was no more than a further endorsement of the failure of that entente. Secondly, his own growing colonial ambitions for Germany appear to have influenced his decisions.[1] He was at this moment busy collaborating (though still in secret) with the German adventurer, Karl Peters, in Zanzibar,[2] and also encouraging the designs of Flegel on the Niger.[3] It was one thing for Germany to lay down extensive rules about effective occupation, so long as she was only a minor colonising power, hoping to profit by the mistakes of others. Should she herself decide to embark on colonial schemes on the grand scale, however, the boot might well be on the other leg, and there is some evidence to show that Bismarck realised this.[4] In any case, whatever the proportions to be allotted to the various motives in his mind, it is clear that his surrender over the third basis, forms the logical complement to the attitude which he adopted over the first and second, since the one like the other involved the recognition of a mistaken anti-British policy.

The Franco-German project on effective occupation was submitted to the conference on January 7th, 1885.[5] It was at once referred to commission,[6] where, after much discussion, it emerged considerably altered in form and content at the end

[1] cf. Königk, p. 161. L.J., Congo, 1885, Engelhardt's Report, p. 26.
[2] cf. Keltie, pp. 224–30. Evans Lewin, pp. 168–76. Johnston, pp. 408–9.
[3] cf. Keltie, p. 271. Johnston, p. 190. Burns, p. 161. Leonard Darwin, British Expansion in Africa, *National Review*, Vol. XXXIII, p. 972. *Encyclopedia Britannica* (11th edn.), Goldie. D. Wellesley, *Goldie*, pp. 35–7.
[4] Königk, p. 161. [*N.B.*—T. V. Lister was therefore not so far wrong when he wrote on Jan. 18, 1885 : " I believe that it (the third basis) was originally started as a protest against what Germany considered to be the shilly-shally proceedings of England, respecting Angra Pequena, but that when the declaration had to be drafted both Germany and France perceived that it might prove inconvenient to their designs in Africa and therefore tried to minimise its effects." (cf. F.O./84/1820/ Malet to Granville, Jan. 18, 1885. Minute, Lister.)]
[5] Protocol VII, Seventh Meeting of Conference, Jan. 7, 1885 : Annex, Project Relative to Formalities to be Observed in order that Future Occupations on the Coasts of Africa shall be Considered Effective. cf. Reeves, p. 45. Banning, p. 44. S.E.D. No. 196, Kasson to Frelinghuysen, Jan. 7, 1885. F.O. /84/1819/ Malet to Granville, Jan. 7, 1885.
[6] Protocol VII. S.E.D. No. 196, Kasson to Frelinghuysen, Jan. 7, 1885.

THE THIRD BASIS

of the month,[1] to be finally ratified by the conference in this new guise, on January 31st.[2] It contained two propositions.[3] The first was that any power in future taking possession of a territory or of a place on the coasts of Africa, situated outside of its existing possessions or which should assume protection of it, should accompany such an act by a simultaneous notification addressed to other powers at the conference, so as to enable them either to recognise it as effective or to establish, if necessary, their objections. The second declared that the said power should also acknowledge the obligation to establish and to maintain in the territories or places occupied or taken under their protection, a jurisdiction sufficient to secure the maintenance of peace, respect for rights acquired and, where necessary, respect for the conditions in which liberty of commerce and of transit should have been guaranteed.

Before either of these propositions was discussed, however, a preliminary inquiry was made in commission by Great Britain (who of course had no knowledge of what had previously passed between France and Germany on this subject) as to whether they could not *both* be extended to the whole continent of Africa, not only to its coasts, as otherwise they would be confined to such a very small extent of territory as to be of little practical utility.[4] The explanation of this proposal, which not only appeared to be, but was in fact directly contrary to Britain's true interests, must be sought, partly in the density of Granville (from whom it originated), who evidently did not realise the clear advantage which would accrue to Great Britain, if the whole project *did* prove of little utility[5]; partly in the strong suspicion entertained at the Foreign Office, that under cover of the apparently restricted scope of the project

---

[1] Protocol VIII : Report of Commission Charged with Examining the Project of Declaration Relative to New Occupations on the Coasts of Africa. L.J., Congo, 1885, Engelhardt's Report, pp. 24-8. S.E.D. No. 196, Kasson to Frelinghuysen, Jan. 12, Feb. 2, 1885. F.O./84/1819/ Malet to Granville, Jan. 15, 1885, Tel. 10. F.O./84/1820/ Malet to Granville, Jan. 16, 1805, Tel. 11 : Jan. 18, Africa, 41 : Jan. 19, Tel. 13 : Jan. 29, Africa, 64.
[2] Protocol IX. F.O./84/1820/ Malet to Granville, Jan. 31, Tel. 21. L.J., Congo, 1885, Engelhardt's Report, p. 28. S.E.D. No. 196, Kasson to Frelinghuysen, Feb. 2, 1885.
[3] cf. text, Protocol VII, Annex.
[4] Protocol VIII, Report of Commission. F.O./84/1819/ Granville to Malet, Jan. 14, 1885, Africa, 24 : Malet to Granville, Jan. 15, 1885, Tel. 10. L.J., Congo, 1885, Engelhardt's Report, p. 24. Banning, p. 44.
[5] F.O./84/1819/ Granville to Malet, Jan. 14, 1885, Africa, 24.

very extensive rules would be laid down regarding effective occupation, which would then be given a wide territorial application, by an elastic interpretation of the word "coasts".[1] It was also feared that inland definitions might have been left purposely vague, in order actually to *assist* a power seizing territory on the coast, to encroach on the possessions of one already established inland.[2]

Both these suspicions appear to have been unfounded. The British proposal was opposed by Germany as well as by France in commission, where it was finally turned down, on the ground that coasts alone were within the programme of the conference.[3] But there is no evidence to show that Germany was actuated by anything more than a desire to be loyal to her commitments with France, unless it were a growing realisation of the complications inherent in any wholesale attempt to lay down rules for effective occupation in Africa.[4] When Malet, acting on instructions from Granville,[5] made inquiries at the German Foreign Office, as to the meaning attached there to the word "coasts",[6] he was told that it was understood to imply "territories bordering on the sea," and that the object of the declaration framed at Berlin had been to minimise a delicate subject. With this assertion Malet, after referring it home, declared himself satisfied, and the matter was then dropped.

The feature of it which most strikes an observer is the evident confusion of issues in the minds both of German and British diplomats and statesmen. The Germans failed throughout to realise the extent to which the restriction to the coasts of Africa invalidated the whole project. In England the full implications of the restriction were only realised half-way through the whole discussion, and even then not by all the responsible people concerned.[7] The situation was of course complicated there by the suspicions entertained of Germany's motives,

---

[1] F.O./84/1819/ Malet to Granville, Jan. 15, 1885, Tel. 10, Minute, Kennedy. F.O./84/1820/ Malet to Granville, Jan. 18, 1885, Tel. 12, Minute, Kennedy.
[2] F.O./84/1820/ Granville to Malet, Jan. 14, 1885, Africa, 24.
[3] Protocol VIII, Report of Commission. F.O./84/1819/Malet to Granville, Jan. 15, 1885, Tel. 10.
[4] Protocol VIII, Report of Commission. cf. F.O./84/1820/ Malet to Granville, Jan. 18, 1885, Tel. 12. L.J., Congo, Engelhardt's Report, p. 24.
[5] F.O./84/1820/ Granville to Malet, Jan. 17, 1885, Tel. 7.
[6] F.O./84/1820/ Malet to Granville, Jan. 1885, Tel. 12.
[7] cf. F.O./84/1819/ Malet to Granville, Jan. 15, 1885, Tel. 10, Minute, Kennedy. F.O./84/1820/ Granville to Malet, Jan. 17, 1885, Tel. 7.

THE THIRD BASIS

suspicions which, though unfounded, were naturally fortified by recollections of recent events in Angra Pequena[1] and New Guinea,[2] and which undoubtedly underlay a second proposal now made by Great Britain in commission that the act of notification itself should be accompanied by an approximate definition of the limits of the territory occupied,[3] as a *precaution* against the extension of any given settlement beyond rational limits.[4] This proposal was also vetoed by the powers, however, also no doubt very happily for the true interests of Great Britain.[5]

She *did* succeed however in effecting an alteration in the notification clause of the project, which made it clear beyond all doubt that the rules to be established would be applied not only to the powers already having possessions in Africa, but also to those settling there for the first time.[6] This amendment was evidently inspired by the same *arrière-pensée* about Angra Pequena and New Guinea as that which had lain behind her previous demands. But since it did not go beyond the "coastal" limits of the third basis, and provoked no opposition either from France or Germany it was able to pass the commission safely.

The question having been settled in this way, the British delegates were now free to devote themselves to what was destined to be their main task in the commission, that of *narrowing* the meaning of the Franco-German proposals. Henceforward the discussion of the third basis assumes in consequence its true and rational aspect, Great Britain emerging clearly as the power most anxious to *restrict* the application of new rules; Germany gradually revealing herself as that most anxious to *extend* them; whilst France takes up a position midway between the two, showing herself ready to support Great Britain over minor but not over major issues.

These were at first the only ones to be discussed, a fact

---

[1] cf. F.O./84/1820/ Malet to Granville, Jan. 18, 1885, Tel. 12, Minute, Lister.
[2] cf. F.O./84/1819/ Report, Herschell, on Effective Occupation, Jan. 2, 1885: Report of L.O.'s, Jan. 7, 1885: Note, Lord Chancellor on this report, Jan. 8, 1885.
[3] F.O./84/1819/ Granville to Malet, Jan. 14, 1885. Protocol VIII, Report of Commission. L.J., Congo, 1885, Engelhardt's Report, p. 24. Banning, p. 44.
[4] F.O./84/1819/ Granville to Malet, Jan. 14, 1885, Africa, 24.
[5] F.O./84/1819/ Malet to Granville, Jan. 15, 1885, Tel. 10. Protocol VIII, Report of Commission. L.J., Congo, 1885, Engelhardt's Report, p. 24.
[6] Protocol VIII, Report of Commission.

which, taken in conjunction with Germany's consideration for France, must be taken to account for the former's initial lack of opposition to them. Thus Malet's demand for a further alteration in the notification clause of the project, definitely ruling out the possibility that notification by an occupying power could be taken to imply the recognition by those notified of the occupation in question, was satisfied, without any difficulty in commission.[1] After this it turned its attention to the second paragraph of the Franco-German project, dealing with the question of jurisdiction.[2] This paragraph had originally been inserted by Germany, somewhat *against* the wishes of France, who would have preferred merely to have a notification clause together with a general, though not very precise provision for the dispatch of an agent to the locality in question, endowed with suitable means of exercising his authority.[3] It represented German views entirely therefore regarding the duties of an occupying power. It is not surprising in these circumstances to find in spite of the modifications already introduced by France before the conference met that it provoked French as well as English criticism in commission.[4] France, however, concerned herself entirely with minor points, where backed up by Great Britain she was successful in pleading her case. In the first place she obtained the substitution of the words " obligation to ensure the establishment of sufficient authority," for " obligation to establish and maintain a sufficient authority," in the opening sentences of the clause, the object of the change being to permit the occupying power to preserve the customs already existing in a district, should she wish to do so, without necessarily imposing her own upon it, a provision which would naturally tend to encourage more indirect methods of control than would otherwise have been possible.[5] Secondly, she succeeded in emphasising to an even greater degree than before, the entirely conditional nature of the free trade proviso at the end of the clause, by the insertion

[1] F.O./84/1819/ Granville to Malet, Jan. 14, 1885, Africa, 24. Malet to Granville, Jan. 15, 1885, Tel. 10. Protocol VIII, Report of Commission. L.J., Congo, 1885, Engelhardt's Report, pp. 24–5.
[2] cf. above, p. 181.
[3] L.J., Congo, 1885, Engelhardt's Report, pp. 23–4.
[4] L.J., Congo, 1885, Engelhardt's Report, pp. 24–5.
[5] Protocol VIII, Report of Commission. L.J., Congo, 1885, Engelhardt's Report, pp. 26–7.

of a stipulation that it should refer only to the "conditions" under which free trade should have been previously agreed upon.[1] Neither of these demands aroused any opposition from Germany. This was reserved for the British proposal now put forward in commission, which was *not* supported by France that there should be no mention of "protectorates" in the project, since these were different to annexations or occupations, and should be exempt from any of the obligations imposed upon them.[2] This distinction between annexations and protectorates was in reality quite in accord with French views, but the French Government took care to lie very low during the whole controversy, and took no active part in it.[3] Germany attacked Great Britain, the rest of the powers followed her lead, and the latter was therefore completely isolated.

German irritation at Great Britain's attitude was increased by the delay caused in the whole proceedings,[4] through the latter's late formulations of her demands.[5] This, however, was due chiefly to the way in which the whole question had been sprung upon her, not only unawares, but also inadequately and incompletely explained before the conference opened.[6] Consequently she came to it with no very clear conception of the problems involved. During the first two months her hands had been too full to consider any other questions besides those actually discussed there, and it was not until the beginning of January 1885 that her experts began seriously to consider the question of effective occupation.

On the 2nd of that month, in response to an inquiry addressed to them by Sir Julian Pauncefote, the law officers of the Crown drew up a long memorandum on the subject.[7] But though they stressed the importance, in general terms, of *limiting* rather than of *extending* the scope of the third basis, they made no

---

[1] L.J., Congo, 1885, Engelhardt's Report, p. 27. Protocol VIII, Report of Commission. (But it does not state that proposal came from France.)
[2] Protocol VIII, Report of Commission. F.O./84/1820/ Malet to Granville, Jan. 16, 1884, Tel. 11.
[3] L.J., Congo, 1885, Engelhardt's Report, p. 26.
[4] F.O./84/1819/ Malet to Granville, Jan. 7, 1885, Tel. 7. F.O./84/1820/ Malet to Granville, Jan. 24, 1885, Tel. 18.
[5] F.O./84/1819/ Granville to Malet, Jan. 13, 1885, Tel. 4.
[6] cf. above, pp. 73-6.
[7] F.O./84/1819/ Henry James to Pauncefote, Jan. 2, 1885.

special mention of protectorates, and it remained to the Lord Chancellor, in commenting on their memorandum next day, to point out the importance of distinguishing them from annexations, and of insisting that they should be exempt from any of the obligations imposed on the latter.[1] Annexation, he defined in the words of a memorandum drawn up by Sir Edward Hertslet in 1883, as "the direct assumption of territorial sovereignty," protection as "the recognition of the right of the aboriginal or other actual inhabitants to their own country, with no further assumption of territorial rights, than is necessary to maintain the paramount authority and discharge the duties of an occupying power."

He was supported in this distinction, once it had been made, by the law-officers of the Crown,[2] but it did not meet with the approval of Pauncefote, who said he was afraid that the abuse which would meet England at the conference, should she attempt to make it, would "upset the coach on the third basis."[3] In view of the strong opinion expressed by the Lord Chancellor, however, he declared himself ready to waive his objections,[4] and Malet was therefore instructed on January 13th to urge the commission to omit the word "protectorates" from the jurisdiction clause of the project on the ground that they did not stand on the same footing as annexations or occupations, and were not within the terms of the third basis.[5] If, it was argued, it were really thought necessary to define the obligations of a protectorate, this should be done in a separate paragraph. But the utmost which the British Government would be prepared to agree to, would be an engagement that the protecting power should use such means as it could dispose of to cause justice to be done to foreigners in any dispute which might arise between them and the natives of the country.

The proposal was submitted to the commission by Malet on January 15th,[6] and discussed there the next day.[7] It at once

---

[1] F.O./84/1819/ Note by Lord Chancellor on Law Officers' Report on Effective Occupation, Jan. 3, 1885.
[2] F.O./84/1819/ Law Officers' Opinion on Third Basis, Jan. 7, 1885.
[3] F.O./84/1819/ Pauncefote to Hill, Jan. 9, 1885.
[4] Ibid.
[5] F.O./84/1819/ Granville to Malet, Jan. 13, 1885, Tel. 11: cf. also, amplification, Granville to Malet, Jan. 14, 1885, Africa, 24.
[6] F.O./84/1819/ Malet to Granville, Jan. 15, 1885, Tel. 10.
[7] F.O./84/1820/ Malet to Granville, Jan. 16, 1885, Tel. 11.

THE THIRD BASIS

encountered strong opposition from the German delegates, however, who did not conceal their suspicion that Britain's chief object in avoiding any definition of the obligations of protectorates was to make treaties that would keep others out without imposing any on herself. The powers gave no support to Malet, and though he was successful in obtaining the consent of the commission to separate *treatment* of the obligations of protectorates he did *not* succeed in obtaining any concessions with regard to these obligations themselves, the commission holding that, except for the possible substitution of the word " authority " for that of " jurisdiction ", these should remain the same as those of an occupying power.

Before the meeting broke up a sub-committee was appointed to draft an additional clause on protectorates in this sense.[1] This clause,[2] however, was merged almost as soon as it had been made with the original one[3] of the Franco-German project,[4] and in this form in which it came to be known as the " eventual proposition ", ran as follows : " The signatory power recognise the obligation to establish and maintain in the territories occupied by it, or taken under its protectorate, an authority sufficient to ensure the maintenance of peace, the administration of justice, respect for rights acquired, and, in case of necessity, freedom of commerce and transit in the conditions in which it shall have been established." ' Close perusal of its wording reveals the fact that it made no concession whatever to the British demands. Though the word " authority " was substituted for that of " jurisdiction " all the previous implications of the latter term were re-introduced in another form by the later insertion of the words " to administer justice."

Great Britain, however, had by no means given up pressing her case. Whilst the sub-committee was at work, Malet, on January 10th, made private representations to Busch for the total omission of the word " protectorates ".[5] This, he said, would settle the matter at once. But Busch declared that he must consult Bismarck, and after doing so, returned with the reply not only that Bismarck had refused to agree to the pro-

---

[1] F.O./84/1820/ Malet to Granville, Jan. 18, 1885, No. 41.
[2] cf. Protocol VIII, Report of Commission, Annex 2, Clause 3.
[3] cf. above, pp. 180–1. Protocol VII, Annex.
[4] Protocol VIII, Annex 3, Eventual Proposition.
[5] F.O./84/1820/ Malet to Granville, Jan. 29, 1885, Africa, 64.

posal, but also that he had couched his refusal in the most uncompromising terms.

Consequently at the committee-meeting held next day, a deadlock was reached, the only helpful proposal being one put forward by France that the words " where they have hoisted their flag," should be substituted in the eventual proposition for " occupied by them or placed under their protection."[1] This proposal, however, still implied the possibility of protectorates being classed with occupations or annexations, and since Malet had received instructions from his government to withhold assent to *any* attempt to place them on the same footing, he was unable to agree to it.[2] Further discussion of the whole question was therefore once more adjourned until it should once more have been considered in London.

Here opinion was divided. Pauncefote, in accordance with his earlier views, was in favour of yielding, and advocated acceptance of the " eventual proposition ", together with that of the French proposal made in commission.[3] Sir William Harcourt, who was also consulted, agreed with him.[4] But they encountered strong opposition from the Lord Chancellor.[5]

In Berlin advice similar to that of Pauncefote was given to Malet, both by Sir Travers Twiss and by his colonial advisers, Meade and Hemming, all of whom were evidently much intimidated by Bismarck.[6] They were convinced, they said, that the British proposal would be turned down by the conference, and that Germany would thus inflict a defeat on the British Government which would be all the more serious as it would be public, whilst the responsibility for the rupture between Great Britain and Germany would of course be blamed on the former. They were in favour therefore of accepting the eventual proposition, pointing out that Great Britain did actually in some cases discharge the required obligations in her protectorates on the African coast.

To this the Lord Chancellor replied that the British diplo-

[1] F.O./84/1820/ Malet to Granville, Jan. 20, 1885, Tel. 14.
[2] F.O./84/1819/ Granville to Malet, Jan. 14, 1885, Africa, 24.
[3] F.O./84/1820/ Pauncefote to Granville, Jan. 23, 1885.
[4] Ibid. cf. also, Sir William Harcourt, Jan. 24, 1885.
[5] F.O./84/1820/ L.C. to Pauncefote, Jan. 23, 1885.
[6] F.O./84/1820/ Malet to Granville, Jan. 21, 1885, Tel. 15: Malet to Granville, Jan. 22, Tel. 17.

matists in Berlin evidently placed the smooth working of the conference above any other considerations connected with the question at issue.[1] He, on the other hand, placed the principles involved and the possible future consequences of a false step above any temporary considerations connected with our being or not being in a minority of one at the conference. He appears to have been supported in his views by Gladstone,[2] but not by the rest of the cabinet,[3] where opinion was partly influenced by the desire for German goodwill in the negotiations at that moment proceeding over Egypt.

This opinion finally prevailed in London, but by a fortunate concatenation of circumstances it was announced so late in Berlin that by the time it reached Bismarck the latter had himself decided to yield. In an interview which he had with the German Chancellor on January 24th, Malet once more urged the British case, repeating what he had said previously to Busch.[4] Bismarck was very curt in his reply, however, threatening to break off negotiations completely if there were much further delay. It was this threat which had induced the British government to give way to him. A special cabinet meeting[5] was called in London as a result of it and at this meeting it was decided to accept the eventual proposition together with the French amendment, the only concession to the Lord Chancellor's point of view being the proposed insertion of a clause, specifically limiting this as well as the first paragraph of the project to the coasts of Africa only.[6]

This decision was telegraphed to Malet on January 26th,[7] and communicated by him to Busch on January 27th.[8] Evidently, however, it crossed with a message from Bismarck to Busch on that day, for to Malet's intense surprise Busch came to him on the 28th, saying that he had just received instructions from Bismarck to consent to the original British proposal and to omit all mention of protectorates from the third basis. It

---

[1] F.O./84/1820/ L.C. to Pauncefote, Jan. 23, 1885.
[2] F.O./84/1820/ L.C. to Granville, Jan. 20, 1885.
[3] F.O./84/1820/ L.C. to Pauncefote, Jan. 23, 1885.
[4] F.O./84/1820/ Malet to Granville, Jan. 24, 1885, Tel. 18 : Malet to Granville, Jan. 29, 1885, Africa, 64.
[5] F.O./84/1820/ Granville to Selborne (no date) : Selborne to Granville.
[6] F.O./84/1820/ Granville to Malet, Jan. 26, 1885, Tel. 12.
[7] Ibid.
[8] F.O./84/1820/ Malet to Granville, Jan. 29, 1885, Africa, 64.

would not therefore be necessary, he said, for Malet even to submit the subsequent proposal made by the British Government to the commission, since he (Busch) would himself state that Germany had accepted the earlier proposal.

This was accordingly done.[1] The proposal was at once accepted by the commission, which followed Bismarck's lead as blindly as it had done earlier, and it was formally ratified by the powers at the eighth meeting of the conference on January 31st.[2] At this meeting it was also agreed that the provisions for effective occupation should be erected into a separate chapter of the final act, which, in accordance with the draft drawn up by the commission now ran as follows:

I. Any Power[3] which henceforth takes possession of a tract of land on the coasts of the African continent outside of its present possessions, or which, being hitherto without such possessions, shall acquire them, as well as the Power which possesses a Protectorate there, shall accompany the respective act with a notification thereof addressed to the other signatory powers of the act, in order to enable them, if need be, to make good any claims of their own.

II. The signatory powers of the present act recognise the obligation to ensure the establishment of authority in regions occupied by them on the coasts of the African continent, sufficient to protect existing rights, and, as the case may be, freedom of trade and of transit under the conditions agreed upon.

The British triumph was thus complete. Not only had the Lord Chancellor carried his point about protectorates and annexations; the restriction to the coasts of Africa, which he had originally proposed should be applied to *both* protectorates and occupations was now left standing and applied to occupations alone.[4] So was the word "authority", instead of the much more definite term "jursidiction", there being this time no further alteration in the wording nullifying its implications.[5] A Belgian amendment striking out the words "to cause peace

---

[1] Ibid. cf. also, Protocol VIII, Report of Commission. L.J., Congo, 1885, Engelhardt's Report, p. 26.
[2] Protocol VIII. F.O./84/1820/ Malet to Granville, Jan. 31, 1885, Tel. 21.
[3] General Act, Chapter vi. Protocol VIII, Report of Commission, Annex 4.
[4] cf- above, p. 189.
[5] cf. above, p. 188.

THE THIRD BASIS

to be administered," from the eventual proposition, completed the series of amputations to which this had been subjected, and finally ensured its utter ineffectuality.[1]

Thus, in the words of Malet's final report,[2] " No attempt was made at the conference to interfere with existing maxims of international law. Dangerous definitions had been avoided, and international duties on the African coast remained such as they had hitherto been understood to be." He could have gone further. In so far as they still continued to haunt the walls of the conference-room, the revengeful ghosts of Angra Pequena, the May dispatch, and the " Monroe doctrine for Africa " had now finally been laid to rest.

[1] Protocol VIII, Report of Commission.
[2] F.O./84/1822/ Malet to Granville, Feb. 21, 1885, Africa, 130. (C. 4284, No. 2, Malet to Granville, Feb. 21, 1885) (full text).

EPILOGUE

A BOOK[1] of historical tables drawn up by the former Kaiser, William II, which has been published since the war, contains the following jotting for the years 1884-5 : " November 15 bis Februar 26—Kongo-Konferenz—Die festländischen Mächte einig in ihrer Politik gegen England." Fuller knowledge of the history of the conference would have corrected such an erroneous statement. Fitzmaurice was nearer the truth when he declared that the British mission to Berlin, which critics began by describing as an English pilgrimage to Canossa, ended by converting opprobrium into victory, and emerged successfully from a difficult position, without loss either of dignity or of any important national interest.[2] This verdict is substantially correct and is endorsed by further study of the conference. In has been argued that Great Britain lost the Congo there.[3] But since it is clear that she never wished to have the Congo, but merely to keep France away from it, it can scarcely be said that she " lost " it. On the other hand she *did* succeed (with the help of Germany) in securing her prime objective on the Congo, which was the exclusion of France. More important still, she also succeeded (again with the help of Germany) in gaining the recognition of the conference for her claims to the lower Niger, claims which were a great deal more valuable to her than any settlement of any kind on the Congo. Over the third basis, the question of effective occupation, she was likewise successful in making her views prevail, to the detriment, this time, of those of Germany. For Great Britain, therefore, the conference was a diplomatic triumph. This is the first important conclusion to be drawn from a study of it.

---

[1] Kaiser Wilhelm II—Vergleichende Geschichtstabellen von 1878 bis zum Kriegsausbruch, 1914.
[2] cf. Fitzmaurice, II, p. 375.
[3] cf. Johnston, *Colonisation*, p. 189.

EPILOGUE

The second, which is related to it, has already been dwelt upon, for it forms the main theme of this study. This was the breakdown, at the conference, of the Franco-German entente which had been responsible for summoning it as well as for drawing up its programme—a breakdown which provides a striking illustration of the futile and mistaken nature of the Anglo-German estrangement which led to the entente. That this breakdown occurred was common knowledge at the time.[1] " The conference ", wrote *The Times* on February 18th, 1885,[2] " was said to be the offspring and the pledge of the growing friendship of Germany and France. It is a proof of friendship no doubt to be able to survive differences of opinion, and so far as we can discover this is the chief proof of the friendship of France and Germany." Since contemporary historians still maintain, however, that the West African Conference was a humiliation for England and a triumph for the entente, it seems worth while emphasising the point.[3]

The entente did not long survive the conference.[4] It came to a sudden end, a month after the latter had closed, with the fall of Tonkin and the resignation of Jules Ferry in March 1885 —never again to be renewed. It must not be supposed, however, that it achieved nothing. Though unsuccessful in West Africa it was successful in Egypt, where, as the result of joint pressure on the part of France and Germany, Great Britain was forced at the beginning of 1885 to accept international regulation not only of the Egyptian debt question, but also of the Suez Canal.[5] This was a triumph for the French, but not for German interests, since Germany, as Bismarck openly admitted at the time, had not the slightest interest in Egypt.[6] The entente therefore benefited France, but not Germany, for France

---

[1] cf. Thomson, pp. 235–6, footnote 3.
[2] Ibid.
[3] cf. Langer, pp. 306–7.
[4] cf. Gooch, *Franco-German Relations*, pp. 23–4. Wienefeld, pp. v, 162–7, 174. Yarnall, pp. 78–9. Adams, p. 238. Townsend, *Rise and Fall*, p. 110.
[5] cf. Wienefeld, pp. 131–5. Yarnall, pp. 52–3. Adams, pp. 237–8. Langer, pp. 305–6.
[6] cf. G.P., IV, No. 758, Bismarck to Münster, Jan. 25, 1885, pp. 96–7. "Ägypten als solches für uns ganz gleichgultig und für uns nur ein Mittel ist den Widerstand Englands gegen unsere Kolonialbestrebungen zu überwinden. Der Kleinste Zipfel von Neu Guinea oder Westafrika, wenn derselbe objectiv auch ganz wertlos sein mag ist gegenwärtig für unsere Politik wichtiger als das gesamten Ägypten und seine Zukunft." cf. also Thomson, pp. 214–15, footnote 5.

gained a good deal from it, Germany nothing, a fact which in itself illustrates the mistaken nature of the policy pursued by Bismarck in forming it.

It is true that to the Anglo-German estrangement, which was the precursor of the entente, Bismarck owed the acquisition of Angra Pequena, Togoland, the Cameroons, part of New Guinea, and Zanzibar—the foundation in fact of Germany's colonial empire, and that the entente, by forging the last link in the isolation of Great Britain at this time, may have assisted him to *confirm* the first three, and possibly to *make* the last two of these acquisitions. But it may be questioned whether this assistance (which was purely moral) was indispensable and therefore very valuable to Bismarck, since he was already in a very strong position without it.

It may also be questioned whether his acquisitions were in themselves desirable. None of them even paid their way as German colonies, and even now, if returned to the Reich, would, as everyone knows, increase its wealth to no appreciable extent. It is natural, however, that Germany should wish to have them back. But the main reason why they *cannot* in fact be handed back to her, is precisely because, founded as they were in a moment of deliberate hostility to England, in territories bordering on her empire, they are (however small in some cases their intrinsic value) of great strategic importance to Great Britain and her Dominions, and cannot safely be entrusted to a power whose friendly intentions are not above suspicion. All this is the fruit of the Anglo-German estrangement of 1884–5, since as has been shown there was no intrinsic reason why Bismarck should have seized these particular territories, and no evidence to show that he *would* have seized them, if it had not been for his quarrel with England.

That he made serious miscalculations in the conduct of his colonial policy during these years is so evident in the light of all the facts, that it scarcely needs elaborating. What *does* call for explanation, however, is how so great a statesman as Bismarck could have committed blunders which manœuvred him into the position in which he found himself at the West African Conference, where in order to save his policy he had completely to reverse its trend. The answer to this question seems to be that Bismarck was a great European, but not a

EPILOGUE

great Colonial statesman. This seems clear both from the way he drifted into a colonial policy and from his subsequent handling of that policy once he had inaugurated it. It should be remembered of course that there was no Colonial Office at that time in Germany, and no trained band of experts therefore on whom he could rely for accurate information on colonial questions. It is true that he had in von Küsserow, the head of the commercial department of the Foreign Office, a very able colonial adviser. But one man, however able, and one newly-created department of an unspecialised nature cannot supply the deficiency of an old-established and highly specialised bureaucracy, and of the tabulated information and knowledge supplied by years of expert acquaintance with local problems that such a bureaucracy supplies. The prime source of Bismarck's errors in 1884 and 1885 was his failure to understand the true nature of Franco-British relations in Africa. Had he been better informed, it is possible that he might have acted differently. It should be remembered also that he was an old man at this time, often in poor health. This too may have had something to do with his colonial miscalculations.

Whatever their cause, there is no doubt about their effects. The legacy of ill-will left by the Anglo-German estrangement of 1884-5 is unfortunately still alive and pregnant of consequences to-day, not only because Germany's claim to her lost colonies constitutes the one concrete grievance which she is able to bring against Great Britain, but also because the bitterness which still clings to the events of 1884 and 1885 has not yet died down. Accurate historical knowledge however should help to quell this bitterness by revealing its artificial character. It was due more than anything else to a "war of words", a war of white-books and blue-books, of press campaigns and speeches in Reichstag and Parliament, which raged between the two countries at the time. This war was initiated by Bismarck as part of a deliberate campaign of colonial propaganda against England, launched in order to secure his *own* position in Germany. Its effect has been to exaggerate, not only at the time, but ever since, the importance of the Anglo-German colonial quarrel of 1884-5. No better illustration of this could be found than the way in which it has obscured the far more important and far-reaching colonial rivalry that existed between England

and France at the same time. Between these two countries there really *were* vital interests in dispute, and tension between them over colonial questions lasted for over twenty years. Yet in spite of frequent hostility and friction, there never arose such a sharp and virulent estrangement of feeling between them as there did between England and Germany in 1884 and 1885. Yet the more Anglo-German differences are studied during these years, the less do they appear to have had any real or necessary foundation, the more does it seem that they were grossly exaggerated and distorted, chiefly to meet the needs of publicity and propaganda in Germany. Is not this at once a warning and a hope for the future?

APPENDIX I

THE TITLE OF THE CONFERENCE, P. 3

THE conference is more popularly known as "The Congo Conference", and this title has been perpetuated in recent studies of it.[1] But the title is misleading because the conference dealt with the Niger as well as with the Congo, and its settlement of the one question was as important as its settlement of the other. It also even, if ineffectually, laid down rules for effective occupation along the coasts of West Africa. For this reason too the title is inadequate. Contemporaries like Stanley and Émile Banning talk of it simply as the "Berlin Conference."[2] So do most subsequent writers on the subject.[3] But this title is also inadequate, because of the danger of confusion with the more famous Berlin Congress of 1878. Moreover, its was not the title officially used at the time. The English, French, and German documents all refer to the "West African Conference". It was of extreme importance that the conference was held in Berlin, however. For this reason the somewhat cumbersome title of "Berlin West African Conference" has been adopted.

APPENDIX II

PORTUGUESE CLAIMS ON THE CONGO, P. 11

PORTUGAL's claim to the south bank of the Congo and the territories bordering it, should be distinguished from her claim to the north bank of the river, and the coast-line contiguous to it up to 5° 12'

[1] H. E. Yarnall, *The Great Powers and the Congo Conference, 1884–5*. G. Königk, *Die Berliner Kongo-Konferenz, 1884–5*.
[2] Stanley, *The Congo*. É. Banning, *Mèmoires : Le Partage Politique de l'Afrique*.
[3] e.g., J. S. Reeves, *The International Beginnings of the Congo Free State*. A. B. Keith, *The Belgian Congo and the Berlin Act*. Evans Lewin, *The Germans and Africa*. J. S. Keltie, *The Partition of Africa*. H. H. Johnston, *The Colonisation of Africa by Alien Races*. E. Fitzmaurice, *Life of Lord Granville*. R. S. Thomson, *Fondation de L'Etat Independent du Congo*.

south latitude. (The modern enclave of Cabinda and Molembo.) Neither claim had, in the nineteenth century, any justification from the point of view of effective occupation, since she was not then established on either the one or the other. But the former did at least have some historical justification, since she had actually been in possession of the south bank at one time, as well as of a considerable stretch of territory in the neighbourhood. Over Cabinda and Molembo she had never, at any time, had any effective control.

The story of her penetration of the Congo begins with the voyage of Diego Cam up the river in 1482.[1] After this her influence spread steadily, there being no competition from other European powers, who were all more interested in America than Africa at this time.[2] In the sixteenth century she founded the kingdom of San Salvador on the south bank of the river.[3] Its boundaries appear from the first to have been co-terminous with those of the native "Kingdom of Congo" founded by Bantu tribes in the fourteenth century, which it superseded.[4] This lay between the Congo River on the north, and the Kwanza on the south. Its eastern limits were uncertain but appear to have lain somewhere between 15° and 16° of longitude.[5] The sovereignty of the kingdom carried with it vague claims to suzerainty over the territories of Cabinda and Molembo, north of the Congo,[6] claims which Portugal inherited but which she appears to have made no effort to substantiate.

In the seventeenth century, after the subjugation of Portugal by Spain, there was trouble with the Dutch, who captured San Salvador and São Paulo de Loanda. But in 1641, after Portugal had regained her independence, peace was made, and her possessions on the Congo were handed back to her.[7] The Portuguese were now reinstated in their kingdom of San Salvador. But towards the end of the century they failed to hold their own, and were expelled by the natives.[8] This was the end of their rule in San Salvador, the kingdom remaining virtually independent down to the year of the Berlin Conference.[9] Thus the seventeenth century closes with the definite retreat south-

---

[1] cf. Keltie, p. 39. Johnston, *Colonisation*, p. 80. Grenfell, I, p. 70. Keith, p. 19. Reeves, p. 8. Thomson, p. 120. Königk, p. 47.
[2] cf. Keltie, pp. 40, 78.
[3] cf. Keltie, pp. 41–2. Johnston, *Colonisation*, pp. 85–7. Grenfell, pp. 69–70. Keith, pp. 19–20. Thomson, pp. 120–1. Königk, p. 47.
[4] cf. Johnston, Grenfell, I, p. 69. Keith, p. 19.
[5] cf. Stanley, I, p. 11. Thomson, p. 120. Keith, p. 20.
[6] cf. Johnston, Grenfell, I, p. 70.
[7] cf. Johnston, Grenfell, I, pp. 71–7. Keltie, pp. 65–6. Keith, p. 20.
[8] cf. Thomson, p. 121. Keith, pp. 20–1. Keltie, p. 42. Johnston, Grenfell, I, pp. 72, 75–6.
[9] cf. Keltie, p. 42.

APPENDICES

wards of the Portuguese towards Angola, and the end of their active influence in any country bordering on the Congo River. During the eighteenth century Portugal held her own with varying degrees of success in the country south of São Paulo de Loanda.[1] But she made no attempt, except at the end of the century, to expand northwards again. During the great wars which rent Europe at this time, she was frequently stripped of her possessions in Africa, but they were as frequently handed back to her. Each time that this happened she made assertions about her claims on the West Coast of Africa, which were remarkable chiefly for their vagueness. This was principally because no one knew exactly what these claims comprised.[2] After the Treaty of Paris in 1763 they were not called into question again until 1734. In that year Portugal suddenly ordered a fort to be built at Cabinda, in order " to protect Portuguese sovereign rights in Africa." This brought the French on the scene. France had long been casting covetous eyes on the Congo, which was one of the most valuable slave-markets of Africa. But she had hitherto been too preoccupied with her wars in Europe, America, and India, to devote any attention to it. Released from these she now seized this opportunity to send a French frigate to Cabinda, which attacked and demolished the fort.[3] The reason she gave for this attack was that its erection threatened to interfere with " that freedom of trade which the subjects of all European nations had long enjoyed on the African coast." The Portuguese protested and a long diplomatic correspondence ensued. After two years Spain was called in as a mediator, and in 1786 a treaty was finally drawn up between the two powers.[4] In this treaty Portugal asserted, France neither contested nor recognised, Portuguese claims to exclusive dominion south of the Congo. At the same time France tacitly implied recognition of these claims by consenting not to let the commerce of her subjects extend south of Cape Padron (at the mouth of the Congo on its southern bank), on condition that other nations should do the same. As for the Cabinda territories up to 5° 12′, over which the dispute had originated, Portugal declared that she had no desire to place obstacles to free trade there ; France that her expedition had not had the intention of in any way troubling, weakening, or diminishing the rights of sovereignty which Portugal still claimed over them. This statement was important because it was later on taken by Portugal to prove that France had recognised

---

[1] cf. Keltie, pp. 74–5.
[2] cf. Reeves, pp. 9–10.
[3] cf. Reeves, p. 10. Keith, p. 22. Johnston, *Grenfell*, I, pp. 74, 76. Königk, p. 48. Thomson, p. 121.
[4] cf. Reeves, pp. 10–11. Königk, p. 48. Thomson, p. 121.

her sovereignty over the coast up to 5° 12'.[1] Be this as it may, there seems little doubt that France would in the next years have asserted her supremacy over the mouth of the Congo and the regions adjoining it, if the French Revolution had not intervened and cut short the policy of encroachment and spoliation which her previous action had foreshadowed.[2]

Portugal's position in the nineteenth century was this. In Angola she extended her rule inland,[3] and had by 1884 carried it north as far as Ambriz,[4] just above 8° south latitude, and south as far as Mossamedes, 15° south latitude.[5] But, with the exception of a brief military raid on San Salvador in 1859, followed by the establishment of a native king on the throne as Dom Pedro V and military occupation of the town which lasted until 1866, but had no further repercussions,[6] she did not penetrate at all into the territories lying between 8° and 5° 12' south latitude which comprised her former kingdom of San Salvador as well as the Cabinda and Molembo district.

That this was so was due chiefly to the action of Great Britain, who, in the course of her efforts to control the slave trade on the coast of West Africa, came in time to assume a defiant attitude towards Portuguese claims, and in the end to keep her out of the territories in question by threats of force. Since Portugal had, by treaty with her in 1810 and 1817, been given the right to carry on the slave trade in her own possessions but not elsewhere in Africa,[7] this clearly was the natural policy to pursue for a power anxious to restrict the trade. There is no doubt that it was at first the sole motive behind Britain's action, though later she added to it the desire to ensure freedom of trade for her merchants near the mouth of the Congo. Sir Harry Johnston in his *Life of Grenfell* (p. 76) states that France at first collaborated with Britain in her efforts. But if this was the case the latter seems very soon to have taken a leading, and finally an exclusive, part both in suppressing the slave trade and in keeping Portugal away from the mouth of the Congo.

It is true that twice, in 1810 and in 1817, she tacitly acknowledged Portugal's claims by permitting her in the treaties drawn up

---

[1] cf. Thomson, p. 122. Reeves, pp. 11–13—but Mr. Reeves seems to interpret the treaty incorrectly.
[2] cf. Keith, p. 22.
[3] cf. Johnson, *Colonisation*, pp. 94–5.
[4] cf. below.
[5] cf. Johnson, *Colonisation*, p. 94.
[6] cf. Johnston, *Grenfell*, I, p. 75. Keith, p. 24.
[7] cf. Appendix III.

APPENDICES

with her in these years, to carry on the slave trade not only in Angola, but also in " the territories of Molembo and Cabinda on the west coast from 5° 12′ to 8° south latitude, over which the King of Portugal asserted rights."[1] But when even this concession provoked infringements of the treaty by Portugal, Great Britain changed her tactics. Henceforward she used threats not bribes to enforce her demands and never once after 1817, until the conclusion of the Anglo-Portuguese Treaty in 1884, did she recognise Portugal's claims to the territories lying between 8° and 5° 12′ south latitude. It was even a concession on her part that Ambriz was allowed to form part of the Portuguese dominions. In the middle of the century the verdict of a court (created at Loanda in 1844) for the adjudication of vessels captured twenty-five miles north of Ambriz (then thought to lie at 8° south latitude), elicited from Palmerston a clear intimation to the Portuguese Government that the claims of the Portuguese Crown to sovereignty over the territory lying between 5° 12′ and 8° south latitude was not recognised by the British Government. A year later, however, geographical research revealed that Ambriz actually lay eight miles north of the parallel of 8° south latitude. The British notification was then extended to cover Ambriz too.[2] Controversy ran high between the two countries. Then in 1855 Portugal occupied Ambriz, contending that the terms of the treaty of 1817 justified her act.[3] Finally Great Britain in 1856 agreed to let her keep it, on condition that its boundary should not be carried beyond the south bank of the Logé, so that " the interests of British merchants should be secured, and that slavery should be abolished." At the same time Lord Clarendon warned the Portuguese Government that " any attempts of the Portuguese authorities in Africa to extend that occupation will be opposed by Her Majesty's naval forces."[4] Further protests from Portugal between 1856 and 1877 were answered in similar terms.[5] Finally, after Lord Derby had, in 1876, gone out of his way to remind the Duke of Saldanha that the order of 1856 was still in force, these protests died down.[6]

[1] cf. Reeves, pp. 13, 14. Keith, pp. 22, 23. Thomson, pp. 123, 124.
[2] cf. Keith, p. 23.
[3] cf. Keith, pp. 23-4. Thomson, p. 25. Keltie, p. 141.
[4] cf. Keith, p. 24. Thomson, p. 126. Keltie, p. 141.
[5] cf. Keith, p. 24. Thomson, p. 126. Keltie, pp. 140-1.
[6] cf. Keltie, pp. 140-1.

APPENDIX III

PORTUGAL AND THE SLAVE TRADE IN THE NINETEENTH CENTURY, P. 12

PORTUGAL'S position with regard to the slave trade in the nineteenth century was as follows : By a treaty of amity and alliance concluded with Great Britain at Rio de Janeiro in 1810, she bound herself to prohibit slave-trading by her subjects in any part of Africa not belonging to Portugal. But she expressly reserved to herself in this treaty the right to buy and sell slaves in her own possessions in Africa.[1] She did not keep this treaty.[2] On January 22nd, 1815, a month before the Congress of Vienna had passed a resolution to abolish the slave trade, she concluded another treaty with Great Britain, in which she renounced the right to carry on the trade north of the Equator, but retained it in all those territories south of the Equator to which the Portuguese Crown had a claim.[3] The exact extent of these territories was defined in an additional convention drawn up with Great Britain at Lisbon in July 1817. In this treaty it was stated that they stretched from Cape Delgado to the Bay of Lourenço Marques on the east coast, and from 5° 12' to 8° south latitude on the west.[4] By the same treaty British cruisers were given powers of search over Portuguese ships and British commissioners were appointed to enforce the treaty stipulations.[5] In spite of this the trade continued to flourish. In 1839 Palmerston passed an Act which allowed British cruisers to search and seize suspected or actual slavers flying the Portuguese flag almost precisely as if they had been British ships.[6] Still the trade continued. Then in 1842, as the result of a threat on the part of the British Government to question Portuguese sovereignty along the entire West Coast of Africa, if Portugal did not take more effective steps to control the slave traffic the latter signed another treaty in which she promised to suppress it altogether.[7] Further threats of a similar nature resulted in yet another treaty between the two powers in 1871. In this Great Britain now declared herself satisfied that

---

[1] cf. Reeves, p. 13. Keith, p. 22. Thomson, p. 123.
[2] Reeves, pp. 13–14.
[3] cf. Reeves, p. 14. Stanley, I, p. 15. Thomson, pp. 123-4.
[4] cf Reeves, p. 14. Keith, p. 23. Thomson, p. 124.
[5] cf. Reeves, p. 14.
[6] cf. Bell, p. 235.
[7] cf. Reeves, p. 15.

APPENDICES

the slave trade was at an end and agreed to withdraw her commissioners.[1] It was not until 1878, however, that Portugal finally abolished the slave trade in all her African dominions.[2]

APPENDIX IV

CAMERON'S OFFER OF THE CONGO TO GREAT BRITAIN, P. 13

NOTHING could illustrate better Great Britain's lack of territorial ambitions on the Congo. Cameron had not confined himself to exploration merely. He had concluded treaties with native chiefs giving the British Government the option of assuming a protectorate over the inner basin of the Congo.[3] Before leaving Africa in 1875 he had even issued a proclamation on his own initiative, taking possession of the basin. But his action was not recognised by Lord Carnarvon, at that time Secretary for the Colonies.[4] Curiously enough commercial circles both in Manchester and Liverpool were opposed to the idea of such a protectorate,[5] just as they were later to the Anglo-Portuguese Treaty,[6] on the ground that the establishment of any political control, even (in this case) that of Great Britain, menaced the complete freedom of trade which actually existed on the Congo.[7] Nevertheless, it is clear that the British Government *could* have annexed the Congo in 1875 had it really wished to do so. The strength of the British fleet had sufficed for years to keep Portugal away from the mouth of the river.[8] It was clearly sufficient to establish Great Britain there herself, should she wish to utilise it for this purpose.

APPENDIX V

THE CONGO NOTE OF MAY 5TH, PP. 28-9

THE evidence direct and indirect for the non-delivery of this note is as follows :

[1] cf. Reeves, p. 15.
[2] cf. Johnston, *Colonisation*, p. 158.
[3] cf. Keith, p. 27. Johnston, *Grenfell*, p. 82.
[4] cf. Fitzmaurice, II, p. 343.
[5] cf. Johnston, *Grenfell*, p. 82. Keith, p. 27.
[6] cf. p. 26.
[7] cf. Keith, p. 27.
[8] cf. Appendix III.

1. There is no record of its delivery *either* in the German White Book on the Congo *or* in the British archives; whereas there *is* evidence of the delivery of the note of April 29th[1] on May 1st, *both* in the German White Book[2] *and* in the British archives.[3]

2. Granville, *both* in a note addressed to the Portuguese Government on May 9th referring to a proposal made by the latter that Great Britain should open negotiations with the powers,[4] *and* in his inquiry of May 26th to the German Government[5] refers specially to Münster's confidential communication of May 1st, but mentions no later one. This, too, would seem to point to his never having had such a communication.

3. That he was anxiously awaiting one from the German Government seems proved both by his note of May 26th and by his repeated minutes on the dispatches from Lisbon. "Consult Germany—Wait for an answer from Berlin."[6]

Comparison of the text of the note of May 5th[7] with that of April 29th[8] reveals a distinct advance in Germany's attitude towards the Anglo-Portuguese Treaty between these two dates. In the note of April 29th she had only stated her objections to the treaty; in the note of May 5th she put forward suggestions as to the nature of the agreement which should take its place. The assurances given by Granville on May 1st regarding negotiations with Portugal for an International instead of an Anglo-Portuguese Commission on the river, were not, it was stated in this note, considered sufficient by the German Government. It was made clear therefore that the procedure for a new agreement must be not *modification* of the existing treaty, but the creation of *an entirely new treaty* in which all the other interested powers should participate. This decision to veto the Anglo-Portuguese Treaty completely was an important one which certainly ought to have been made known to the British Government. Had this been done it seems probable that Granville would at once have scrapped the treaty, acceding as promptly to Bismarck's demands in May, as he did later in June, as soon as he knew them.[9] In that case Germany might never have taken up the idea of a conference,

---

[1] cf. p. 28.
[2] W.B., Congo, No. 18, Münster to Bismarck, May, 1, 1884: No. 23, Hatzfeldt to Münster, May 5, 1884.
[3] F.O./84/1811/ Granville to Ampthill, May 1, 1884, Africa, 3.
[4] cf. p. 28, F.O./84/1811/ Granville to Petre, May 9, 1884, Africa 40b.
[5] cf. p. 32, F.O./84/1811/ Granville to Ampthill, May 26, 1884—also in C. 4205, No. 1.
[6] cf. pp. 31-2.
[7] W.B., Congo, No. 17, Hatzfeldt to Münster, May 5, 1884.
[8] W.B., Congo, No. 17, Hatzfeldt to Münster, April 29, 1884.
[9] cf. pp. 31-2.

APPENDICES 205

or at any rate not in conjunction with France without telling England. It is of course impossible to prove this without further evidence, but it is certainly a possibility which cannot be ignored. Without further evidence, too, the reason for Münster's nondelivery of the note must remain a mystery, a mystery which is doubly baffling because the date of the note is the same as that of a much more famous one concerning Anglo-German relations as a whole, which was also not delivered by Münster.[1] This note was signed by Bismarck, the Congo note of May 5th by Hatzfeldt. There can be no question therefore of their having formed part of the same dispatch. But as they were sent off on the same day they presumably arrived on the same day. It looks like something more than coincidence that neither of them were delivered. Münster's excuse for not delivering the note concerning Anglo-German relations generally, was that he did not understand its meaning, an excuse which is justified by perusal of the note.[2] But, unless ambiguities have been cut out of the Congo note given in the German White Book (which is quite possible as it is admittedly only an extract), the same excuse does not hold good in this case as its terms are perfectly clear and explicit. The problem is one which can only be solved probably by a thorough perusal of the German archives.

APPENDIX VI

THE PORTUGUESE PROPOSAL FOR A CONFERENCE, PP. 29-30

THIS is commented on with some surprise by Keltie (p. 208). It is only very briefly mentioned by Keith (p. 55), Reeves (p. 64), and Yarnall (p. 41). Their information is derived from an English Blue Book,[3] and from the German White Book on the Congo, of 1885 This information is meagre and does not in itself explain the proposal. All that the English Blue Book contains is :

1. A reference to the conference in Bismarck's note of June 7th to Granville,[4] in which he states that " the Portuguese Government itself seems . . . as a consequence of the communications it has received from other powers to have become convinced of the necessity

[1] cf. pp. 51-5—also Appendix X.
[2] cf. pp. 52-5.
[3] *Accounts and Papers*, LV, 1884-5, C. 4205.
[4] cf. p. 52.

of making the Congo question the subject of an international agreement, and has therefore put before certain powers a suggestion for a conference."

2. A dispatch from Lord Lyons, the British ambassador in Paris, to Granville, on July 16th, 1884, in which he states that Ferry, in an interview which he had had with him that afternoon had told him that " Prince Bismarck had suggested that a conference should be held on the Congo question."

3. A dispatch written by Lord Ampthill, the British ambassador in Berlin, to Granville, on July 25th, in which he says that when acting on instructions from Granville he went to see Count Hatzfeldt and made inquiries about the proposal, he learnt from the latter that " the proposal did not come from the German Government, but from the Portuguese Government, as stated by Prince Bismarck in his dispatch of June 7th."

In the German White Book on the Congo there is only a passing reference to the origin of the conference in a note, written by Bülow, the German chargé d'affaires at Paris, to Bismarck on May 29th, in which he reports Ferry's willingness to participate in an international conference whose object it would be to ensure to all nations free navigation and equal rights on the river.

In view of this scanty evidence it is not surprising that the whole question has hitherto assumed a slightly mysterious air, in published accounts of the Congo negotiations. It is now possible to review it in the light of further evidence.

1. *The German Archives as used by Thomson (pp. 201-3) (Acta Betreffend Allgemeines Angelegenheiten des Congo Gebiets Band III).*

These give direct evidence that on May 13th, 1884, Portugal made a proposal for a conference through a circular to her ambassadors, whose contents were at once delivered to the German and French Governments, and possibly to those of other powers too. Bismarck's reason for taking up the proposal was that if Portugal were allowed to make it, the initiative would pass from her hands to those of England.

2. *The Protocols of the Conference (Accounts and Papers, LV, 1884-5, C. 4361).*

These are of course old publications, but Thomson's information throws light (though he himself does not seem to have noticed this) upon a reference in Protocol II, recording the second meeting of the conference on November 19th, 1884. This is a reference, in the speech of the Marquis de Penafiel, one of the Portuguese delegates, to a circular dispatch sent by the Portuguese Government to Berlin, Paris, Brussels, the Hague, Madrid, Rome, and Vienna on May 13th, 1884. This dispatch he qualifies with the remark that " there was expressed for the first time the desire to unite the powers interested in the questions pending on the West Coast of Africa."

This is quite clearly the same circular as that mentioned in the German archives. It is, that is to say, the proposal for a conference, though Penafiel was evidently careful to leave out any direct mention of it in his speech.

3. *The British Archives (Slave Trade Papers, F.O./84/1811/1812).*

These give the background of the proposal. They make it clear that it was not a proposal in the air, since it was at the beginning only suggested by Portugal as an *alternative* to what both the British and Portuguese Governments considered by this time to be *in any case* a necessity, namely, some sort of approach to the powers, in order to obtain their assent to modifications in the Anglo-Portuguese Treaty. Great Britain differed from Portugal in considering that separate negotiations would be better for this purpose than a conference. This was on account of her fear of France.

Portugal cannot be exonerated from a charge of double-dealing in her relations with Britain, since it is clear that two days after she had made a confidential proposal for a conference to *her* (May 11th), she then sent one to all the major powers of Europe (May 13th), without even informing the British Government that she had done so. After repeated inquiries from Granville, following the latter's reception of Bismarck's note of June 7th, with its unexpected revelations about the proposal, du Bocage, the Portuguese Foreign Minister, finally admitted on June 29th that such a proposal had indeed been " alluded to . . . as a suggestion made to the British Government," in conversations with the French and German ministers at Lisbon. He gave no date.[1] Since the statements of Portuguese diplomatists at this time have to be treated in the opposite manner to the numerical calculations of mediaeval chroniclers, doubled, that is to say, instead of halved in intensity, if a fair estimate of their truth is to be gained, this statement may be taken as tantamount to an admission that the proposal had actually been made by Portugal both to France and to Germany.

[1] F.O./84/1812/ Petre to Granville, June 29, 1884, Africa, 73.

APPENDIX VII

GERMAN INTERESTS ON THE CONGO OF A SECONDARY NATURE, P. 34

THE tardiness of Bismarck's protest against the Anglo-Portuguese Treaty is itself significant. The implication that the Congo was for him a question of secondary importance seems borne out by a consideration of the position there. According to the statement of the Solingen Chambers of Commerce in 1884, German interests on the Congo were " in some cases . . . second only to the English ".[1] English interests, that is to say, were admittedly greater than German there. Yet even England, who could undoubtedly have annexed the Congo in 1875,[2] or again in 1882 and 1883,[3] had she wished, evidently did not consider the trade of sufficient value there to warrant more than indirect control, at the cost of a tariff, through her influence over Portugal. It seems clear that the Congo, both for England and for Germany was a question of secondary importance in 1884.

APPENDIX VIII

BISMARCK'S INQUIRY OF FEBRUARY 1883, P. 40

THE text of this inquiry is given in the German White Book on Angra Pequena of 1885.[4] But Mr. Aydelotte[5] has shown that this published text contains two important omissions.

1. A passage in which the German Government made it clear that if it granted protection to Lüderitz it would be merely " in the manner and in the degree in which the empire generally allows it (protection) to extend to the interests of its citizens living abroad."

---

[1] W.B., Congo, 1884, No. 5, Report of Solingen Chambers of Commerce, April 1, 1884.
[2] cf. Appendix IV.
[3] cf. pp. 17-18.
[4] W.B., Angra Pequena, No. 2, Hatzfeldt to Herbert Bismarck, Feb. 4, 1883.
[5] W. O. Aydelotte, *Bismarck and British Colonial Policy*, pp. 28-31.

APPENDICES

2. Count Herbert Bismarck was also asked to say that "now, as formerly, we have no thought of any oversea projects, and especially of any interference in existing British interests in South Africa, so that we would only be too pleased to permit her effectual occupation to extend to German settlers in those regions."

That Herbert Bismarck delivered this part of his message seems proved by a minute written on February 7th at Walmer by Sir Julian Pauncefote.[1] Germany, Sir Julian Pauncefote was told, "had not the least desire to establish a footing in Africa."

The effect of the dispatch was naturally to create the impression that the German Government was anxious for British protection of Lüderitz's settlement. This impression remained as the dispatch was never contradicted.

APPENDIX IX

THE GERMAN TELEGRAM OF APRIL 24TH, P. 41

The ambiguity of the telegram of April 24th has been very forcibly demonstrated by Mr. Aydelotte in his recent study of the Angra Pequena negotiations.[2] The telegram ordered the German consul at Cape Town to declare the establishments of Herr Lüderitz north of the Orange River "to be under the protection of the Reich." But the German term "protection" was an extremely vague one. Bismarck himself appears to have attached different meanings to it at different times. In the past it had been used by the German Government to signify assistance from the nearest German consul, and sometimes from a German warship as well. So understood it had been granted to German traders for many years without causing any political complications. The announcement of April 24th was evidently meant to imply something more definite. But Bismarck himself did not accompany it by any definition of the new meaning he now attached to the word "protection". Consequently both the British Government and the Cape authorities, as well as his own ambassador in London failed to understand it.

That there was genuine misunderstanding on the part of the British Government and the Cape authorities is clear from their

---

[1] Quoted by Miss Adams in her unpublished thesis on "The British Attitude to German Colonial Development, 1880–5," pp. 85–6.
[2] W. O. Aydelotte, *Bismarck and British Colonial Policy, 1883–5*, pp. 59–60, 83.

reception of the telegram. When Granville was informed of its contents on April 25th all he said in reply was that he would immediately communicate with the Colonial Office about it.[1] When Scanlen, the Cape premier, received the message of the German consul on the 24th he merely remarked " with some astonishment " that he could not see " what could have impelled the Imperial Government to this communication ".[2] When Sir Hercules Robinson, the Governor of the Cape, forwarded the German consul's note to London, the only comment he made was that he had not yet heard from the Cape's ministers whether they would accept Lord Derby's invitation to take control of Angra Pequena or not[3]; whilst in a minute written on this dispatch (it arrived in London on May 22nd), Sir Robert Herbert, a Colonial Office official, declared that he saw " no objection to the statement that the German subject and his establishment were under the protection of the German Empire, if provisional protection pending inquiry is meant ".[4] Evidently he, and with him responsible Colonial Office opinion, thought that this was what *was meant*.

The ignorance of the Foreign Office and the Colonial Office of Bismarck's real intentions in Angra Pequena is further exemplified in public statements made at this time both by Lord Granville and by Lord Derby.[5] Münster did not help to enlighten this ignorance; on the contrary he aggravated it for the simple reason that his own was as great. He did not actually deliver the message of April 24th, which was communicated to Granville by Baron von Plessen, the German chargé d'affaires in London,[6] as Münster was away at the time on leave. But he returned a fortnight later and was responsible for handling the rest of the correspondence concerning it.[7] It seems impossible, however, to blame him for his misunderstanding of the situation, not only because of the ambiguity of the telegram, but also because his instructions of February and December 1883[8] were never contradicted, and on one occasion at least, in the very same note in which he was requested to press the contents of the telegram

[1] cf. C. 4190, No. 43, Foreign Office to Colonial Office, April 25, 1884. Aydelotte, p. 55.
[2] cf. W.B., Angra Pequena, No. 18, Lippert to Bismarck, April 28, 1884. Aydelotte, p. 69.
[3] cf. C. 4190, No. 50, Robinson to Derby, April 29, 1884. Aydelotte, p. 60.
[4] cf. Adams, p. 97.
[5] cf. W.B., Angra Pequena, No. 14, Münster to Bismarck, May 17, 1884. No. 19, Münster to Bismarck, May 26, 1884. Aydelotte, pp. 64–5, 73. Adams, pp. 98–100. Keltie, pp. 187–8.
[6] cf. C. 4190, No. 43, Foreign Office to Colonial Office, April 25, 1884. Adams, p. 97.
[7] cf. Aydelotte, p. 59.
[8] cf. p. 40.

of April 24th on the British Government, he was also requested to press for a reply to these earlier notes, asking whether the British Government would itself assume protection over Lüderitz's settlement. A kind of Humpty Dumpty correspondence, all at cross purposes, ensued in this way between Münster and Berlin, which makes it clear that Münster saw no discrepancy between the instructions of December 27th and the telegram of April 24th.[1] Not only did Bismarck make no effort to point this out to him,[2] there is also evidence recently brought to light by Mr. Aydelotte from the German archives that after a certain date the German Chancellor deliberately withheld information from his ambassador in London concerning the German Government's intentions in Angra Pequena. When Hatzfeldt on May 29th suggested that Lord Granville should be informed that Angra Pequena was one of the questions in which Germany awaited an obliging policy from England in return for Germany's kindness in other fields, Bismarck did, it is true, agree to this, but when Hatzfeldt further suggested that Count Münster should be "very confidentially informed of our intentions so far as is necessary so that he does not underestimate the importance which we attach to this matter," he declared, " No. On no account anyone who does not *of necessity* take part."

Thus the more the question is studied, the more does it appear that the responsibility for the failure of the British Government to understand the message of April 24th devolves upon Bismarck and upon Bismarck alone. This is doubly important because it lay *behind* their failure to understand the more important dispatch of May 5th,[3] a point which seems to have escaped attention so far in published comments on these events.

APPENDIX X

THE MAY 5TH DISPATCH, PP. 51–2

CONTROVERSY centres on two questions connected with this dispatch :
 I. The Question of its non-delivery.
 II. Bismarck's subsequent use of it.

---

[1] cf. Aydelotte, pp. 67–8, 70. W.B., Angra Pequena, No. 15, Bismarck to Münster, May 21, 1884 (but N.B. this is shown by Mr. Aydelotte to be incomplete) : No. 16, Münster to Bismarck, May 21, 1884 : No. 17, Hatzfeldt to Münster, May 24, 1884 (but Mr. Aydelotte points out that this only contains part of the telegram). Keltie, pp. 187–8.
[2] Aydelotte, p. 67.
[3] cf. Appendix X.

212 THE BERLIN WEST AFRICAN CONFERENCE

I. *The Question of its Non-Delivery.*

Evidence of this is as follows :

(1) *The Course of the Subsequent Correspondence between Bismarck and Münster.*

Münster's side of the correspondence makes it clear that he did not understand Bismarck's intentions and thought that he was merely meant to make representations about Heligoland. After he had been told *not* to do this, he thought that he was meant to do nothing at all—and did nothing. Bismarck's side of the correspondence shows that he was becoming increasingly aware that Münster was not carrying out his instructions properly.[1] By June 1st at least Bismarck had a strong suspicion that the note had not been delivered, for on that day he wrote to Münster, " ich bin im Zweifel darüber ob Ew. die Instruktionen vom 5. und 11. Mai in ihrem ganzen Umfange zur Ausführung gebracht oder sich durch Befürchtung eines unerfreundlichen Eindrucks haben davon abhalten lassen den Lord Granville vor die Alternative za stellen, sich durch eine mindestens gerechte, wenn auch vielleicht nicht wohlwollende Haltung gegenüber unseren überseeischen Interessen unsere politische Unterstützung zu sichern oder zu sehen, dass wir die Förderung unserer Interessen in dem Zusammengehen mit anderen Mächten suchten. Ew. pp. ersuche ich ergebenst, mich über diesen Zweifel aufklären zu wollen."[2]

(2) *Lack of any Record in the British Archives.*

There is no record either in the Foreign Office archives or in the Granville Papers of the delivery of such a note, although there *does* exist a memorandum of Granville's in the Granville Papers, dated May 17th, recording a long conversation which he had with Münster on that day, about Heligoland.[3]

(3) *Count Herbert Bismarck's Conversations with Granville, June 1884.*

Count Herbert Bismarck's conversations with Granville on June 14th, 17th, and 22nd, 1884, as recorded in the *Grosse Politik* and the German White Book on Angra Pequena,[4] themselves reveal

---

[1] cf. pp. 55–7. G.P., IV, Nos. 738–44. W.B., Angra Pequena, Nos. 22, 24. Aydelotte, pp. 62–4, 70–4, 76, 79–80. Adams, pp. 104–16, 118. Lovell, pp. 102–3. Langer, pp. 294–5. Thomson, pp. 193–4. Taylor, pp. 33–5.
[2] G.P., IV, No. 743, p. 60.
[3] cf. Fitzmaurice, II, p. 351. Adams, pp. 107–9. Aydelotte, p. 64. Lovell, p. 103.
[4] G.P., IV, Nos. 745, 746, 747. W.B., Angra Pequena, No. 25.

APPENDICES

beyond all doubt that Granville was in complete ignorance of the importance now attached by the German Government to colonial questions; for on Herbert Bismarck's own showing he repeatedly stated during these conversations that this was the first time that it had been made clear to him.[1] There is a report of the conversation of June 14th in an English Blue Book,[2] in which Granville states that " It was evident that there had been some misunderstanding on both sides." Actually the original wording was much stronger. It ran : " Count Bismarck admitted that the views of the German Government had not perhaps been quite so clearly stated as might have been done." But at Bismarck's special request this passage was omitted from the published version of the dispatch.[3] There seems little doubt however that Herbert Bismarck must have made some admission of this kind, for Granville's statement is corroborated by an unpublished letter written by Herbert Bismarck to his father on June 24th, 1884, in which he states that, " It is a fact that Münster, to whom one never writes clearly enough, did not find what he should have found in his instructions ; he asked Granville if England would not extend her protectorate to Angra Pequena, and on this account one cannot charge the present cabinet with *mala fides* from the outset."[4]

(4) *Bismarck's own Subsequent Statements.*

On January 24th, 1885, Bismarck told Sir Edward Malet, the British ambassador in Berlin, that " Not being satisfied with the result (of the May 5th dispatch), he sent his son, Count Herbert Bismarck, to England in the hope that he might succeed where Count Münster had failed."[5] On February 3rd, 1885, Bismarck wrote to Münster himself : " Ich kann . . . den wiederholten Ausdruck meiner Uberzeugung nicht zurückhalten, dass die unerfreuliche Gestaltung unseres Verhältnisses zu England nicht eingetreten sei würde, wenn Ew. die Alternative, unseren Kolonialbestrebungen freundlich entgegenzukommen oder unserer Gegnerschaft auf jedem für uns erreichbaren Felde der Politik sicher zu sein, mit der Schärfe und Beharrlichkeit vertreten hätten, welche durch meine Instruktion angezeigt war."[6]

[1] cf. also Adams, pp. 116–17, 131, 133. Aydelotte, pp. 91–8. Fitzmaurice, II, pp. 353–4. Lovell, pp. 95–7. Thomson, pp. 195–6. Yarnall, pp. 28–30. Taylor, pp. 41–2.
[2] C. 4190, No. 69, Foreign Office to Colonial Office, July 14, 1884 (Enclosure, Granville to Ampthill, June 14, 1884).
[3] cf. Adams, p. 130.
[4] cf. Adams, p. 118 ; Lovell, p. 94 ; Aydelotte, p. 80—short reference.
[5] *A. and P.*, LIV, 1884–5 : C. 4273, No. 148a, Malet to Granville, January 24, 1885. cf. also Adams, p. 118. Aydelotte, p. 71—short reference.
[6] G.P., IV, No. 759, p. 100. cf. Adams, pp. 114–15.

214 THE BERLIN WEST AFRICAN CONFERENCE

(5) *Granville and Münster, 1885.*

Granville says that when he showed Münster Malet's report of his conversation of January 24th with Bismarck, Münster " was frightened out of his wits and went home to consult his archives. He found the famous dispatch, but a telegram not to act upon it, and begged me to keep this secret." The " telegram not to act upon it " was evidently Bismarck's note of May 25th, instructing Münster to say no more about Heligoland.[1]

Granville's account therefore tallies with the internal evidence supplied by the correspondence of Bismarck and Münster itself, as well as by Granville's memorandum of May 17th, that all that Münster ever talked to Granville about was Heligoland.

(6) *An Admission of Hatzfeldt's.*

On May 24th, 1884, Hatzfeldt told the Crown Prince that Münster had not yet reported on the reception of the May 5th overture, therefore he, Hatzfeldt, could not satisfy the Crown Prince's especial interest in the colonial negotiations with England. The terms of his report of this interview are in themselves interesting, as they show the extreme secrecy that surrounded the overtures of May 5th. " Da Eure Durchlaucht," he wrote to Bismarck, " mich nicht ermächtigt hatten, von der speziellen Unterhandlung zu sprechen, mit welcher Graf Münster beauftragt ist so habe ich jede Erwähnung derselben unterlassen. Die Frage des Kronprinzen (nur Kolonialfragen ?) berechtigt vielleicht zu der Vermutung, dass Seiner Kaiserlichen Hoheit Andeutungen aus England zugegangen sind. Ob es sich unter diesen Umstanden empfiehlt Seiner Kaiserlichen Hoheit schon jetzt und solange noch kein Bericht des Grafen Münster über die Aufnahme unseres Vorschlages vorliegt über denselben Vortrag zu halten, darf ich Eurer Durchlaucht Entscheidung anheimstellen." Needless to say Bismarck's answer was " No ".[2]

(7) *Subsequent Assertions of Gladstone as well as of Granville.*

After the receipt of Malet's report of his conversation of January 24th with Bismarck, Gladstone wrote to Granville on January 29th, " Unless memory fails me wholly, which is not impossible, this remarkable dispatch of May 5th is to me a perfect mystery. I suppose that if Münster's fate is yet trembling in the balance you would not (supposing me to be right) like me to show him up. But when he is gone you might think the case ought to be cleared."[3] Speak-

---

[1] cf. p. 55. Adams, p. 125.
[2] G.P., IV, No. 742, p. 58. cf. also Adams, p. 112.
[3] cf. Adams, p. 124.

APPENDICES

ing in the House of Commons on March 12th, 1885, Gladstone said, " I remember that upon hearing of that dispatch I immediately said to Earl Granville I could not believe my memory had so entirely and absolutely gone that I should not recollect such a dispatch. Earl Granville said, ' I am in the same position ; I have no recollection of it.' It is no wonder, because we have been in communication with the representative of Germany on the subject, and it appears that it had never been communicated."[1]

In spite of this weight of evidence the German historian, Herr Thimme,[2] whose views are supported by Professor Langer,[3] maintains that the fault was entirely on the English side in not understanding Münster's representations. He bases his case on an unpublished dispatch written on June 6th by Münster to Bismarck, in answer to Bismarck's note of June 1st expressing the latter's doubt as to whether Münster had carried out his instructions of May 5th and May 11th in their entirety. " Count Münster ", Thimme declares, " replied not with the pretext that the dispatch had been withdrawn : on the contrary he maintained that in accordance with the instructions imparted to him, he had emphatically demonstrated the seriousness of the situation to Lord Granville."[4] Thimme adduces this as evidence that Münster had from the beginning understood his instructions, and that the British Government were au fait as regarded the general situation. It was sheer blindness and perversity on their part therefore that they did not foresee the consequences. He ignores not only the rest of the evidence, which is all against such a supposition, but also the date of the dispatch. Even if Münster *had* (though again the evidence is against this) made some representation in the sense desired by Bismarck between June 1st and June 6th, *after* his receipt of Bismarck's strongly worded dispatch of June 1st, this would be no proof that he had done so earlier. Moreover, the value of Münster's assertions is questionable. He had also declared at the end of May that he had made clear the contents of the telegram of April 24th,[5] though it was evident that he had not done so. More serious still Herr Thimme appears deliberately to have repressed those parts of the dispatch of June 6th which invalidate his own argument. This is clear from extracts published by Mr. Aydelotte.[6] Mr. Aydelotte does

---

[1] cf. Adams, p. 125. Fitzmaurice, p. 428. Lovell, p. 106.
[2] F. Thimme, " Das Berühmte Schwindeldokument E. A. Crowes," *Berliner Monatshefte*, September 1929.
[3] W. L. Langer, *European Alliances and Alignments*, p. 296.
[4] cf. Thimme, p. 975, note. cf. also Adams, pp. 114, 124.
[5] cf. Appendix IX, p. 209.
[6] Aydelotte, pp. 80–1.

not concern himself with Herr Thimme's article, but his extracts are so damning to the latter's arguments that it seems worth while relating the two. It appears that Münster opened the dispatch of June 6th by quoting the instructions to Count Herbert Bismarck of February 4th, 1883.[1] " The explanation ", he wrote, " which Count Herbert Bismarck gave, at the beginning, of the negotiations over Angra Pequena has not been without influence on the policy and the views of the British Government. . . . Lord Granville and Lord Derby are still under the impression that the Imperial Government wishes to found a German colony at Angra Pequena. Our right to found colonies has been disputed so far as I know, by neither of them." A little later he added, " As far as concerns my personal attitude towards the German colonial attempts . . . I have always believed that I stood in the same position as Your Serene Highness. The above-quoted passage from the instructions of February 4th last year, ' that now as formerly we have no thought of oversea projects,' had strengthened me in this belief." It seems impossible in these circumstances to take Herr Thimme's argument seriously.

II. *Bismarck's Subsequent use of the Dispatch.*

This was very unscrupulous. Although it is clear that Bismarck must have known, at any rate by the end of June 1884, after his son had talked to Granville, that the dispatch of May 5th had not been delivered, he did not hestitate a few months later to use it in recriminations both public and private against the British Government, as part of an intensive campaign of colonial propaganda which he was carrying on against her.

On January 24th, 1885, he spoke at great length to Sir Edward Malet, the British ambassador at Berlin, about the circumstances which had led to the political estrangement between the two countries. " At every point ", he said, " at which Germany had endeavoured to found a colony, England had closed in, making new acquisitions, so as to restrict Germany's power of expansion." " In order to show ", Malet reported, " how different were their relations only a year ago and how much he had desired that the good relations then subsisting should continue," he then read portions of the May dispatch to the British ambassador. Although admitting, as has been seen,[2] that Münster had *not* delivered his messages properly, he at the same time reproached the British Government because it " had entirely failed to appreciate the importance which his

---

[1] cf. Aydelotte, pp. 80–1 ; also Appendix VIII.
[2] cf. above, p. 213.

APPENDICES

government attached to the question, as he did not suppose that if Granville had understood it, the successive annoyances to which Germany had been exposed would not have been averted." When Malet asked if there were any differences at that moment outstanding between the two countries, and whether his government could do anything to remedy them, Bismarck replied that "the understanding which he had arrived at with France in consequence of his failure to come to one with us, put it out of his power to take up the question now, as he had expounded it on May 5th."[1]

Granville wrote back on February 7th that the "misunderstanding" referred to "was due to the suddenness with which the British Government became acquainted with the departure by Germany from her traditional policy in regard to colonisation. The misconception", he stated, "which had produced a change of attitude on the part of Prince Bismarck towards this country can only be attributed to causes for which Her Majesty's Government are not responsible. The dispatch of Prince Bismarck to Count Münster was never communicated to me."[2]

In spite of this denial, and in spite of his own knowledge of the situation, Bismarck made public use of the dispatch in his propaganda against England. Great controversy has arisen over this question because several false statements have actually been made on the English side concerning it. These can all be traced to Fitzmaurice, who, in his *Life of Granville*, states[3] that Bismarck in a speech to the Reichstag on March 2nd, 1885, (1) referred to the May dispatch; (2) "brandished it before the eyes of the German parliament." Neither of these statements is true. The latter, in view of the fact that Bismarck *did* refer in his speech to dispatches in the German White Book on Angra Pequena, which he had with him, has further been taken to imply that a full text of the dispatch was published in the German White Book.[4] Actually Bismarck did *not* produce the May 5th dispatch in the Reichstag, nor did he refer to it directly, though he *did* refer to it *indirectly* in a protest which he made against the publication in English Blue Books of his confidential conversation of January 24th with Malet, a protest which incidentally would seem to reflect his guilty conscience.[5] The

---

[1] C. 4273, No. 148a, Malet to Granville, January 24, 1885. cf. also Adams, p. 118. Aydlotte, p. 71—short reference.
[2] C. 4273, No. 176, Granville to Malet, February 7, 1885. Adams, pp. 121–2.
[3] Fitzmaurice, *Life of Granville*, Vol. II, p. 427.
[4] cf. Gooch and Temperley, *Documents on the Origin of the War*, Vol. III, Memo. E. A. Crowe, January 1, 1907, p. 408. E. T. S. Dugdale, *German Diplomatc Documents*, Vol. I, Preface, Sir Rennell Rodd, p. vii. *Rennell Rodd Memoirs, 1884–93*, p. 67.
[5] cf. Fitzmaurice, II, p. 427. Adams, p. 120.

dispatch was *not* published at the time and appears in no German White Book. It was published for the first time in 1922 in the *Grosse Politik*.[1]

Much has been made of these mistakes by German writers since the War, and particularly by Herr Thimme, whose long and tendacious arguments have done much to obscure the more important issue of the non-delivery of the dispatch.[2] Thimme, followed by Langer,[3] goes so far as to accuse subsequent writers on the subject of wilful misrepresentation of the facts, whereas as a glance at Fitzmaurice's book is sufficient to indicate where the source of the error lies. Fitzmaurice gives chapter and verse for his statements.[4] As his book is an authoritative work to which anyone interested in the history of the dispatch is bound to refer, it was not only natural but inevitable that subsequent discussions of it should at first have accepted his statements as they stood.

The question arises what the source of Fitzmaurice's error was. There has been some conjecture about this.[5] It has remained for Miss Adams, in her unpublished study of " The British Attitude to German Colonial Development, 1880–5," to produce an entirely plausible and convincing explanation. Though Bismarck did not refer specifically to the May dispatch in his Reichstag speech of March 2nd she has discovered that articles were published in the *Norddeutsche Allgemeine Zeitung* on March 2nd, 3rd, and 4th, 1885, enlarging on Germany's grievances against England. These articles were not signed by the chancellor, but were generally accepted as officially inspired. One of them referred to the communication of May 5th, and stated that it had been left unanswered. It seems clear therefore that Fitzmaurice confused this article with the reported text of Bismarck's speech.[6] His mistake was not such a big one after all.

It seems impossible in conclusion to exonerate Bismarck, in this as in other matters connected with his colonial policy in 1884 and 1885, from a charge of deliberate—and provocative—duplicity.

---

[1] G.P., IV, No. 738.
[2] F. Thimme, " Das Berühmte Schwindeldokument E. A. Crowes "—as above.
[3] Langer, *European Alliances and Alignments, 1871–90*, p. 296.
[4] p. 427, footnote reference to Bismarck's speeches, " Reden der Minister Präsidenten und Reichskanzler Fürsten von Bismarck, ii, 61, March 2, 1885.
[5] cf. Adams, pp. 120–1, 125–7. Aydelotte, pp. 70–1. Thimme, p. 846.
[6] Adams, pp. 120–1.

APPENDICES

APPENDIX XI

BISMARCK AND "THE EQUILIBRIUM ON THE SEAS," P. 68

As far back as April 25th, 1884, Bismarck had spoken to Courcel of the possibility of a sort of Napoleonic Armed Neutrality of the other commercial nations against England.[1] In July he mentioned it to General von Schweinitz.[2] At the beginning of August, as has been seen, he referred to it again (p. 81). Then in September he enlarged still further on the subject (p. 88).

The question of naval supremacy never emerged into the foreground during the colonial dispute between England and Germany. Nevertheless, it played a significant if hidden part in it.[3] Not only was the possibility of this co-operation in itself formidable: the British Navy was also sadly out of date. The other powers had been out-building Britain not only in numbers, but in type of craft. The recent improvements in machinery, and the invention of new weapons like the torpedo had upset the old standards completely. In the years after 1870 all the leading Continental powers, with France in the van, had made great efforts to build up a modern fighting force. In 1882 England had 20 first-class ships as against 32 possessed by France, Germany, Italy, Austria, and Russia. France alone had 16 and Germany 9, so that these two powers together outnumbered England. The British naval authorities had been slow in increasing appropriations for construction and hesitant about introducing new designs and armament. Only when it was too late, in the autumn of 1884, did the question first arouse public attention, so that in December five and a half million pounds were voted for construction during the following years. There is no doubt therefore that if the Franco-German entente had resulted in a naval combination against England, it would have constituted a very serious menace to her position.[4] Actually there was little likelihood of this happening. There was never any real danger of war between England and Germany in 1884 and 1885, because the colonial issues between them were not of sufficient importance to cause one.[5] Bismarck only used the naval strength of his allies potentially—but with good results. To it he owed the foundation of Germany's colonial empire.

[1] D.D.F., V, No. 249, Courcel to Ferry, April 25, 1884. cf. also Adams, p. 42.
[2] Langer, p. 301.
[3] cf. Aydelotte, p. 133.
[4] cf. Langer, pp. 302–3.
[5] cf. Aydelotte, p. 133.

APPENDIX XII

THE INVITATIONS TO THE CONFERENCE, P. 69

The first series of invitations comprised Great Britain, Belgium, the Netherlands, Portugal, Spain, and the United States.[1] They were issued on October 8th.[2] The second series comprised Austria, Russia, Italy, Denmark, and Sweden and Norway.[3] They were issued on October 18th.[4] Finally Turkey, in response to her claim that the area under discussion touched on her dominions, was also included in the invitations.[5]

Although Bismarck was anxious to get the conference called before the German elections at the end of October,[6] he did not succeed in doing so, not, as might have been thought from the acrimonious tone of his correspondence with her, on account of *Great Britain's* delay in answering his invitation, but on account of that of the *United States*.[7] It was France who had first suggested inviting the latter,[8] but the idea was eagerly taken up by Bismarck, who already in May had sounded the American Government as to the possibility of its participation in some sort of international regulation of the Congo question.[9] On October 17th the United States government accorded a provisional acceptance to the invitation to the conference. But by the 28th Kasson, the American ambassador in Berlin, was still without his instructions. Hatzfeldt inquired therefore how long it would take him to get them, and as the result of his inquiry the date of the conference was then fixed

---

[1] cf. W.B., Congo, 1885, No. 36, Bismarck to Courcel, September 30, 1884 : No. 37, Courcel to Bismarck, October 2, 1884 : No. 38, Note on Invitations. L.J., Congo, 1884, No. 27, Bismarck to Courcel, September 30, 1884 : No. 28, Courcel to Bismarck, October 2, 1884 : D.D.F., V, No. 406, Courcel to Ferry,. September 22, 1884 : No. 414, Courcel to Ferry, October 1, 1884. Yarnall, p. 56.
[2] cf. W.B., Congo, 1885, No. 38. F.O./84/1813/Plessen to Granville, October 8, 1884 (C. 4205, No. 10). Yarnall, p. 56.
[3] cf. L.J., Congo, 1884, Nos. 27, 28. D.D.F., V, Nos. 406, 414. Yarnall, p. 56.
[4] cf. F.O./84/1813/Granville to Malet, October 18, 1884, Africa, 39a (C. 4205, No. 19—but important omissions). Yarnall, p. 56.
[5] cf. W.B., Congo, 1885, No. 38, footnote. Yarnall, p. 56.
[6] cf. D.D.F., V, No. 406. Yarnall, p. 64.
[7] cf. Yarnall, pp. 62-4.
[8] cf. Yarnall, p. 61.
[9] cf. W.B., Congo, 1885, No. 21, Hatzfeldt to Eisendecher, May 4, 1884. Yarnall, p. 61.

for November 15th,[1] a circular being issued to this effect, on November 3rd, by the German Government.[2] Reeves maintains that Bismarck's idea in inviting so many powers was to veil as much as possible the political intent of the conference.[3] This may be, though he has actually no evidence for it. It is suspicious, however, that Bismarck gave different reasons to England and to France for inviting the second series of powers. At the beginning of October he told Courcel that he was in favour of inviting them " in order to give the greatest validity possible to the resolutions of the conference."[4] In the middle of the month he instructed Plessen to tell Granville that it had been decided to ask them " in consequence of some annoyance having been expressed by the Italian Government at the circumstance that Italy had not been included among the powers invited to take part in the . . . conference."[5] Whatever his motives, however, the effect of the invitations was certainly to gather together a large number of powers with no colonial possessions in Africa and little direct interest in the issues at stake.

APPENDIX XIII

THE OIL RIVERS CORRESPONDENCE AND THE ACTIVITIES OF GREAT BRITAIN, FRANCE, AND GERMANY ON THE GUINEA GULF, 1880–5, P. 125

THE fact that Bismarck used publicity as a weapon in his political campaign against England in 1884 and 1885, and published controversial White Books on colonial questions, which in turn provoked controversial Blue Books from the British Government, has tended to give undue historical prominence to the Anglo-German colonial quarrel of those years, and to distract attention from the far more serious and far-reaching Anglo-French colonial rivalry that existed at the same time all over the world—not least on the coasts of West Africa.

A clear illustration of this is the history of English, French, and

[1] cf. Yarnall, p. 64.
[2] cf. W.B., Congo, 1885. L.J., Congo, 1885, No. 2, Rotenhan to Ferry, November 3, 1884 : No. 3, Ferry to Rotenhan, November 4, 1884. F.O./84/1814/ Münster to Granville, November 3, 1884 (C. 4205, No. 31). Yarnall, p. 64.
[3] cf. Reeves, pp. 30–1.
[4] D.D.F., V, No. 414, Courcel to Ferry, October 1, 1884.
[5] F.O./84/1814/ Granville to Malet, October 18, 1884, Africa, 39a.

German activities on the Guinea Gulf from 1880 to 1885. The English Blue Book on the Cameroons,[1] which together with the German White Book[2] is the only published source on the subject, is part of a large unpublished volume of papers entitled "Correspondence Respecting Affairs in the Oil Rivers District on the West Coast of Africa, and the Question of the British Protectorate," which exists in the Record Office, in the form of confidential prints, both in the Foreign Office archives,[3] and in the Granville Papers.[4] Perusal of these shows that the Cameroons Blue Book *under-emphasises* the friction which existed between France and Britain on the West Coast of Africa prior to the appearance of Germany on the scene in 1884. Moreover, the extent to which the negotiation of treaties of protection with the chiefs of the Cameroons formed part of a *general* scheme embracing the whole of the Niger delta, and the coast from Lagos to Ambas Bay is not fully brought out.

This is important not only in view of Hewett's subsequent action on the Niger, but also because of the later history of the Cameroons under German rule. This illustrates the difficulty found by the Germans in making their enterprises prosper, on account of their lack of easy access to the interior along a navigable river, the Cameroons River itself being a small stream affording no navigable highway far inland.[5] The point of the *British* attempt to seize the Cameroons was that they offered a healthy and convenient place of residence for a consul working jointly for the Niger and Cameroons districts.[6] There is no doubt that as a healthy outpost of a Niger protectorate, such as Great Britain had originally intended to make of them enjoying all the facilities offered by the Niger itself, the Cameroons would have proved of far more value than isolated, by themselves, as the Germans procured them. Thus, when Hewett secured the whole of the Niger delta and the rest of the Oil Rivers, after Nachtigal had forestalled him further south, he not only obtained for Great Britain the part of the coast that was of paramount importance, he also (although this does not appear to have been recognised at the time) severely handicapped the future German colony.

The most important omission in the Blue Book is its failure to give any adequate account of Hewett's activities on the Niger after

[1] *Accounts and Papers, 1884–5*, Vol. LV, C. 4279.
[2] W. B. Kamerun, 1885.
[3] Embassy Archives, France, F.O./146/.
[4] G.D./29/269/.
[5] cf. G. L. Beer, *African Questions at the Peace Conference*, p. 22.
[6] cf. Oil Rivers Correspondence, C.P. 4955, No. 4, Memorandum, Lister, October 4, 1883.

APPENDICES

Nachtigal had forestalled him in the Cameroons. These are only passingly alluded to, and the only treaties made by him which are mentioned are those covering the strip of coast just north of the Cameroons (south of the Niger delta), between Old Calabar and Victoria.[1] Thus the small extent to which the original British programme was spoilt by Nachtigal's annexations is minimised, as well as the successful way in which Hewett, by retaliating on the Niger, carried out the main part of his programme. The impression is given in this way that the Germans achieved a much bigger success than was actually the case.

Later the fact that Great Britain *had* secured the coast from Lagos to the Rio del Rey was made known in an official notification of the British protectorate issued after the Berlin conference had recognised the Lower Niger as British on June 5th, 1885. This notification which correctly defined the limits of the protectorate was published in the *London Gazette* of that day.[2] It can also be found in Sir Edward Hertslet's *Map of Africa by Treaty*.[3] Hertslet likewise gives a list of treaties concluded between the Royal Niger Company and native chiefs between 1882 and 1884.[4] But these do not help to reconstruct the history of Hewett's movements in 1884 and 1885, or to give any idea of what he achieved. In the first place all those treaties of the company which were afterwards held as valid, had to be ratified by him later. Their dates, therefore, are no indication of his movements. Secondly, those treaties of Hewett's which were *not* preceded by preliminary treaties of the company are not given at all, though these were some of the most important which he made. They are all to be found, however, together with full details of how and when they were made in the Oil Rivers Correspondence.[5] So far they appear to have been unnoticed there, for they have never found their way into print, nor are they given as references in any printed sources.

[1] cf. C. 4279, No. 25, Admiralty to Foreign Office, August 26, 1884 : No. 48, Admiralty to Foreign Office, October 14, 1884 : No. 62, Hewett to Granville, September 24, 1884.
[2] cf. Burns, p. 157.
[3] Hertslet, Vol. I, p. 123.
[4] Hertslet, Vol. I, pp. 131–53.
[5] C.P. 5021, Nos. 31, 39, 52, 74 : C.P. 5063, Nos. 15–28.

NOTE ON SOURCES

Unpublished Sources

THE backbone of the unpublished material used for this study is contained in the Slave Trade Papers for 1884–5 (cf. Bibliography), which are to be found in the Public Record Office. They give a full account both of the events leading up to the conference and of its history while it sat, and are of course the source from which such published information as exists in contemporary blue books has been drawn. These unpublished papers have never before been used by any writer on the conference. Care has been taken to correlate the information contained in them with whatever exists in the blue books, and wherever a reference is found both in a blue book and in an unpublished dispatch this has in every case been stated. Important omissions and expurgations in the blue books have also been specifically mentioned where relevant. Volumes of the Granville correspondence, likewise to be found in the Record Office, have also been used. A good deal of this correspondence has already been referred to by other writers on German colonial developments during these years.[1] A good deal of it has not been used by other writers. In each case it has been specifically stated in the footnotes when this was the case and when it was not. Access to the unpublished volumes of the Dilke Papers at the British Museum was very kindly given me by Miss Tuckwell. I did not find much there that was of any use to the present study, but they were illuminating on one or two points. As will be seen from the Bibliography I have also made use of the private correspondence of my grandfather, Sir Joseph Archer Crowe, who was one of the delegates to the

---

[1] e.g., M. A. Adams, "The British Attitude to German Colonial Development, 1880–5". W. O. Aydelotte, *Bismarck and British Colonial Policy, 1883–5*. W. H. Scotter, "International Rivalry in the Bights of Benin and Biafra, 1815-85."

conference. It is of only minor importance, however, containing for the most part little more than an endorsement of the fuller official information contained in the Slave Trade Papers. There are, however, one or two interesting expressions of general points of view, and records of conversations, which space has not permitted me to bring into prominence. The official correspondence on the Niger and Oil Rivers from 1879 to 1884[1] is, I think, of great interest and value. I should I feel mention at the start, the debt of gratitude I am under to Professor Newton for so kindly helping me to trace this correspondence himself at the Record Office. It is not easy to find, as it is not indexed at all under the heading " Niger ", or even under that of " Oil Rivers ". Finally I succeeded in tracing it through the references given in the unpublished thesis of a former pupil of Professor Newton's, Mr. W. H. Scotter, on " International Rivalry in the Bights of Benin and Biafra " (referred to in Bibliography). As can be seen in the Bibiography the correspondence is in the form of confidential prints. As far as I can ascertain the manuscript sources on which these prints are based do not exist in full at the Record Office. I have found one or two dispatches in their original form in other volumes there, but not the whole correspondence. This is rather mysterious, but everything connected with the Niger at this time is mysterious. Taubmann-Goldie, as recounted in Dorothy Wellesley's biography,[2] destroyed his own papers at the outbreak of the Great War. All the officials of the National African Company were bound to the strictest secrecy. I have been told by Miss Fegan (former librarian of Girton College), who has lived many years in Nigeria and knows it well, that A. C. Burns, the author of the best standard history of Nigeria (cf. Bibliography), once told her of the extreme difficulty that he had in writing it when it came to the history of British activities there in the third quarter of the nineteenth century, owing to the fact that not only the National African Company, but also any of the other commercial companies that had ever existed on the river had destroyed their own archives. He himself does not

---

[1] Confidential Prints—Correspondence Respecting the Oil Rivers District and the Question of a British Protectorate, 1879–84.
[2] D. Wellesley, *Sir George Goldie—Founder of Nigeria.*

appear to have discovered the Oil Rivers Correspondence in the Record Office. In fact, the only writer to have utilised it so far, is, as far as I can make out, Mr. Scotter. In these circumstances it would appear to be of particular significance. The use made of it by Mr. Scotter differs somewhat from mine. His work is a long historical survey beginning in the year 1815, and deals very briefly with the years 1884-5, with which my whole study is concerned. He hardly touches on the points that are of particular interest to me.

These are the unpublished sources that I have used. It is obvious that at a conference where practically every power in Europe, as well as the United States, was present, the unpublished archives of each one of them would be of assistance in writing its history. It is equally obvious however that it would be mentally and physically impossible to read and digest them in four years. Seeing the volume and scope of the British archives, the published British, French, German, and American official documents alone, and of the secondary sources dealing with the subject, it would I think have been impossible, in any case in the time, to have studied even the archives of the other countries, who, besides Great Britain, were mainly concerned in it: Germany, that is to say, France, Portugal, Belgium, and the United States. Even had there been time to attack those of Germany and France it is not certain that this would have been possible, for whereas our official documents are open to the public up to 1885, those of France and Germany are closed after 1870. Special permission would have had to be obtained to have access to them. In the case of Germany at any rate it seems doubtful whether this would have been granted. In France, too, I should imagine that difficulty might have been experienced. With regard to the German archives, however, Mr. R. S. Thomson's study of the Foundation of the Congo Free State (cf. Bibliography) has been of great assistance, as he himself had access to these before 1933, and has embodied much valuable information from them in his work. In general it may be said of this information, as far as the immediate history of the conference is concerned, that it corroborates the information which I have myself derived from the British archives, even more than it adds to it.

NOTE ON SOURCES

Published Official Sources

A very thorough perusal has been made of all the British blue books dealing in any way with Anglo-German colonial relation in Africa between 1884 and 1885, as well as with those bearing directly on the conference itself. A list of these is given in the Bibliography. As stated above, they have been carefully compared with the unpublished official correspondence from which they are drawn, and checked against it in detail in the footnotes. Quite a good deal of use has also been made of two French yellow books on the Congo, published in 1884 and 1885, which I obtained from the Foreign Office library. Considerable use has also been made of the French Documents on the Origin of the Great War, edited by Bourgeois and Pagès. (cf. Bibliography). The documents to which I have referred here cover in many cases the same ground as those to which I have also referred in the *Grosse Politik*, Vols. III and IV. In each case they have been checked against each other in the footnotes. I have endeavoured to make it clear when these documents have been used by other writers and when by myself alone. Two German white books on Angra Pequena and the Congo, respectively, have also been used. These, too, I obtained from the Foreign Office library. The United States Senate Executive Document, No. 196 (cf. Bibliography) containing published correspondence of some importance bearing on the conference has also been used. It is to be found in the British Museum. Here again care has been taken to make it clear in the footnotes when the dispatches quoted have been referred to by other authorities, and when they have not.

I made great efforts to obtain the Portuguese white book on the Congo negotiations of this date, which is of some value. But my efforts were not successful. It does not exist in any library, and it is not obtainable in England. Through a student who was studying two years ago in the Lisbon archives, under the auspices of Professor Newton, I endeavoured to procure a copy in Portugal. But it appears that it cannot be obtained there either as it is out of print. Extracts from it are, however, given in the French yellow book on the Congo of 1884, and these have been utilised to the full.

Very extensive use has been made in the second half of this

study of the protocols of the conference. These are to be found in an English blue book (cf. Bibliography), in Hertslet's *Map of Africa by Treaty*, Vol. II, in the French yellow book on the Congo of 1885, in the German white book on the Congo of the same year, and in the Senate Executive Document, No. 196. These are the only references that have actually been handled by me. But they are also to be found in State Papers, and, doubtless, in the published official documents of every power that attended the conference. In spite of the fact, however, that they have been open to the public since 1885, their bulk and formidable technical character seem to have succeeded in frightening off all subsequent writers on the conference from a thorough study of them. Yet they are well worth such a study, and, even without the aid of other documents, form a valuable contribution to its understanding. Every effort has been made here to utilise them to the full.

Unpublished Theses

Of the two unpublished theses which I have mentioned, that of Mr. Scotter has chiefly been of value to me on account of its bibliography, which, as stated above, helped me to trace the Oil Rivers Correspondence of 1879–84 : that of Miss Adams has proved of great assistance to me in many ways. My debt to her has been acknowledged in detail in footnotes and appendices. I must leave my references to speak for themselves. As with other authorities I have taken pains never to omit her name when she mentions anything to which I refer, whether I have had direct access to the documents she uses or not. Her work seems to me an exceptionally able and penetrating study of Anglo-German relations during these years, which would, if published, I am sure, attract many readers.

Besides her thesis and that of Mr. Scotter, I have also read through that of Mr. Aydelotte on " Bismarck and British Colonial Policy, 1883–5", in the Cambridge University Library. But since his book came out about two months later, I have referred to this and not to the thesis in my Bibliography. I have made full use of it with regard to the Angra Pequena negotiations of 1882–5 between England and Germany, on

NOTE ON SOURCES

which he is the latest and the most competent authority. This has been fully acknowledged in footnotes and appendices.

Secondary Sources

With regard to these, I must again leave my Bibliography and footnotes to speak in the main for themselves. Great care has been taken throughout this study never to omit a reference to any secondary authority known to me, who has touched on the points that I have raised, whether or not I have myself had access to fuller information concerning them. My idea in doing this has been to try and give a clear conception to anyone reading what I have written, as and when they read it, to what extent it is based on original documents alone, to what extent on the work of others, and to what extent on both. It is of course impossible to explain in numerous footnotes the relative importance to be attached to two or more references on one point, in each footnote. But it is obvious that when an original source and a secondary source are given, the original source is the fuller one. Whenever special importance is to be attached to a particular source, an attempt has been made to indicate this very briefly. If fuller information is required the reader must be referred to the references themselves. The reason why I have devoted a good deal of time and trouble to them is that they supply a need which I have myself frequently felt in reading both the published and unpublished work of others, to know not only the source used to illustrate a particular point, but also all the other possible sources which throw any light on this point. A procedure which I find particularly baffling, and which seems to occur very frequently in the kind of subject about which I have been writing, which has already been partially but not wholly worked over, is when the author, basing his or her work mainly on unpublished sources, uses and refers to these sources only, in cases where they have already been embodied in another published work, this work being either intentionally or unintentionally ignored altogether. This is very muddling to anyone not intimately acquainted with the subject. Above all it places obstacles in the way of a student anxious to make further acquaintance with it. In endeavouring to avoid such a procedure, therefore, I have to a certain extent anticipated what would, in other circumstances, be my own difficulties, and trust, that in doing so, I have not misread those of others. To the best of my ability I have tried to mention every source known to me of which I have made the slightest use in my statements, or which has given me the slightest help in formulating them.

Perhaps the single work of another author which has been most invaluable to me is Professor Thomson's study of the conference in its relation to the founding of the Congo Free State (cf. Bibliography). He has had access to practically every important published and unpublished source on the subject of the Congo during these years, *except* the British archives which I have used. As has been stated above, he has in particular had access to the German archives whose results he embodies in his book.

The two most recent accounts of the conference itself are those of H. E. Yarnall[1] and Georg Königk.[2] Mr. Yarnall is an American of markedly pro-German sympathies who wrote and published his book in Germany (although it is written in English) under German direction. I had great difficulty in obtaining it, as no English bookseller was able to procure it for me. Eventually, however, I succeeded in procuring it myself, from a Heidelberg bookseller, during a visit to Germany. It is of small value, however, being slight in size and superficial in its treatment of the subject. The work of Herr Königk was sent to me by a friend in Germany. Considering that it is published under the auspices of the Nazi government it is surprisingly moderate in tone, although it contains occasional startling assertions about the aims of British policy. The author has read Professor Thomson's book and has himself had access to some of the German documents. Judging from the results, however, this must have been rather restricted. At any rate he produces no information of any special value from them. He has in general nothing very new to say, but the work is well put together and is very readable. It is on a much bigger scale than Mr. Yarnall's.

---

[1] H. E. Yarnall, *The Great Powers and the Congo Conference, 1884 and 1885*, Göttingen, 1934.
[2] G. Königk, *Die Berliner Kongo Konferenz, 1884–5—Ein Beitrag zur Kolonialpolitik Bismarcks*, Essen, 1938.

NOTE ON SOURCES

The oldest monograph on the conference is that of J. S. Reeves—*The International Beginnings of the Congo Free State*—published in 1894 (cf. Bibliography). Apart from this there are short accounts of it in Émile Banning's *Mémoires*, in Stanley's books on the Congo, and in the histories of Keith, Keltie, and Koschitzky (cf. Bibliography). There is a short but erroneous interpretation of it in W. L. Langer's *European Alliances and Alignments*, and chapters on it in the theses both of Miss Adams and Mr. Scotter. None of these accounts are adequate either in scope, treatment, or documentation. The best and most up-to-date account is probably Professor Thomson's. But the latter makes no attempt, as he himself states, to make a detailed study of it. He is mainly concerned with its relations to the policy and ambitions of Leopold of the Belgians. He has for instance nothing to say about the discussions which took place over the Niger at the conference.

Claims to Originality

My claims to originality in this study are as follows:

1. The use of unpublished English sources never before used.
2. Special value of these in regard to the Niger, which has not been adequately treated in any previous history of the conference.
3. Fuller use of the already available official material, notably the protocols of the conference, than has ever before been made.
4. Treatment of the subject and correlation of the general trend and meaning of Anglo-German policy at this time with the diplomatic history of the conference.

BIBLIOGRAPHY

UNPUBLISHED DOCUMENTS.

SLAVE TRADE PAPERS RELATING TO THE CONGO AND THE WEST AFRICAN CONFERENCE (In P.R.O.), 1884–5, Vols. 1809–22.

F.O./84/1809. Jan. 1—March 20, 1884.
1810. March 21—April 30, 1884.
1811. May 1—June 20, 1884.
1812. June 21—Sept. 30, 1884.
1813. Oct. 1—Oct. 22, 1884.
1814. Oct. 23—Nov. 15, 1884.
1815. Nov. 16—Nov. 27, 1884.
1816. Nov. 28—Dec. 9, 1884.
1817. Dec. 10—Dec. 18, 1884.
1818. Dec. 19—Dec. 31, 1884.
1819. Jan. 1—Jan. 15, 1885.
1820. Jan. 16—Jan. 31, 1885.
1821. Feb. 1—Feb. 15, 1885.
1822. Feb. 16—Feb. 28, 1885.

GRANVILLE PAPERS (P.R.O.).
G.D./29/22. Correspondence: Cabinet, Political, and Various, 1855–85.
28. Correspondence: Cabinet, Political, and Various, 1884–5.
122. Correspondence with Dilke, 1882–5.
128. Correspondence: Gladstone, 1884.
156. Belgium and Holland, 1880–5, Misc. 1.
198. Drafts: Belgium, 1880–5.
178. Correspondence: Ampthill—German Embassy—1882–4.
179. Correspondence: Malet—German Embassy—1884–5.

CONFIDENTIAL PRINTS—CORRESPONDENCE RESPECTING THE OIL RIVERS DISTRICT, AND THE QUESTION OF A BRITISH PROTECTORATE, 1879–84 (to be found both in Foreign Office Archives—Embassy Archives, France, F.O./146/ and in the Granville Papers—G.D./29/269/.

BIBLIOGRAPHY

F.O./146/   C.P. 4824.   Jan. 1879—Nov. 1882.
G.D./29/269/   4825.   Dec. 1882—June 1883.
                   4869.   June—Oct. 1883.
                   4955.   Oct.—Nov. 1883.
                   5004.   Nov. 1883—June 1884.
                   5021.   July—Oct. 1884.
                   5063.   Nov.—Dec. 1884.

DILKE PAPERS (British Museum). (Access by kind permission of Miss Tuckwell).
General Correspondence (Political Series), 1884.
Memoir, Chapters xxi, xxiv, xxv.

PRIVATE CORRESPONDENCE, JOSEPH ARCHER CROWE WITH HIS WIFE, 1884-5. (In my possession.)

PUBLISHED DOCUMENTS.

I. GREAT BRITAIN.

G. P. GOOCH and H. V. TEMPERLEY (Editors). *British Documents on the Origins of the War*, Vol. III. H.M. Stationery Office, 1928.

E. HERTSLET. *Map of Africa by Treaty*, 3 Vols. H.M. Stationery Office, 1894.

BLUE BOOKS—ACCOUNTS AND PAPERS.

THE ANGLO-PORTUGUESE TREATY.
Vol. LVI, 1884 :
    C. 3885.   Correspondence Relating to Negotiations between the Governments of Great Britain and Portugal for the Conclusion of the Congo Treaty, 1882-4.
    C. 3886.   Dispatch to Her Majesty's Minister at Lisbon, enclosing the Congo Treaty, signed February 26, 1884, and Corrected Translation of the Mozambique Tariff.
    C. 4203.   Further Papers Relating to the Treaty connected with the Negotiations with Portugal for a Treaty Respecting the Congo River and the Adjacent Coast.

ANGRA PEQUENA.
Vol. LVI, 1884 :
    C. 4190.   Correspondence respecting the Settlement at Angra Pequena on the South-West Coast of Africa.

THE CAMEROONS.
Vol. LV, 1885 :
C. 4279. Correspondence respecting Affairs in the Cameroons.

THE WEST AFRICAN CONFERENCE.
Vol. LV, 1884-5 :
C. 4205. Correspondence respecting the West African Conference.
C. 4241. Further Correspondence respecting the West African Conference.
C. 4284. Correspondence with Her Majesty's Ambassàdor in Berlin respecting the West African Conference.
C. 4360. Further Correspondence respecting the West African Conference.
C. 4361. Protocols and General Act of the West African Conference.
C. 4739. General Act of the Conference of Berlin, February 26, 1885.

II. FRANCE.

BOURGEOIS ET PAGÈS (Editors). *Documents Diplomatiques Français, 1871-1914—Origines de la Guerre de 1914*, Serie I, Vols. IV and V. Paris, 1933.

BOURGEOIS ET PAGÈS. *Origines et Responsabilités de la Grande Guerre 4° partie Documents Secrets des Archives Françaises et Allemandes*. Paris, 1921.

YELLOW BOOKS—DOCUMENTS DIPLOMATIQUES.
Affaires du Congo et de l'Afrique Occidentale, 1884 and 1885.

III. GERMANY.

LEPSIUS and THIMME (Editors). *Die Grosse Politik der Europäischen Kabinette, 1871-1914, Sammlung der Diplomatischen Akten der Auswärtigen Amter*, Vols. III and IV. Berlin, 1922.
cf. also E. T. S. DUGDALE, *German Diplomatic Documents, 1871-1914* (English selected translation), Vol. I, *Bismarck, Relations with England, 1871-90*. London, 1928.
(But—very important—not advisable to use without reference to original published German documents.)

BIBLIOGRAPHY

WHITE BOOKS—STENOGRAPHISCHE BERICHTE ÜBER DIE VERHANDLUNGEN DES REICHSTAGS.
Angra Pequena, 1884.
Aktenstücke Betreffend die Kongo Frage, 1885.

IV. UNITED STATES.

UNITED STATES SENATE EXECUTIVE DOCUMENT, No. 196. 49th Congress, 1st Session. Washington, 1886.

UNPUBLISHED THESES.

M. A. ADAMS. *The British Attitude to German Colonial Development, 1880–5.* (M.A., London, 1935).
W. H. SCOTTER. *International Rivalry in the Bights of Benin and Biafra, 1815–85.* (London, Ph.D., 1933).

SECONDARY WORKS.

W. O. AYDELOTTE. *Bismarck and British Colonial Policy. The Problem of South West Africa, 1883–5.* University of Pennsylvania Press, 1937.
J. BAINVILLE. *Bismarck et la France d'Après les Mémoires du Prince Hohenlohe.* Paris, 1907.
É. BANNING. *Le Partage Politique de l'Afrique.* Brussels, 1888.
Mémoires Politiques et Diplomatiques—Comment Fut Fondé Le Congo Belge. Paris–Brussels, 1927.
G. L. BEER. *African Questions at the Peace Conference.* New York, 1923.
H. C. F. BELL. *Life of Palmerston*, 2 vols. London, 1936.
BOURGEOIS ET PAGÈS. *Les Origines et les Responsabilités de la Grande Guerre.* Paris, 1921.
A. C. BURNS. *History of Nigeria.* London, 1936.
E. DAUDET. *La France et l'Allemagne Après le Congrès de Berlin.* Paris, 1919.
E. FITZMAURICE. *Life of Lord Granville*, 2 vols. London, 1905.
W. M. GEARY. *Nigeria under British Rule.* London, 1927.

G. P. Gooch. *Franco-German Relations, 1871–1914*. London, 1923.
History of Modern Europe, 1878–1919. London, 1924.
A. J. Grant and H. Temperley. *Europe in the Nineteenth Century* (Third Edition). London, 1931.
S. L. Gwynn and G. M. Tuckwell. *Life of Sir Charles Dilke*, 2 vols. London, 1901.
A. L. Hodge. *Angra Pequena*. Edinburgh–Munich, 1936.
H. H. Johnston. *History of the Colonisation of Africa by Alien Races* (New Edition). Cambridge University Press, 1913.
George Grenfell and the Congo, 2 vols.
A. B. Keith. *The Belgian Congo and the Berlin Act*. Oxford, 1919.
J. Scott-Keltie. *The Partition of Africa*. London, 1893.
G. König. *Die Berliner Kongo Konferenz, 1884–5 (Ein Beitrag zur Kolonialpolitik Bismarcks)*. Essen, 1938.
M. Koschitzky. *Deutsche Kolonialgeschichte*, 2 vols. Leipzig, 1887–8.
W. L. Langer. *European Alliances and Alignments, 1871–90*. New York, 1931.
Evans Lewin. *The Germans and Africa (Their Aims on the Dark Continent and How They Acquired their African Colonies)*. London, 1915.
R. I. Lovell. *The Struggle for South Africa, 1875–99*. New York, 1934.
Sylvia Masterman. *The Origins of International Rivalry in Samoa*. London, 1934.
J. S. Reeves. *The International Beginnings of the Congo Free State* (Johns Hopkins University Studies, Baltimore, 1894).
Holland Rose. *The Development of European Nations, 1870–1900*. London, 1923.
H. M. Stanley. *The Congo and the Founding of its Free State*, 2 vols. London, 1885.
G. H. Scholefield. *The Pacific—Its Past and Future and the Policy of the Great Powers from the Eighteenth Century*. London, 1919.
A. J. P. Taylor. *Germany's First Bid for Colonies, 1884–5*. London, 1933.
R. S. Thomson. *Fondation de l'Etat Indépendant du Congo (Un Chapitre de l'Histoire du Partage de l'Afrique)*. Brussels. 1933.
M. E. Townsend. *The Origins of Modern German Colonisation*. New York, 1921. *Rise and Fall of Germany's Colonial Empire*. New York, 1930.
D. V. Wellesley. *Sir George Goldie—Founder of Nigeria*. London, 1934.

BIBLIOGRAPHY 237

R. H. WIENEFELD. *Franco-German Relations, 1878–85.* (Johns Hopkins University Studies, Baltimore, 1929.)
KAISER WILHELM II. *Vergleichende Geschichtstabellen Von 1878 bis zum Kriegsausbruch, 1914.* Leipzig, 1922.
H. E. YARNALL. *The Great Powers and the Congo Conference, 1884 and 1885.* Göttingen, 1934.

ARTICLES AND ESSAYS.

LEONARD DARWIN. " British Expansion in Africa " (*National Review*, Vol. XXXIII, March–August, 1899).
H. ONCKEN. " The German Empire " (*Cambridge Modern History*, Vol. XII, Chapter vi).
F. M. SANDWITH. " Egypt and the Egyptian Sudan, 1845–1907 " (*Cambridge Modern History*, Vol. XII, Chapter xv).
F. THIMME. " Das Berühmte Schwindeldokument, E. A. Crowes " (*Berliner Monatshefte*, September 1929, Vol. VII).
UNSIGNED ARTICLE. " Taubmann Goldie " (*Encyclopedia Britannica*, Eleventh Edition, Vol. XII).

INDEX

Alsace Lorraine: French demands *re*, in West African negotiations with Germany, 65

Ampthill, Lord, stresses Bismarck's assurances that Germany does not want colonies, 41 ; and British recognition of German protectorate in Angra Pequena, 59 ; and Bismarck's refusal to discuss with Granville the International Association of the Congo, 87 ; and Portuguese proposal for a conference, 206

Anderson, Mr. H. P.: and Portuguese proposal for a conference, 32 ; note of to Bismarck about International Association of Congo, 88 ; member of British delegation to conference, 99 ; and territorial negotiations at conference, 161

Anglo-German estrangement: relation of to history of conference, 6–7 ; origin of, 34–49 ; Bismarck no wish for before 1884, 46 ; based on misunderstandings, 49 ; widening of, 50–8 ; Bismarck owes foundation of Germany's colonial empire to, 194 ; legacy of ill-will between England and Germany left by, 195–6

Anglo-Portuguese Treaty: relation of to origin of conference, 11 ; territorial acquisitions of De Brazza responsible for, 15, 17 ; terms of, 16 ; negotiations for, 16–20 ; suggestions of Morier *re*, 16 ; British and Portuguese motives for, 17, 20 ; vacillating policy of Portugal over, 18–19, 21 ; Portuguese negotiations with France carried on at same time as, 18–19, 25 ; point of controversy between Great Britain and Portugal over, 20 ; and Anglo-Portuguese Commission on Congo, 21, 24–5, 56, 64 ; non-ratification of, 11, 23, 27, 32–3, 57 ; opposition of Powers to, 23–4; French opposition to, 24, 34, 56 ; discussions for modification of by Britain and Portugal, 24, 25–8 ; British suggestion that Portugal should ratify, 25–7 ; Portugal refuses to ratify, 27 ; attitude of Germany to, 23–4, 30, 31–3, 34, 51 ; Granville and Germany's attitude to, 28–9, 31–3 ; abandoned by Great Britain, 32–3, 57 ; and May 5th dispatch, 54 ; Bismarck unaware of origin of in Britain's fear of a French monopoly, 63 ; not directed against International Association of Congo, 78 ; Granville's relations with Leopold during negotiations for, 78–9 ; efforts of Leopold to invalidate, 78–87; effects of shelving of on general diplomatic situation, 82–3 ; effect of Leopold's opposition to on British attitude to International Association, 86–7 ; irony of Bismarck's situation *re*, after his destruction of, 83 ; and Congo note of May 5th, 203–5

Angra Pequena: and origin of Anglo-German estrangement, 37, 38–49 ; and origin of Berlin West African Conference, 37–8 ; Sir W. Harcourt ignorant of whereabouts of, 39 ; reasons for German interest in, 38–9 ; British strategic interest in, 39 ; Bismarck asks for British protection of Lüderitz's settlement in, 40 ; Bismarck decides to annex, 40 ; and evolution of Bismarck's colonial policy, 50–1, 53–5 ; and May 5th dispatch, 52–3, 216 ; negotiations *re* deal last blow to Anglo-German understanding, 56–9 ; British Government recognises German protectorate over Lüderitz's settlement in, 57 ; British Government recognises German

INDEX 239

protectorate over all German establishments on coast of, 59 ; Lord Derby's attempt to make further annexations in, 59–60 ; British proceedings in cause Bismarck to formulate third basis, 180, footnote 4 ; ghost of laid to rest at conference, 191 ; and German inquiry of February, 1883, 208–9 ; and telegram of April 24th, 209–11

d'Antas, Senhor: and negotiations for Anglo-Portuguese Treaty, 17, 26 ; and modifications in Anglo-Portuguese Treaty, 28, 30–1, 32 ; and Bismarck's protest against Anglo-Portuguese Treaty, 32

Armed neutrality: Bismarck's conception of for coercion of Great Britain, 63, 219

Banana: Portuguese claims to, 167 ; Portuguese attempts at seizure of, 172–3 ; Portuguese demand for at conference not made seriously, 173 ; International Association gains by convention with France and Portugal re, 174

Banning, Emile: sent by Leopold as special envoy to conference, 96 ; supports Sanford's railway proposition, 131 ; support for International Commission of Congo at conference, 132, 134 ; responsible for neutrality clause in Berlin Act, 139 ; and territorial negotiations, 164–6 ; and title of conference, 197

Bechuanaland: Cape Parliament's resolution in favour of annexation of, 59–60

Belgium: forms national committee of International African Association, 13–14 ; commercial character of Comité d'Études du Haut Congo loudly advertised in, 15 ; small part played by in Leopold's Congo ambitions, 96 ; hostility of to Leopold's ambitions, 96 ; Lambermont and Banning revolutionise attitude of at conference, 96; representation of at conference, 101 ; representation of interests of International Association in delegation of at conference, 95–6, 98 ; recognises International Association of Congo, 149

Benue River: Lokoja consulate at junction of Niger with, 122 ; Hewett's treaties with chiefs on, 125

Berlin West African Conference: legal importance of exaggerated, 3–5 ; political significance of, 5–7 ; at first only concerned with Congo, 11 ; summoned by France and Germany to check British ambitions in Africa, 21–2 ; origin of in Angra Pequena quarrel, 37 ; connection with Anglo-German estrangement and Franco-German entente, 49; repercussions of Angra Pequena negotiations on, 60 ; Niger included in discussions leading up to, 61 ; French propositions official bases of, 66 ; three bases of, 67 ; invitations to, 67, 69, 95, 226–7 ; British invitation to, 73–7 ; attitude of Great Britain towards, 74–5 ; rumour regarding Bismarck's plans for, 87 ; problems and personalities of, 95–104 ; procedure of, 101–2 ; discussion of first basis at, 105–18 ; discussion of second basis at, 119–41 ; recognition of International Association of Congo at, 142–51 ; international negotiations connected with, 152–5 ; discussion of third basis at, 176–91 ; summary of diplomacy of, 192–3 ; title of, 198

Bismarck: and Anglo-German estrangement, 34–49, 50–8, 194–6 ; and Anglo-Portuguese Treaty, 29, 31–3, 51, 54–5, 63, 83, 141, 208 ; and Angra Pequena, 38–49, 50–1, 53–5, 56–60, 208–9, 209–11, 216 ; and armed neutrality against Britain, 63, 219 ; and British claims on Niger, 75, 76, 98, 120, 126–7, 147 ; and British recognition of International Association, 91, 126–7, 143–7 ; colonial policy of, 7, 34–58, 194–5, 211–18, 221–3 ; and Congo note of May 5th, 31–2, 51, 53–5, 203–5 ; and effective occupation, 64, 75, 178–80, 188, 189–91 ; and Egypt, 46, 48, 51, 52–3, 60–1, 62, 63, 69–71, 72, 77, 193 ; and equilibrium on seas, 68, 219 ; and expedition to South Seas, 56 ; and Fiji land claims of German settlers, 36, 50–1, 57; and Flegel's designs on Niger, 180; and Franco-German entente, 51, 52, 55–6, 58, 61, 62, 71, 72–7, 83, 90–1, 126–7, 141, 151, 154, 156, 162–3, 176, 180, 193–4; and French preemption treaty with International Association, 83–4; and German colonial movement 43–6, 48–9, 195; and German designs on Congo, 84; and German recognition of International Association, 77, 83–6, 142, 144–5; heads German delegation to conference, 96, 100; and invitation to conference, 67, 69, 70, 220–1; and May 5th dispatch, 51–5, 211–18; and Dr. Nachtigal's expedition to West Africa, 50, 56, 66; and Portuguese proposal for conference, 30, 32, 55–6; and Samoa, 35–6, 43; seizes Togoland, 35–6, 43; supports Kasson's neutrality proposal at conference, 136–9; supports International Association at conference, 90–1, 107, 126–9, 139–40, 140–1, 143–7, 151, 154, 156–6, 162–3, 176; and telegram of April 24th, 41, 50, 209–11; and territorial negotiations at conference, 76–7, 102, 151, 152–3, 154–5, 162–3, 168

Brandenburg, Count: and German recognition of International Association, 84–5

Brazza, H. Savorgan De: travels of on Congo, 13; rivalry of with Stanley on Congo, 14–15, 158; political character of mission to Congo concealed from French public, 15; territorial acquisitions of responsible for Anglo-Portuguese Treaty, 15, 17, 18; French assurances re treaties of to Portuguese Government, 19; conflicting claims of France and International Association following expedition of, 158; and Makoko treaties, 158

Busch, Herr: member of German delegation to conference, 100–1; supports Malet over first basis, 115; reproaches of Courcel to re Franco-German entente, 137; and effective occupation, 187–8, 189–90

Cabinda: Portugal never any effective control of before 1884, 198–200; French attack on Portuguese fort at, 1764, 199; French and Portuguese assertions re in 1786, 200; Portuguese claims to, 168–70, 200–1; Leopold's readiness to make concessions to Portugal in, 170–1; goes to Portugal by treaty with International Association, 173; possibly lost to International Association by Bismarck's failure to mediate with France, 175

Cameron, Capt. V. L.: effect of discoveries of on international rivalry on Congo, 13; offers Congo to Great Britain, 13, 201

Cameroons: part of included in Conventional Basin of Congo, 4; British and German interests in, 37; and Anglo-German estrangement, 37; Bismarck's seizure of, 37; Nachtigal ordered to annex by Bismarck, 56; Nachtigal forestalls Hewett in, 125; Bismarck owes acquisition of to Franco-German entente, 194; British motive in attempting to seize 128; effect of Hewett's annexations on German colony of, 222–3

Clarendon, Lord: and Portuguese claims on Congo, 201

"Combinaison," the: origin of, 160–1; lack of practical success of, 161–4

Comité d'Études du Haut Congo: formation of, 14; Stanley becomes agent of, 14; political character of concealed by Leopold, 15; dissolution of, 15; turns into International Association of Congo, 15

Congo: at first only basis of discussion for conference, 6, 11; attitude of powers to when nineteenth century opens, 11–12; Anglo-Portuguese Treaty considered to establish veiled British protectorate over, 16; Bismarck goes out of his way to oppose Great Britain in, 5; Bismarck misreads French and British policy in, 63; Cameron and, 13, 201; delimitation of basin of, 108–14; freedom of commerce in basin of, 63, 65, 75–6, 84, 86, 98; free naviga-

INDEX 241

tion of, 3, 67, 102, 119–20, 128–41; and French pre-emption treaty with International Association re, 82–3; French penetration in, 17; German designs on, 84; German interests of secondary nature in, 51, 208; Great Britain excludes France from, 192; interest of powers in after 1850, 12–13; Leopold placed in as result of German and British policy, 90, 155, 156, 175; neutralisation of, 138; Portuguese claims on, 11, 18, 19, 24, 197–201; Portuguese proposal for conference on, 29–30, 30–2, 55–6, 205–7; rivalry of Stanley and De Brazza on, 14–15, 158; scene of some of worst brutalities in colonial history, 3–4; territorial settlement of 1884–5, 4, 73, 76–7, 102, 151, 152, 175

Congo, Conventional Basin of: delimitation and extent of, 4, 108–14; freedom of commerce in, 3, 98, 105–6, 114–18, 184–5; import duties in, 116–18; neutralisation of, 4, 135–9
Congo Free State: neutralisation of, 4; transformation of International Association of Congo into, 149–50
Congo, International Association of: cf. International Association of Congo
Congo, International Commission of: cf. International Commission of Congo
Congo note of May 5th: not delivered by Münster, 28–9, 51, 203–5; effect of non-delivery on Bismarck and Granville, 31–2, 54; does not help Münster to understand Bismarck's colonial policy, 53–5
Courcel, Baron de: and negotiations for Franco-German entente, 62–4, 66, 67–8, 69–70, 219; instructions of to conference, 73; heads French delegation to conference, 100; friction of with Bismarck at conference, 73, 77, 110, 137, 162–3; and delimitation of geographical basin of Congo, 107–8; and delimitation of Conventional Basin of Congo, 110, 113, 114; and twenty years' limit on restriction of import duties in Congo, 117; agrees to separate treatment of Niger and Congo, 127–8; and Kasson's neutrality proposal, 137–8; on preoccupation of delegates at conference with International Association, 143; and territorial negotiations between Portugal and International Association, 170

Crowe, Sir J. A.: member of British delegation to Berlin, 99; private correspondence of, 224–5

Delagoa Bay: Morier suggests cession of, in return for Portuguese concessions on Congo, 16
Derby, Lord: and Cape government's decision to control coastline of South West Africa, 56–7; attempt to seize part of coast of Angra Pequena not yet occupied by Germans, 59; and Portuguese claims on Congo, 201; ignorance of Bismarck's real intentions in Angra Pequena, 210
Du Bocage, Senhor: succeeds de Serpa and carries through the Anglo-Portuguese Treaty, 19; and admission of France and Holland to Anglo-Portuguese commission on Congo, 25, 28; and ratification of Anglo-Portuguese Treaty, 26–7, 32–3; and Portuguese proposal for a conference, 29, 30–1
Du Bocage, Senhor Carlos: mission of to Paris regarding territorial negotiations on Congo, 166–7; first interview with Ferry, 166; refuses to recognise claims of International Association, 167

Effective occupation: inadequacy of ruler laid down concerning, 4, 190; German proposal that principle of free trade should be linked to, 64, 178; becomes third basis of conference, 67; French and German attitude towards before conference, 65–6; British attitude towards before conference, 75, 76; assurance of Bismarck to Great Britain re, 75; discussion of at conference, 176–96; only three powers at conference really concerned with, 176-7; attitude of Great Britain towards at conference, 177; attitude of Germany towards at conference, 177-8; origin of proposals *re* in Bismarck's annoyance over Angra Pequena, 178; Bismarck recognises mistake of anti-British policy *re*, 180; Franco-German project on, 180-1; memorandum of English law officers on, 185-6; eventual proposition *re*, 187-9, 190-1; views of Lord Selborne on, 179, 186, 188-9, 190; views of Gladstone on, 189; triumph of British distinction between protectorates and annexations *re*, 179, 185, 186-90; British claims prevail over German in, 190-1, 192

Egypt: Bismarck supports Britain in, 46-8; Bismarck brings pressure on Great Britain in to enforce German colonial demands 51, 52; London conference on, 60-1; question of, united to that of West Africa in Franco-German entente, 61; the part of the entente that France cares about, 63; the part of the entente that Germany does not care about, 63; small measure of agreement *re* between France and Germany, 69-70; Bismarck anxious for peaceful solution of problem of, 72; British desire for German goodwill in reacts on policy *re* effective occupation, 193; Franco-German entente powerful in, 193; Germany not slightest interest in 193, footnote 6

England: cf. Great Britain

Equilibrium on seas: Bismarck and, 68, 219

Fernando Po: headquarters of British consul planned at, 112

Ferry, Jules: and Franco-German entente, 62, 64, 65, 67, 69; suggests cession of Alsace-Lorraine to France, 65; disinclination of for exact definition of Congo Basin, 107; and territorial negotiations at conference, 164-8; anxious for France to treat alone with International Association, 164; accepts suggestion of Pirmez for lottery, 165; intrigues with Portuguese, 166; breaks off negotiations with International Association, 167-8; asks for Bismarck's mediation in territorial negotiations. 68; re-opens terriroitial negotiations with International Association, 168; Tonkin episode and fall from power, 193; and Portuguese proposal for conference, 206

Fiji: and Anglo-German estrangement, 36; place of German protests *re* in Bismarck's colonial policy, 50-1; mixed commission appointed to inquire into German land claims in, 57

First basis of conference: formulation of, 67; discussion of, 105-18; cf. also free trade—in geographical basin of Congo—in Conventional Basin of Congo

Fitzmaurice, Lord Edmond: and ratification of Anglo-Portuguese Treaty, 25-7; estimate of success of British policy at Berlin West African Conference, 192; and May 5th dispatch, 217-18

Flegel, Joseph: unofficial adviser to German delegation at conference, 101; designs of on Niger encouraged by Bismarck, 180

France: and Anglo-Portuguese Treaty, 12, 17-25, 34, 56; attitude at conference, 95, 105-6, 119, 176-8; Bismarck's attitude to before 1884, 47-8; colonial rivalry of with England, 195-6, 221; and effective occupation, 64-5, 176, 177, 178-9, 181, 182, 184, 185, 188; and Egypt, 60-1, 63, 69, 70, 72, 193; and Franco-German entente: cf. Franco-German entente; and free trade, 64-5, 73, 114-18, 178; and free navigation of Congo, 128-9, 135, 192; and first basis of conference, 105-6, 108, 109, 112, 114-15, 116-18; and German traders in West Africa, 37; and Guinea Gulf, 66, 120, 122, 124, 221-2; importance of at conference, 5, 95; and International African Association, 14-15; and Niger, 119-20, 122-4, 125-8, 140, 153, 221-2; and neutralisation of Congo, 133;

INDEX

pre-emption treaty of with International Association, 79–81, 81–3, 142, 158; recognition of flag of International Association, 81–2, 142; representation of at conference, 101; territorial gains at conference, 156, 174; and territorial negotiations at conference, 73, 95, 102, 105–6, 119, 176, 177

Franco-German entente: relation of to history of conference, 6; origin of, 50–8; and May 5th dispatch, 52; and Münster's failure to communicate his messages, 55; no development in during period of Anglo-German reconciliation, 58; fresh repercussions of Angra Pequena negotiations on, 60; cementing of, 61–71; and London Egyptian conference, 61; Courcel real author of on French side, 62; and Skiernewice meeting, 68; Hohenlohe on, 71; weakening of, 72–7; French and German differences over re Egypt, 72; French and German differences over, re West Africa, 72–3; French reserves re, 73; Bismarck's reproaches to Courcel re, 73; bearing of Leopold's policy on, 77; Bismarck continues to support after French pre-emption treaty with International Association, 83; British suspicious of, 90; effect of Bismarck's growing dissatisfaction with an attitude to British claims on Niger, 90–1, 126–7; collapse of at conference, 95, 176, 193; French and German dissatisfaction with at conference, 137, 140, 162–3, 180; Bismarck's contradictory position regarding at time of its formation, 141; effect of Bismarck's attitude on to territorial questions at conference, 154, 156; effect of on Bismarck's attitude to third basis, 180; end of after conference, 193; lack of success in West Africa but success of in Egypt, 193; value to Bismarck of in foundation of German colonial empire, 194

Franco-Portuguese entente: suspicions of Leopold's adherents of, 157, 161–2

Free trade: Germany anxious for establishment of in Africa, 63, 64; France suspicious of principle of, 63; Leopold determined but hypocritical champion of, 80–1, 86; Bismarck forced to divorce principle of from effective occupation, 64, 65, 178, 184–5; in geographical basin of Congo, 63, 65, 75–6, 84, 86, 98; in Conventional Basin of Congo, 3, 98, 105–6, 114–18, 184–5; Germany, Britain and International Association support principle of at conference, 98, 105–6, 114–15; France and Portugal oppose principle of at conference, 98, 105–6, 114–15, 184–5; Italy supports principle of at conference, 98; Holland supports principle of at conference, 98; Russia opposes principle of at conference, 98

German colonial movement: characteristics of, 41–3, 45–6, 48; evolution of 1880 ff., 43

German East Africa: part of included in Conventional Basin of Congo, 4; Bismarck's seizure of, 38

German designs on Congo: Bismarck and, 84

German recognition of International Association of Congo: cf. International Association of Congo, German recognition of

Germany: and Anglo-German estrangement; cf. Anglo-German estrangement; and Anglo-Portuguese Treaty, 23–4, 30, 31–3, 34, 51, 63, 83; and Angra Pequena, 37, 38–49, 50–5, 56–9, 60, 180, 208–9, 209–11, 216; attitude of at conference, 22, 95, 98, 105–6, 119, 176–7; colonial movement in: cf. German colonial movement; and effective occupation, 64, 75, 178–80, 188, 189–91; and Egypt, 46, 48, 51, 52–3, 60–1, 62, 63, 69–71, 72, 77, 193; and Franco-German entente: cf. Franco-German entente; and free trade in Congo, 22, 185–6, 114–15, 116–17; importance of at conference, 5, 6–7; and International African Association, 14; and International Association of Congo, 22, 77, 83–6, 90–1, 107, 126, 127,

INDEX

128-9, 139-40, 140-7, 151, 154, 155-6, 162-3, 168, 175, 176; and neutralisation of Congo, 135-9; and Niger, 75, 76, 90-1, 120, 147; and Portuguese proposal for a conference, 30, 32, 55-6, 205-7; representation of at conference, 100-1; strong position of 1884, 46-7; and territorial negotiations on Congo, 76-7, 154, 155, 156-7, 162-3 168

Gladstone: views on effective occupation, 189; and May 5th dispatch, 214-15

Goldie, Sir George Taubmann: unofficial representative at conference, 100; buys out British and French firms on Niger, 123-4, 126; destruction of papers of, 225

Granville, Lord: and Anglo-Portuguese Treaty, 17, 26-7, 27-8, 29; difficulties with Germany over Anglo-Portuguese Treaty, 28-9, 32; and Congo note of May 5th, 29, 32, 54, 203-5; and May 5th dispatch, 53, 54-5, 212-13, 214-15, 216, 217; and Portuguese proposal for a conference, 31, 32, 207; and non-ratification of Anglo-Portuguese Treaty, 32; discussion of colonial questions with Herbert Bismarck, 57; and German invitation to conference, 74-5; relations with Leopold during and after negotiations for Anglo-Portuguese Treaty, 78-9; conversation with Münster on Congo, 88-9; and British recognition of International Association, 80, 89, 143-4, 146, 147; and effective occupation, 181-2; and telegram of April 24th, 210, 211

Great Britain: and Anglo-German estrangement: cf. Anglo-German estrangement; and Anglo-Portuguese Treaty, 11, 16, 20, 21, 24-8, 28-9, 31-3, 54, 56, 57, 65, 78-9, 86-7, 203-5; and Angra Pequena, 37, 38-49, 40, 52-3, 56-9, 59-60, 180, 191, 208-9, 209-11, 216; attitude of at conference, 23, 95, 98, 105-6, 119, 176-8; Cameron's offer of Congo to, 13, 203; colonial rivalry of with France, 195-6, 221; and effective occupation, 75, 76, 176-7, 178, 179, 180, 185-6, 187-9, 190-1, 192; and Egypt, 46-8, 51, 52, 60-1, 196; and free trade in Congo, 75, 98, 105-6, 109-10, 112, 114-18; importance of at conference, 5-6; and International African Association, 13-14; and International Association of Congo, 78-9, 86-7, 90-1, 143-9; and International Commission of Congo, 21, 24-5, 32, 132-3; and neutralisation of Congo, 135-9; and Niger, 75-6, 90-1, 120-6, 140, 147, 153, 192, 127-8, 222-3; representation of at conference, 99-100; and Portuguese claims on Congo, 17-18, 19, 197-201; and Portuguese proposal for a conference, 29-30, 30-1, 32, 55-6, 205-7; and Portuguese slave trade, 12, 200-1, 202-3; success of diplomacy of at conference, 192

Guinea, Gulf of: French activities in, 66, 120, 122, 124, 221-2; British fear of French activities in leads to decision to make annexations in Niger district, 124; German respect for French interests in, 66; activities of Britain, France and Germany in 1880-5, 221-3

Harcourt, Sir W. V.: ignorance of whereabouts of Angra Pequena, 39, footnote 6; and effective occupation, 188

Hatzfeldt, Count: author of Congo note of May 5th, 28, footnote 7, 205; and Franco-German entente, 62-3, 70, 137, 162-3; permanent member of German delegation to conference, 100-1; conducts meetings of conference when Bismarck not present, 100; and territorial negotiations at conference, 157, 160-2, 168; and origin of "Combinaison", 161; suggests Münster should be taken into Bismarck's confidence over Angra Pequena, 211; and May 5th dispatch, 214

Heligoland: figures largely in May 5th dispatch, 52; misleads Münster in May 5th dispatch, 54-5, 212, 214

INDEX

Herbert, Sir Robert: and telegram of April 24th, 210
Hertslet, Sir. F.: formulates distinction between annexations and protectorates, 186
Hewett, consul: told to secure protectorate over Niger's oil rivers district, 124–5 ; forestalled by Nachtigal in Cameroons, 125 ; treaties in Niger and oil rivers district, 125–6, 222–3 ; debt of British delegates at conference to, 126 ; annexations of handicap German colony in Cameroons, 222 ; small extent to which programme of spoilt by Nachtigal's annexations, 222–3
Hohenlohe, Count: and Franco-German entente, 62, 71 ; and territorial negotiations at conference, 165
Holland: opposition to Anglo-Portuguese Treaty, 23 ; question of admission of to International Commission on Congo, 24–5, 28; invitation to conference, 98, 220 ; supports free trade in Congo at conference, 98 ; recognises International Association of Congo, 149
Humanitarian questions at conference: slave trade only one of importance discussed at, 3 ; small place occupied by at, 103–4

International African Association: formation of, 13 ; stimulates international rivalry in Africa, 14 ; national committees of, 13–14 ; De Brazza and French national committee of, 14–15
International Association of Congo: evolved out of International African Association, 13 ; Comité d'Études du Haut Congo turns into, 15 ; Germany's recognition of, 77, 83–6, 142, 144–5 ; general belief in beneficent and non-political character of, 78 ; Granville's relations with during and after negotiations for Anglo-Portuguese Treaty, 78–9; U.S.A. recognises flag of, 79–81, 142 ; France recognises flag of and signs pre-emption treaty with, 79–81, 81–3, 142, 158 ; British antagonism to, 86–7 ; British attitude to on entering conference, 87–8, 90–1 ; representation of at conference, 142–3 ; vital bearing of status of on issues of conference, 142–3 ; Bismarck's support of at conference, 90–1, 107, 126, 127, 128–9, 139–40, 140–1, 143–7, 151, 154, 155–6, 162–3, 176 ; recognition of by powers at conference, 102–3, 142–51, 155–6 ; Great Britain's recognition of, 143–9 ; Bismarck's threat about Niger responsible for British recognition of, 90–1, 147 ; supplants International Commission of Congo as medium for Leopold's ambitions, 132 ; neutralisation of, 139 ; and territorial questions at conference, 102, 126, 150, 154–6, 157–60, 168, 169–70, 170–5 ; France signs territorial agreement with, 149–50 ; Portugal signs territorial agreement with 149–50 ; territorial gains of at conference, 154–5, 174
International Commission of Congo: formed by International African Association, 13 ; Great Britain's demand for in Anglo-Portuguese Treaty, 21 ; Great Britain always advocates, 25 ; Granville asks for German co-operation re, 32 ; France shows necessity for, 56 ; German proposals to France re, 64 ; hostility of France and Portugal to at conference, 131–2 ; Germany, Great Britain and International Association support at conference, 132–3 ; Russian opposition to, 133 ; International Association substituted for by Leopold as medium for his ambitions, 132 ; question of sovereignty of over river, 133–4 ; financial powers of, 134–5
Import duties in Congo Basin: twenty years' limit in restriction of, 116–17 ; differences between France and Germany re, 116–17 ; Germany's agreement with France and International Association re, 117; attitude of Great Britain to, 117–18
Italy: and International African Association, 14 ; and invitation to conference, 95, 220, 221; friendly attitude of to Great

Britain at conference, 98 ; supports free trade in Congo at conference, 98

Kasson, Mr. John A.: co-opts Stanley and Sanford on to his staff at conference, 97 ; ardent champion of liberal principles at conference, but fails to ratify final act of, 97–8 ; and west coast extension of Congo Basin, 113 ; neutralisation proposal of, 135–7

Lambermont, Baron de: sent as Leopold's special envoy to conference, 96, 101 ; supports Sanford's railway proposition, 131 ; supports International Commission on Congo, 132 ; and territorial negotiations at conference, 157, 160–2, 164

Lagos: Great Britain appoints consul to, 122 ; Great Britain annexes, 122

Leopold II, King of Belgians: International Association of Congo cloak to hide ambitions of, 5–7 ; important part played by at conference, 7 ; effect on of discoveries of Cameron, 13 ; forms International African Association at Brussels, 13 ; and Brussels conferences, 1876 and 1877, 13 ; elected head of International Commission of Congo, 13 ; and Comité d'Études du Haut Congo, 14–15 ; driving power behind International Association of Congo, 15 ; ambitions of on Congo not suspected by powers, 78 ; and Anglo-Portuguese Treaty, 78–9; and agreements with U.S.A., France and Germany, 79–80 ; and American recognition of flag of International Association 79, 80–1 ; and pre-emption treaty with France, 79, 81–3 ; and German recognition of International Association, 83, 84–7, 144–5 ; British distrust of, 86–7, 87–8 ; delegates of to conference, 96 ; Kasson's sympathy with designs of, 97 ; substitutes International Association for International Commission of Congo as medium of ambitions, 132 ; failure of powers and his own adherents to understand policy of, 132 ; support of Bismarck for, 132, 155, 162–3 ; and neutralisation of Congo, 139, 143 ; and territorial questions at conference, 154, 155, 159, 162–3, 165, 166, 170, 175

Liquor traffic: not discussed at conference, 103

Lister, T. V.: Portuguese sympathies of and hostility to International Association, 88 ; arguments against recognition of International Association, 145 ; correct estimate of origin of Bismarck's proposal for conference in his annoyance over Angra Pequena, 180, footnote 4

Livingstone, David: Cameron's search for and effects on international rivalry in Congo, 13

Lüderitz, Herr: and protection of settlement of at Angra Pequena Bay, 40, 44, 50, 57 ; place of Bismarck's support of in history of German colonial movement, 43–4 ; Lord Derby attempts to occupy parts of South West Africa not occupied by, 59

Lyons, Lord: and territorial negotiations at conference, 165 ; and Portuguese proposal for a conference, 206

Makoko: French claims to empire of, 159

Makoko treaties: ratification of, 17; De Brazza annexes right bank of Stanley Pool by, 158 ; French claims by refuted by International Association, 160

Malet, Sir E.: interview with Bismarck on eve of conference, 76; instructions to conference, 75–6, 90 ; heads British delegation to conference, 99 ; argues successfully against an International Commission on Niger, 127–8 ; and effective occupation, 75, 182, 184, 186–7, 187–8, 189–90, 191 ; and Sette Camma question, 111 ; proposal for freedom of navigation on all rivers of Africa, 129–30 ; and British recognition of International Association, 144–5, 146, 146–7 ; and territoria negotiations on Congo, 160–2

163 ʯ and May 5th dispatch, 213, 214, 216–8
May 5th dispatch: contents and non-delivery of, 51–5, 211, 218; ghost of laid at conference, 191
Monopolies: introduction of in Congo Basin, 118
Morier, Sir Robert: negotiations with Portugal for settlement on Congo, 16
Münster, Count: misleads British government about Bismarck's decision to annex Herr Lübernitz's settlement, 111; responsibility for Anglo-German estrangement, 45; and Congo note of May 5th, 28–9, 51, 53–4, 55, 203–5; delivers German protest against Anglo-Portuguese Treaty, 28; and May 5th dispatch, 51–5, 217–24; told not to recognise British claims in Angra Pequena, 56–7; Bismarck realises incompetence of, 57; and German recognition of International Association, 87; conversation with Granville about Congo, 88–9; and telegram of April 24th, 41, 211–12

Nachtigal, Dr.: expedition of to West Africa, 50; alteration in instructions of, 56; German pledges to France *re* annexations of, 66; forestalls Hewett in Cameroons, 125; small extent to which British programme spoilt by annexations of, 222–3
New Guinea: Bismarck's seizure of, 38; expedition of Dr. Finsch to, 56
Niari Kwilu: Stanley annexes districts watered by, 15, 158; rights of International Association to recognised by France in pre-emption treaty, 158; new French claims to, 159; negotiations between International Association and France for, 160, 164–5; France receives by convention with International Association, 169–70, 174; lost to Association, through Bismarck's failure to mediate with France, 175
Niger: France responsible for discussion of at conference, 61, 120, 153; French demand for free navigation on, 65; and second basis of conference, 67; British objection to international control of, 75–6; British readiness to guarantee free trade and free navigation on, 75; Bismarck disputes British claims to, 75; Bismarck accedes to British claims to, 76, 120, 126–8; differences between France and Germany help to place Great Britain on, 90–1, 126–7, 128; British interests in, 120–2; British exploration of, 121; French expansion on, 122–3; Anglo-French commercial competition on, 123–4, 126; British plans for protectorate over made through fear of France, 124–5, 221–2; Hewett's treaties with chiefs on, 125–6, 222–3; claims of British delegation at conference to, 126; disappointment of French hopes *re*, 128, 140, 153; triumph of Great Britain over, 128, 153, 192; pledges of France and Great Britain *re*, 140; Bismarck's threats regarding, responsible for British recognition of International Association, 90–1, 147

Oil rivers: British Government decides on annexations, 124–5; correspondence *re* and activities of Great Britain, France and Germany in 1880–5, 221–3

Pauncefote, Sir Julian: and British recognition of International Association, 145, 147, 148; and effective occupation, 185–6
Penafiel, Marquis de: and Portuguese proposal for conference, 206–7; member of Portuguese delegation to conference, 101; and Portuguese convention with International Association, 171–3
Petre, Mr. George G.: and question of modifications in Anglo-Portuguese Treaty, 25, 27–8, 29; and ratification of Anglo-Portuguese Treaty, 27, 32–3; and Portuguese proposal for a conference, 32
Pirmez, M. Eugène: and territorial negotiations at conference, 164–8

INDEX

Plessen, Baron: delivers telegram of April 24th, 210

Ponthoz, Count van der Straten: member of Belgian delegation to conference, 96, 101

Portugal: and Anglo-Portuguese Treaty, 13–33 ; attitude of at conference, 95, 105–6, 119, 176; attitude to England and France on Congo, 118 ; claims of on Congo, 11, 18, 19, 24, 197–201 ; and Franco-Portuguese entente: cf. Franco-Portuguese entente ; and free trade in Congo, 98, 105–6, 114, 184–5 ; importance of at conference, 5, 95 ; and International African Association, 13–14 ; and International Association of Congo, 156–7, 161–2, 163, 166–75 ; and International Commission of Congo, 21, 24–5, 131–2, 133, 135 ; and neutralisation of Congo, 136–7 ; proposal of for conference: cf. Portuguese proposal for a conference ; recognises International Association of Congo, 150–1 ; representation of at conference, 101 ; and slave trade, 11–12, 200–1, 202–3 ; and territorial negotiations at conference, 154–8, 160, 175 ; territorial gains of at conference, 156, 174–5

Portuguese proposal for a conference: Du Bocage and, 29–30, 30–1 ; evidence for, 205–7 ; Bismarck takes up, 30, 55–6 ; British Government informed of by Bismarck, 32

Protectorates and annexations: British distinction between, 179, 185 ; distinction formulated by Hertslet, 186 ; views of Selborne and Pauncefote on, 186 ; opposition at conference to British proposal for, 186–7 ; private representations of Malet to Busch *re*, 187–8 ; Bismarck agrees to British distinction between, 189–90 ; triumph for view of Lord Selborne *re*, 191

Robinson, Sir Hercules: and telegram of April 24th, 210

Rohlfs, Gerhard: and German annexation of Congo, 84

Royal Geographical Society: foundation of by Great Britain, 4

Russia: opposed to free trade in Congo, 98 ; opposed to International Commission on Congo, 133

Samoa: and Anglo-German estrangement, 35–6 ; German Subsidy Bill *re*, 43

Sanford, Colonel: and American recognition of International Association, 80 ; co-opted on to staff of American delegation to conference, 97 ; railway proposal of, 130–1 ; French reproaches to Bismarck *re*, 162

Scanlon, Sir Robert: and telegram of April 24th, 210

Second basis of conference: formulation of, 67 ; discussion of, 119–41 : cf. also Congo, free navigation of, and of Niger

Selborne, Lord: and effective occupation, 179, 186, 188–90 ; and British recognition of International Association, 145–6

Senegal: Bismarck excludes from propositions *re* free trade and effective occupation made to France, 64 ; French activities in, 122–3

Serpa (de Pimentel), Senhor: and Anglo-Portuguese Treaty, 17, 19 ; member of Portuguese delegation to conference, 101 ; and territorial negotiations at conference, 161, 167

Sette Camma: accepted by French as limit of Conventional Basin of Congo, 109 ; Courcel's difficulties with Germany *re*, 110 ; acceptance of as frontier boundary by powers, 110–12

Skiernewice: Franco-German entente strengthened by meeting of three emperors at, 68 ; French fears *re* meeting at, 67 ; Bismarck sees Courcel after meeting at, 67

Slave trade: only important humanitarian question discussed at conference, 3 ; resolution of Congress of Vienna for suppression of, 11–12 ; ineffective clauses in final act of conference *re*, 103 ; Portugal and, 11–12, 106–7, 108–9 ; Great Britain and on Niger, 120–1

Stanley, Henry Morton: journeys of on Congo, 13 ; rivalry with De Brazza on Congo, 14–15, 158 ; becomes agent of " Comité d'Études du Haut Congo," 14 ;

ride of U.S.A. in American citizenship of, 80 ; places interests of Leopold before those of U.S.A., 81, 97 ; and British recognition of International Association, 89 ; co-opted on to staff of American delegation to conference, 97, 101 ; and delimitation of Conventional Basin of Congo, 109, 110, 113 ; and territorial negotiations at conference, 157, 158, 159

Stanley Pool: right bank of annexed by De Brazza, 158 ; left bank of annexed by Stanley, 158 ; Stanley's annexation not recognised by French, 159 ; French claim to right bank of not recognised by International Association, 160 ; International Association claims both banks of, 160 ; French demand for Niari Kwilu in exchange for, 164

Strauch, Colonel: unofficial representation of at conference, 95–6 ; and recognition of International Association by powers at conference, 150 ; and territorial negotiations on Congo, 157, 161–2

Territorial negotiations at conference: officially outside programme of conference, 4 ; French stipulate exclusion of from discussions of conference, 73, 102, 152 ; Bismarck proposes discussion of at conference, 76–7 ; discussed during conference as a result of Bismarck's insistence, 102 ; Bismarck's difficulties in helping International Association over, 151, 152–3 ; history of, 151–75; territorial settlement of Niger, 153 ; territorial negotiations over Congo, 153–75 ; first phase of negotiations, 157–64 ; second phase of negotiations, 164–9 ; third phase of negotiations, 169–75 ; Bismarck realises importance of discussion of, 152–3; Bismarck refuses to bring pressure to bear on France in, 162–3 ; French reproaches to Bismarck *re*, 162–3 ; conference adjourned on account of, 164

Telegram of April 24th: terms and delivery of, 209–11 ; Münster belittles importance of, 42 ; date of marks " birthday " of German colonial empire, 50

Thimme, Herr F.: and May 5th dispatch, 215–16, 218

Third basis of conference: formulation of, 67 ; discussion of, 176–91 : cf. also effective occupation

Togoland: Bismarck's seizure of, 37–8

Twiss, Travers, Sir: unofficial member of British delegation to conference, 99 ; and International Commission of Congo, 134 ; and German recognition of International Association, 144, note 3; and British recognition of International Association, 147 ; and effective occupation, 188

Turkey: attitude of at conference, 99 ; late recognition of International Association, 150

U.S.A.: opposition of to Anglo-Portuguese Treaty, 23 ; recognises flag of International Association of Congo, 79–81 ; invitation to conference, 69, 95, 220–1 ; representation of at conference, 101 ; representation of interests of International Association in delegation of, 95–6, 97 ; attitude of at conference, 97–8 ; and effective occupation, 177

William II, Kaiser: erroneous estimate of diplomacy of conference, 192

Woermann, Herr Adolf: advises German delegation at conference over first basis, 101 ; and twenty years' limit on restriction of import duties in Congo, 117

Zanzibar: part of comprised in Conventional Basin of Congo, 4 ; interests of France and England in, 112 ; and east coast extension of Conventional Basin of Congo, 112